SOUND AND HORROR IN THE GIALLO FILM

ICONS OF HORROR
Marc Olivier, series editor

SOUND AND HORROR IN THE GIALLO FILM

—⁂—

DAMIEN POLLARD

INDIANA UNIVERSITY PRESS

This book is a publication of

Indiana University Press
Office of Scholarly Publishing
Herman B Wells Library 350
1320 East 10th Street
Bloomington, Indiana 47405 USA

iupress.org

© 2025 by Damien Pollard

All rights reserved
No part of this book may be reproduced or utilized in any form or by any means, electronic or mechanical, including photocopying and recording, or by any information storage and retrieval system, without permission in writing from the publisher.

First Printing 2025

Library of Congress Cataloging-in-Publication Data

Names: Pollard, Damien author
Title: Sound and horror in the giallo film / Damien Pollard.
Description: Bloomington, Indiana : Indiana University Press, 2025. | Series: Icons of horror | Includes bibliographical references and index.
Identifiers: LCCN 2025018928 (print) | LCCN 2025018929 (ebook) | ISBN 9780253073907 hardback | ISBN 9780253073914 paperback | ISBN 9780253073938 ebook | ISBN 9780253073921 adobe pdf
Subjects: LCSH: Horror films—Italy—History and criticism | Motion pictures—Italy—History—20th century | Sound in motion pictures | LCGFT: Film criticism
Classification: LCC PN1995.9.H6 P6 2025 (print) | LCC PN1995.9.H6 (ebook) | DDC 791.43/61640945—dc23/eng/20250423
LC record available at https://lccn.loc.gov/2025018928
LC ebook record available at https://lccn.loc.gov/2025018929

*To Jemima, Dexter, Sebastian, Brontë, and Ottilie.
I'll show you the films when you're older.*

CONTENTS

Acknowledgments   ix

Introduction: Eavesdropping on History   1
1. Intertextual Voices: *The Girl Who Knew Too Much*   33
2. Directorial Voices: *The Bird with the Crystal Plumage*   53
3. Ideological Voices: *Short Night of Glass Dolls*   73
4. National Voices: *Don't Torture a Duckling* and *Torso*   94
5. Economic Voices: *The New York Ripper* and *Tenebrae*   116

Conclusion: The Voice as a Process   142

Bibliography   157

Index   167

ACKNOWLEDGMENTS

APPROPRIATELY ENOUGH FOR A BOOK concerned with voices, *Sound and Horror in the Giallo Film* is deeply indebted to the countless conversations that I have enjoyed with other scholars, as well as film critics and filmmakers, and the resulting work would not have come together without their generosity and input.

Since my earliest days as a postgraduate student, John David Rhodes has been an invaluable guide and mentor. His ability to attend to the finest of details while keeping the big picture in mind has been a constant source of inspiration for me, and his encouragement and insight are stamped on all the pages that follow. Thank you, JD. My sincere thanks are due to Robert Gordon and Kay Dickinson as well for their patient support throughout the life of this project, for opening my eyes (or, more often, ears) to new perspectives and new questions, and for the constant good humor. Marc Olivier has also been an invaluable source of encouragement and wisdom as this book has come together; his discerning feedback—sometimes offered via email, sometimes over ramen—and his blend of enthusiasm and rigor have shaped *Sound and Horror in the Giallo Film* deeply and always for the best.

I am very grateful to giallo screenwriter and director Luigi Cozzi, who agreed to be interviewed by me on a sweltering morning in Rome, back in June 2019. The value of Cozzi's firsthand knowledge of giallo production is huge, and I hope that I have done justice to the insights he has afforded me. My thanks go to Mark Kermode, too, for his interest in my work and for the contacts with whom he very kindly offered to put me in touch. My sincere thanks, in turn, go to one of those contacts: Alan Jones. Alan's encyclopedic knowledge of the giallo and his long-standing personal relationship with Dario Argento make him an incomparable resource for research like mine. His willingness to share his experiences and knowledge has been of great benefit to this project and has allowed me to fill gaps in my understanding that are not covered in the existing literature. I am also very grateful to Michael Siegel for the help he gave me early in this journey and to Charles Leavitt and Zygmunt Barański for the welcome and support they gave me while I was visiting the University of Notre Dame in the first few months of 2019.

Sound and Horror in the Giallo Film would also not have come into the world were it not for the incredible generosity of Keith Sykes, who supported my postgraduate studies and was a source of emboldening words as I set off on the path that has led to this book. I will always be grateful for both. Throughout that journey, I have been bolstered by the input of friends and colleagues at the University of Cambridge's Centre for Film and Screen and its Italian Section and Northumbria University's School of Design, Arts and Creative Industries (particularly those involved in Northumbria's Horror Studies Research Group). Since we were PhD students, Jules O'Dwyer has been a constant companion and a vital source of both humor and perspective, often at the same time. I am also grateful to Matyáš Moravecz, Silvia Pergetti, and Edward Bowen for helping to make my research so much more enjoyable and so much less lonely.

The professionals at Indiana University Press have been a joy to work with on *Sound and Horror in the Giallo Film*, and I owe a great debt of gratitude to Allison Chaplin, Sophia Hebert, Darja Malcolm-Clarke, and Vickrutha Sudharsan for their thoroughness, attention, professionalism, and approachability as they deftly guided the manuscript through the publication process. I am also grateful to the book's two anonymous peer reviewers for their wonderful suggestions and galvanizing words.

Finally, I must record, with love, my gratitude to my parents, Glenda and Steve; my siblings Jenna and Dominic; my siblings-in-law Leon and Bea; and my five nieces and nephews. Without your excited encouragement, this work would not have been possible.

Much of the research that makes up *Sound and Horror in the Giallo Film* was conducted while I was a doctoral student at the University of Cambridge and was generously funded by Cambridge's Arts and Humanities Research Council Doctoral Training Partnership (award number AH/L503897/1).

Parts of chapter 3 have been previously published as:
Pollard, Damien. 2020. "'Can't You Hear Me?' Ideologies of the Voice in *Giallo* Cinema." *Screen* 61, no. 3:385–402. *Screen* is published by Oxford University Press.

SOUND AND HORROR IN THE GIALLO FILM

INTRODUCTION

Eavesdropping on History

BLOOD AND BLACK LACE (*Sei donne per l'assassino*, 1964) ends with a shot of a red telephone swinging quietly on its cord. As the phone sways and the camera moves toward it, the handset remains as silent as the two corpses heaped in front of it (fig. 0.1). Like a chalk outline of a body at a crime scene, the silence of the phone emphasizes what used to be there but is now gone or perhaps what should be there but is missing. Sound—particularly the human voice—haunts the end of this film; it is an absent presence that commands and demands our attention. The final shot of *Blood and Black Lace* asks us—*forces* us—to listen attentively.

But listen to what? *Blood and Black Lace* is a film with an almost obsessive interest in the visual. The opening credits show each of the principal cast members standing motionless next to mannequins in pools of brightly colored light as if they were no more than objects to be looked at. Colored light is used throughout the film and is rarely explained by the story's events; it is purely a source of pleasure for the eye. The mannequins signify the film's setting: a haute couture fashion atelier, itself a sort of temple to that-which-can-be-seen. Surely, sound is a minor concern in this film? Yet, following the opening sequence, the first shot is of the atelier's sign swinging in a storm before breaking its chain. It squeaks loudly several times. Critics have noted the visual parallels between the swinging sign and the swinging phone (see Lucas 2007, 566), but the squawk of the former and the silence of the latter form auditory bookends for the film too. These moments reveal that while *Blood and Black Lace* is insistent in the importance it grants to the visual, it is also persistent in the importance it grants to sound. Questions of sound, and especially voice, are vital to *Blood and Black Lace*'s narrative structure; its thematic preoccupation with Italy's postwar

Figure 0.1. *Blood and Black Lace* (Mario Bava, 1964) concludes with a telephone swinging silently behind two corpses.

modernity; and even the multinational, multilingual mode of production by which it came to be made. If we listen to the film closely—from an aesthetic perspective but also with an ear to the historical and industrial aspects of its sound design—it has much to tell us.

FIRST WORDS: *FILONE* CINEMA AND THE *GIALLO*

Blood and Black Lace is one of the earliest examples of a *giallo* film, a type of murder mystery horror film made in Italy—often with international collaboration—between the early 1960s and the late 1980s (these films are known as *gialli* in the plural). To understand the giallo, it is helpful to consider the broader Italian notion of *filone* cinema. The filone (*filoni* in the plural) has no direct equivalent in Anglophone cinema; it is often compared to the idea of the subgenre but is perhaps more accurately described as "formula" (Wagstaff 1992, 248). A cinematic filone denotes a body of texts that replicate the formula of a successful film—sometimes domestic, sometimes foreign (and often American)—to capitalize quickly on its popularity and financial success. As giallo screenwriter and director Luigi Cozzi famously summarized in the early 1980s, "In Italy . . . when you bring a script to a producer, the first question he asks is not 'what is your film like?' but 'what *film* is your film like?'" (quoted in Church 2015, 11, original emphasis). Filone cinema thus falls under the wider rubric of "exploitation" cinema (a form of cinema in which films are produced to exploit the popularity of a certain film, genre, or star, for example).[1] Paolo Albiero and Giacomo Cacciatore (2015, 14) summarize: "[Filoni] could run their course in a few films or in hundreds. Each filone shared a series of characteristic elements that defined it: historical and geographical setting; thematic and narrative features; often a particular cinematographic language.... Filoni were often born from the sensational, and sometimes surprising, success of a single film. To ride the wave of this success, variations—more or less imaginative—emerged. For the same reason, these films were also made very quickly."[2] Austin Fisher (2019, 17) has similarly framed filone film production in terms of a twofold aim: "Firstly, to create speculations in an attempt to predict where the next cycle might lie, informed by previous patterns; and secondly, to exploit the short-lived favourable market conditions of profitable cycles." The major postwar filoni produced (at least in part) in Italy include the *peplum* (sword-and-sandal) epic (1950s and 1960s); the Italian-style comedy (1950s–1980s); the gothic horror (1960s); the James Bond–style spy adventure (1960s); the Italian (or, "Spaghetti") Western (1960s and 1970s); the giallo (1960s to 1980s); the *poliziottesco* film in which crimes are tackled by members of state-run police forces (1970s); the zombie horror (1970s and 1980s); and the cannibal horror (1970s and 1980s).[3] The filone's need to chase trends in pursuit of continued sales caused its defining features to change over time. As formulas evolved, new selling points were incorporated, and neighboring filone cross-pollinated. Films produced under the filone model had a close connection to their industrial contexts, and there was a bond between the commercial imperatives that governed their production and the formal characteristics of the films themselves.[4]

The industry that produced filone films was populated by small and often short-lived production companies. Although major Italian producers like Galatea turned out films in several filoni, it was medium-sized companies like Seda Spettacoli, Dania Film, and Fulvia Film that produced most filone films, along with small fly-by-night operators. Albiero and Cacciatore (2015, 14) summarize: "The key figures of this celluloid underworld were speculative producers, seduced by the lure of easy money and the possibility of breaking into the golden world of entertainment, and they left the most varied professions to do so. Hence, there were swarms of small production companies with a few thousand lire in share capital and lifespans as short as a single film, shamelessly imitating the most popular narratives." Producers were also lured into the filone market by the promise of generous subsidies from the Italian government, that existed to protect and nurture the country's film industry. Small production companies would often recoup their money by selling (or preselling, if production had not yet finished) their films to distributors. The money they could access up front lowered the point at which a film might become profitable. Further, a great number of filone films were made as transnational coproductions. According to this model, production companies from two or more countries (typically European) would share the financial burden of a film in exchange for exclusive distribution rights in their respective home markets and a stipulated share of sales to other territories. This arrangement allowed producers to access financial incentives in multiple countries at once, further lowering the financial risk involved in production. It also meant that casts and crews were composed of an international mix of professionals.[5] Over half of Italy's film output in the 1960s was produced through coproduction, and this included huge numbers of filone films as well as much of the "art" cinema the country was producing in the same period. Even a short and limited theatrical release became a profitable prospect, and the ground was laid for a cinematic gold rush. With cheap, sellable films rendered lucrative regardless of their artistic merits, they were made in their thousands (see interview with Ian McCulloch in Thrower 2017, 17). The reliance on international coproduction within the filone system makes it difficult to label these films as simply "Italian." Giallo films, at least, were almost always directed and produced by Italians and featured Italian cast members in key roles. Much of the production and postproduction was done at Rome's extensive film production facilities as well. It is therefore valid to refer to the giallo (and many of the other filoni listed above) as Italian, but we must remember that Italian cinema in the postwar decades was actively international and relied on lines of collaboration and influence that extended across Europe and often beyond. As I discuss throughout this book, this was an international Italian cinema anchored in an increasingly international Italy.

The small-scale industrial practice that supported most filone production also meant that such films were made according to an artisanal model. Although several filone directors have been reclaimed as cult figures after the fact (including Sergio Corbucci, Mario Bava, Lucio Fulci, Umberto Lenzi, and Ruggero Deodato), many took pride in approaching filmmaking as a craft and a job. Lucio Fulci once asked, "Do I consider myself an artist or an artisan? An artisan, definitely" (quoted in Albiero and Cacciatore 2015, 14). Mario Bava has spoken similarly: "I am a craftsman, a romantic craftsman like those who have disappeared. I make films like I was making chairs" (quoted in Pezzotta 1997, 9). To be clear, a small number of filone directors—for various reasons—did work in a way that resembled the artistically autonomous and visionary style of the "auteur." Key among these are Sergio Leone and Dario Argento (the latter the leading figure in the history of the giallo). These directors are important exceptions to the dominant filone production practice. Many other filone practitioners developed their own distinctive styles, but a good director in the filone paradigm—one who found consistent work and could sustain a living—was primarily one who met commercial demands. Evidence of this trend is found in the fact that almost all filone directors (and writers) hopped between filoni; they were guns for hire or occasionally producer-directors with a keen sense of market trends. The result is that filone cinema often seems to stage a negotiation in which the artistic predilections of the creative personnel must find a way to fit within rigid commercial strictures. In Leon Hunt's (2022, 70) words, "As producers and short-lived production companies tried to second guess public taste—and often foreign taste—artisans tried to keep things interesting for themselves and the audience."

The production factors behind the filone model can help us better understand these films, and some have argued that the same is true of their exhibition. A new perspective has emerged regarding filone cinema, suggesting that these films can be interpreted through the social dynamics in Italy's low-end cinemas. Cozzi (interview with author 2019) estimates that in 1970, Italy had around thirty thousand cinemas. These venues could be divided into first-, second-, and third-run cinemas (known in Italian as *prima*, *seconda*, and *terza visione* cinemas).[6] The first-run theaters were mostly found in cities, featured luxurious decors, and were expensive to attend. They tended to screen high-budget and prestige films, both Italian and foreign. Second-run theaters were cheaper and would screen prestige films after their first run as well as some films destined purely for the second-run circuit. Third-run cinemas, found mostly in rural areas and working-class urban zones, screened high-budget films long after their original release and low-budget filone films that were shown only in these venues (Koven 2006, 27). Christopher Wagstaff (1992) writes that the typical mode of spectatorship in third-run venues bore little resemblance to the norms of mainstream twenty-first-century cinema spectatorship in Europe and was, in fact, more like television spectatorship. The viewer (typically male) might visit the cinema after dinner without knowing what was showing, arrive after the film had started, drink heavily, pay more attention to conversations with friends than the screen, and only watch the film during high-impact set pieces that were designed to impress independently from the films in which they featured (such as shoot-outs in the Western, murders in the giallo, and sex scenes in the sex comedy [see also Koven 2006, 123–39]). Cozzi's recollection of Roman cinemas in the 1970s matches this description; he has spoken of the Giulio Cesare cinema in Rome, which was known for being rowdy. Cozzi (interview with author 2019) claims that the cigarette smoke was sometimes so thick that the screen was almost totally obscured and that audience members would occasionally bring in musical instruments to play during scenes of sex or violence. In his words, "the audience was a spectacle by itself."[7] Wagstaff (1992, 253) argues that this context directly shaped the formal qualities of filoni produced for the third-run market. He explains, "The viewer was being offered either one or a combination of three pay-offs: laughter, thrill, titillation. They are, as it were, three physiological responses, provoked not by whole films, but by items or moments in films. Italian formula cinema simply juggled with plot items to produce the required recipe." It is tempting to read formulaic filone films purely as attempts to entertain the distracted audiences of third-run cinemas. The validity of doing so has been challenged recently, however. Andreas Ehrenreich (2017, 114) has conducted archival research into the giallo showing that "gialli were screened in all kinds of venues including *prima visione* cinemas and, in some cases, profited from major marketing campaigns." Indeed, higher-profile filone films such as Leone's Westerns and Argento's gialli were released in first-run theaters along with some lower-budget gialli directed by Bava, Fulci, Martino, and others (Kannas 2020, 42–43). Ehrenreich acknowledges that many giallo films were made with the second- and third-run circuits in front of mind—a point also made by Leon Hunt (2022, 56)—but he points out that "it is important to abandon generalisations about this highly heterogeneous series of films" (Ehrenreich 2017, 123). It is surely the case that much filone cinema was particularly well adapted to the sort of distracted spectatorship that is often aligned with third- (and sometimes second-) run venues, but it is important to recognize that these films could also circulate more broadly through Italy's cinemas, not to mention those of other countries. The risk in understanding these films purely as entertainment for Italy's small, rowdy cinemas is that we overlook the possible extent of their participation in a broader social landscape.

Taken together, the above issues highlight how inseparable filone texts are from the specific industrial contexts that bore them. The "cultification" of much filone cinema—and its directors and stars—in the decades since these films were made demonstrates that a distinct creative vision does often shine through in many cases. Yet the ways the films were made show that commercial interests dominated filone cinema. At the simplest level, filone texts were objects produced for profit, commercially conceived and manufactured. In this sense, they differ from the art films that emerged at the same time, expressively idiosyncratic texts that often won awards at international festivals but lost money (indeed, the profitability of the filone system in postwar Italy helped to bankroll the country's entire film industry [Koven 2006, 11–12]).[8] Framing the giallo in terms of filone cinema brings the conditions of its production to the fore, and it also mitigates some of the complexities involved in thinking of it primarily as "popular" cinema. Although *popular* may seem like a convenient synonym for "entertainment," "profit-driven," or "not reserved for the arthouse," it raises a lot of tricky questions. Wagstaff (2013) points out, for example, that it is often unclear whether popularity refers to the conditions of a film's origins or its reception (which may change over time), and whether it is a matter of production or form. It is also unclear whether popularity should be measured qualitatively (how much audiences seem to like a film, which may also change over time) or quantitatively (how many tickets, DVDs, or online rentals have been sold, and over what period). It is also a term that is both translated and used differently in different periods and different national contexts. These questions are important and inform this book, but framing the giallo primarily in terms of filone cinema helps us better understand the relationship between these films and the historically and geographically specific industry (or industries) that produced them. The commercial imperatives underpinning filone films are evident in the texts themselves in the multiple, profound ways they work to organize form; industrial context is tightly woven into the fabric of filone cinema. By extension, a given filone film may be shaped by the wider economic, social, cultural, and even political issues influencing the Italian film industry at the time of its production. In short, one of the great appeals of filone films is that they proclaim their historicity (their status as documents produced in and by a specific historical moment) by always pointing back to the industry that made them.

After the Italian Western, the giallo film was Italy's second-most prolific postwar filone.[9] It takes its name—*yellow*—from the yellow-covered paperback detective novels (often translated from English and German) that had been published in Italy by Mondadori since 1929 and that served as the giallo's initial inspiration. Once it moved onto film, the giallo became an altogether darker object, frequently combining explosive violence and outlandish mystery narratives with highly stylized visual and aural aesthetics. The giallo draws clear influence from the films of Alfred Hitchcock, West German *krimi* films (crime films that were produced in West Germany and were roughly contemporaneous with the giallo), the antirealist aesthetics of German expressionism, and long-form comic books (known as *fumetti* in Italy).[10] Gialli almost always feature an amateur detective investigating a murder or series of murders in which they are somehow implicated. By default, they are set in the present, graphically violent, highly sexualized, and stylistically striking. They are often characterized by elaborate camerawork, crash zooms, baroque color palettes, and jarring music. Notably, giallo protagonists tend to be people out of place, foreigners in Italy or Italians abroad (Needham 2002). Baschiera and Di Chiara (2010, 34) outline how the internationalism of giallo coproduction (which was very common) was distinct in leading to a consistently international aesthetic *within* the texts. Here, the giallo takes a different path from both its art and filone cinema contemporaries: gialli were often set within "realistic" international settings unlike the international but mythical settings of the Western and peplum or the typically more nationally circumscribed settings of art cinema. As with all filone, the giallo often intersected with other filone and more widespread genres (particularly the closely related horror and poliziottesco filoni but also science fiction and even soft-core pornography). Gialli tend to differ in how they pick and choose from the filone's main features so that the edges of the giallo corpus are blurry and often difficult to clearly define. The body of films we might reasonably label giallo today has in part been assembled retrospectively by critics, fans, and scholars. Yet while a categorical account of what constitutes a giallo may be elusive, Claudio Bartolini (2017, 20) outlines a four-pointed definition of the giallo that I mention here because it captures these films' generally accepted qualities without being overly restrictive. According to Bartolini, a giallo must convey suspense in both its narrative and its staging; proceed according to an essentially rational base (the confirmed presence of supernatural agents marks a move into the horror filone); take crime as the fulcrum of its narrative; and ensure the dominance of these three qualities over any other characteristics that may be present; for example, they cannot be overpowered by the presence of comedy.

The openness of the giallo's formal definition means that attempts to date its emergence and dissolution are problematic. The evolution of the giallo and the debates surrounding this topic are discussed throughout this book, but I adhere to a critically established chronology by which the first giallo is identified (with some caveats) as Mario Bava's 1963 *The Girl Who Knew Too Much* (*La ragazza che sapeva troppo*). The filone is believed to begin with the success of Dario Argento's first films in the early 1970s and its endpoint is dated (more nebulously) to the late 1980s. Finally, it should be noted that the term *giallo* signifies something slightly different in Italian and in English. In the Anglophone context, it refers to the relatively narrow set of cinematic texts outlined above, which today are generally seen to fall under the wider umbrella of horror cinema. In Italian, *giallo* refers to crime and mystery literature, television, and cinema much more broadly. I use the term in its Anglophone sense, but it should be noted that the filone to which this usage refers is nonetheless recognized as distinct in the Italian context, in which it is sometimes referred to as the *giallo all'italiana* (see Sabelli 2013, 15).

To return to *Blood and Black Lace*, the film is illustrative of the giallo even if that filone would not fully emerge for several more years. It was directed by Mario Bava, a prolific director and cinematographer in Italy both before and after the war. The setting is an atelier in Rome run by a countess named Cristiana and her business partner Massimo. Isabella, one of the young models who works there, is murdered in the opening moments by an assailant who wears a leather trench coat, leather gloves, a fedora, and a white cloth mask that covers his entire face. Inspector Silvestri arrives and begins to investigate while three more models are murdered and a complex web of intrigue is spun. The killer is eventually revealed to be Massimo; he and Cristiana had worked together earlier to kill the latter's late husband so that they might marry, and Isabella had been blackmailing them. Cristiana now dons the coat-and-mask disguise and murders a fifth model named Tao-Li. Hearing the police approaching as she leaves Tao-Li's apartment, she tries to escape through a window. She falls to the ground below but survives and returns to Massimo to find him looting her belongings; she realizes their marriage was a ploy for him to raid her wealth, and she kills him. She then reaches for the phone to call the police but dies almost as soon as she dials the number. The camera moves in on that swinging red phone.

Blood and Black Lace's plot is fairly typical of the gialli that would follow in that it is at once reasonably straightforward and yet oddly convoluted. Logical simplicity in the giallo always runs up against the complexity of repressed histories and desires. Watching these films, one always senses that there is another twist to come, another secret to surface. The film also uses many of the giallo's dominant stylistic traits. The murders are graphic: Isabella is strangled, Nicole is struck in the face with a spiked glove, Peggy is burned to death in a furnace, Greta is smothered, and Tao-Li is drowned before her wrists are slit. These murders are also imbued with sexual overtones; the women's bodies are arranged into erotic displays after death, and they are often scantily clad. As Alberto Pezzotta (1997, 46) has argued, the murder scenes themselves have a pornographic element. They are drawn out and filmed in sumptuous detail so that they exist as spectacles in themselves, quite in excess of their narrative value to the film. In this way, these scenes are early examples of the violent set piece that would become a key feature of much giallo cinema. *Blood and Black Lace* is also a strikingly colorful film, with red, purple, and blue gels giving the lighting in many scenes an uncanny and unnatural tenor, and the camera seems to move around the atelier like a character in itself. In terms of both narrative and style, this giallo, like its descendants, often hovers somewhere between nightmare and fever dream.

The question remains as to why such a visually opulent film ends with a moment that emphasizes sound. According to Roberto Curti (2019, 115, original emphasis), the dangling phone may be little more than a joke. It "childishly remains *alive and swinging* when everyone else is dead" and asks us not to invest too much emotion in the film's human characters. For what it is worth, the endlessly self-effacing Bava often claimed not to remember how the film ended (see 2019, 7). But in this book, I want to ask what might be gained if we take the film's final shot at face value, as an invitation to lean in and listen closely to the giallo.

A GROWING CONVERSATION: HISTORICIZING THE GIALLO

I argue in this book that paying close attention to giallo films' use of sound—and the voice in particular—allows us to hear how these films gave form to much bigger social, cultural, economic, and political phenomena. The use of sound in the giallo helps us understand how these films both responded to and participated in much broader historical processes. *Sound and Horror in the Giallo Film* seeks to build on the highly productive sociohistorical research undertaken regarding the giallo since the turn of the millennium. A key text is Mikel Koven's *La Dolce Morte: Vernacular Cinema and the Italian Giallo Film* (2006), which argues that the giallo should be understood as a "vernacular" cinematic form, a self-perpetuating model composed of culturally specific narrative and stylistic components that can only be correctly read by members of a certain cultural group (in this case, young blue-collar Italian men of the 1970s). Ultimately, Koven argues that these films express a deep ambivalence toward Italy's experience of a modernity characterized by easy international travel, the instability of "the nation," increased consumerism, increased industrialization, and an increasing divide between Italy's industrial North and rural South (2006, 16). Some believe that *La Dolce Morte* is slightly too uniform in its presentation of the giallo and its modes of production and exhibition (including Ehrenreich, mentioned above). However, the book has been critical in encouraging a deeper understanding of the giallo beyond its aesthetics or status as a cult object, positioning it as a type of cinema that speaks of and to Italy's postwar modernization. This perspective has been taken up by others, including Alexia Kannas in *Giallo! Genre, Modernity, and Detection in Italian Horror Cinema* (2020). Kannas gives a detailed history of the giallo and its complex patterns of circulation. She then considers how it challenges traditional views of genre and explores important themes including modernity, tourism, and violence. Like Koven, Kannas stresses that these films cannot be understood aside from the specific historical and geographical contexts that created them. The research represented by these two books places the giallo in Italy's much broader sociohistorical landscape. This matters because it helps us to better understand both the films and the contexts they interact with.

Koven and Kannas are both sensitive to the specific industrial conditions of giallo film production, and this context informs their discussions and analyses. Other scholars have taken up the question of how the material aspects of these films (the nuts-and-bolts way in which they are put together) are shaped by industrial considerations in a way that binds text to context at a very tangible level. For example, Stefano Baschiera and Francesco Di Chiara's article "Once Upon a Time in Italy: Transnational Features of Genre Production" (2010) argues that the giallo's stylistic features can be partly understood in terms of its dependence on coproduction arrangements between companies located around Europe. In this way, the giallo's thematic interest in international modernity seems less a reflection of social attitudes than a practical consequence of Italy's increasingly international film industry and economy. Baschiera and Di Chiara's essay is significant because it shows how the production processes and commercial structures that underlay the giallo both reflect the changing social landscape of Italy and Europe and become part of the films.

In a similar vein, Austin Fisher's *Blood in the Streets: Histories of Violence in Italian Crime Cinema* (2019) contends that Italy's divisive wartime history can be seen reemerging in Italian crime films of the 1970s (including gialli) in minor scene-setting details and throwaway lines of dialogue that refer to historical events. For Fisher (2019, 39), these gestures signal the legacy of Italy's wartime history in everyday postwar discourse because the filone system "necessitated the efficient anticipation of [films'] target audiences' levels of prior knowledge [and] tell[s] us much about the assumed preoccupations of the 'here and now.'" By reading the historicity of these films in the conditions of their production, Fisher convincingly illustrates how tightly society, industry, text, and audience are bound together in the production of filone cinema. Fisher's book is roughly contemporaneous with Valentina Vitali's *Capital and Popular Cinema: The Dollars Are Coming!* (2016), which contains a long chapter on the giallo (centered around Bava's *The Girl Who Knew Too Much*). Vitali (2016, 61–62) argues that the economic conditions under which a popular genre is produced leave their "mark on the production of the films and, inevitably, on their aesthetics." She contends that, in the giallo's case, the dominant economic factor was the rise of speculative capitalism in Italian genre film production (and in the country more widely), and she reveals that the commercial imperatives behind the production of *The Girl Who Knew Too Much* exerted tangible influence on a range of basic material details including the film's use of location, costume, and camera angle. For Vitali (2016, 158), "a film inevitably stages the socio-economic conditions of its own production." Social, economic, and political context influences a given film industry and thus affects the form of the films that the industry produces. For Vitali, historical context is not an external matter that films straightforwardly reflect or allegorize; it is something that exists *inside* the text because it determines how films are put together.

The industrially oriented methodological approaches used by Fisher, Vitali, and others are powerful. To be clear, it is not that thematic readings of films are invalid. On the contrary, the organization of form and content in a film invariably means that certain patterns and preoccupations rise to the fore, and interrogating these patterns can help us better understand how a film is entangled in wider social or political issues. But an analysis of the giallo's relationship to its historical moment(s) that is also aware of the concrete factors that shaped the production of the films allows for the interaction of text and context to be traced and interrogated further. In fact, as Vitali indicates, it allows us to fundamentally rethink the neat division of text and context. When gialli (and perhaps all films) are examined in terms of their specific industrial preconditions, historical context no longer seems to be a factor that operates outside of the text but is something that sits at the heart of film form. What is missing, however, from recent industrial-historical research into the giallo is a sustained focus on these films' use of sound and the voice. This is unfortunate because, on the one hand, the voice is a cornerstone of a film's auditory form, so it is often vital to how films express thematic preoccupations. On the other hand, the cinematic voice is a precise, tangible, and complex product of the postproduction process, which leads to questions about a film's industrial construction. Both thematically and materially, the voice in film always stages a conversation between text and context.

VIVA VOCE: THE VOICE AND THE GIALLO

The human voice is perhaps best defined by how it breaks down borders instead of being limited by them. Attempts to delineate the voice often fall short because it straddles categories and locations by its very nature. For example, it stems from the deep body, yet it is also a product of the mind; it spans both yet belongs to neither. It is a vehicle for the expression of thought, yet it always seems to express emotion. It is intimately shaped by the mouth of the utterer, yet it only truly becomes a voice once it reaches the ear of a listener. It originates in the deep recesses of the body yet only fully materializes as it spreads out around the body. Although we think of the voice as a vehicle for language, as *sound*, it performs a far greater role—it becomes the bearer of desire, emotion, and selfhood. In *Dumbstruck: A Cultural History of Ventriloquism*, Steven Connor (2000, 3, 7) argues that the voice works to join the individual to the physical and social spaces they occupy: "giving voice is the process which simultaneously produces articulate sound, and produces myself, as a self-producing being ... there is no other feature of my self whose nature it is thus to move from me to the world, and to move me into the world." Connor (2000, 4) emphasizes that the voice is intimately bound to the individual and, at the same time, exists outside of the individual: "It is my way of being me in my going out from myself." Our voices are ours, so much so that they can define us in the same way that our faces do. Yet as soon as the voice becomes audible, it dissipates outward and becomes somehow separate from us, part of something bigger. This describes the voice as a way for the individual and their environment to relate to each other: "The voice may be grasped as the mediation between the phenomenological body and its social and cultural contexts" (2000, 12). Connor's theorization illustrates that the negotiation between individual and society staged by the voice is performed afresh with every utterance. The voice's production and projection of a "me" is dynamic: always provisional and always in progress, from one sound to the next. In *A Voice and Nothing More* (2006), Mladen Dolar similarly asserts that the voice bears a profound and irrefutable connection both to the person from whom it stems and to the communities of which they are a part, such that it forms "the intimate kernel of subjectivity" and "stands at the axis of our social bonds" (2006, 14). As in Connor's theorization, the voice is too spatially and socially expansive to be contained in neat categories. Dolar uses a series of Venn diagrams to demonstrate that the voice always seems to span categories like subject/other and body/language, yet it also slips between them. The voice naturally connects the individual to wider social structures, placing it at the center of linguistic, ethical, political, and sociocultural questions (many of which he discusses in depth). This element of the voice is also discussed by Italian philosopher Adriana Cavarero in *For More Than One Voice* ([2003] 2005). Cavarero outlines how the voice has been approached in Western philosophy, art, and politics from the classical period through the twentieth century, asserting that this history proceeds according to a fundamental separation of *logos* (thought or language) and *phonos* (sound). This is a division that has subordinated the unique, sonorous elements of the voice to the depersonalized, semantic content (language) that it transmits. For Cavarero, there are serious consequences to this way of approaching the voice. One is that it perpetuates and undergirds gender inequality because the history of Western art and thought has tended to gender cognitive logos as male, and corporeal (and frivolous) phonos as female. Another is that the emphasis on logos is an emphasis on the abstract, universal, and dehumanized. The tendency of Western thought to veer toward this schema, Cavarero argues, has contributed to the decline of pluralism. More extremely, it has fed into the atrocities of the twentieth century. The voice, which Cavarero equates with phonos, becomes both a metaphor and a vehicle for an alternative politics. The voice as such creates situations in which individuals express their uniqueness and form bonds of reciprocal relation in which each recognizes the uniqueness of the other. This is, at heart, an ethical and political issue for Cavarero because "the political, the exclusively human sphere of the world, consists in the 'in-between,' in what relates and separates men at the same time, revealing their plural condition" ([2003] 2005, 192). For Cavarero, and for Connor and Dolar, the stakes are high when it comes to the voice. The voice possesses a sort of paradoxical magic: while it both expresses and stands in for the irrefutable uniqueness of the individual, it also proves the inseparability of the individual from the groups and spaces around them. It brings difference into contact, and this contact has the potential to be both constructive and destructive.

The three considerations of the voice that I have mentioned here sit among many others that speak from a range of disciplinary perspectives, including film and media studies. In the 1970s and 1980s, film scholars including Rick Altman, Mary Ann Doane, and Christian Metz published articles theorizing film sound in its own right and as a component of cinema's wider ideological operations. While this body of work devotes frequent attention to the voice, one of the first sustained considerations of the topic was Michel Chion's *The Voice in Cinema* ([1982] 1999). Like most theorists of the voice, Chion warns against confusing the voice with speech alone, as that overlooks the voice's rich materiality as a complex and dynamic sound ([1982] 1999, 1). The voice in its full complexity requires careful study, according to Chion, because cinema is "vococentric." He explains, "In actual movies, for real spectators, there are not *all the sounds including the human voice. There are voices, and then everything else.* In other words, in every audio mix, the presence of a human voice instantly sets up a hierarchy of perception" ([1982] 1999, 5, original emphasis). Chion argues that soundtracks are designed accordingly, with the voice—"speech, shouts, sighs or whispers"—prioritized above all other sounds ([1982] 1999, 6). This is partly because the voice carries dialogue and its intelligibility is thus crucial for the communication of a film's narrative, but it is also because "the ear is inevitably carried toward" the voice thanks to the huge social significance that we know it to bear ([1982] 1999, 5). Like the philosophers and theorists mentioned previously, Chion stresses that the voice is not so much a *facet* of human subjectivity and sociality but a *foundation* of each. This is shown in the prime position the voice assumes in films' formal hierarchies and in the effect it can have on how audiences engage with and experience a text (the term *audience* appropriately comes from the Latin *audire*, "to listen"). In his exploration of this idea, Chion coins several concepts that have been mainstays of the study of the voice in film ever since. Prime among these is his theory of the *acousmêtre*, the voice without a visible source on-screen that floats unbounded in the liminal space between screen and proscenium, suggesting malevolence and possessing the ominous powers of omnipresence, panopticism, omniscience, and omnipotence ([1982] 1999, 17–47).

The implications of Chion's analysis go beyond the revelation of the voice's great formal importance. If the theorists mentioned show that the personal, social, and political stakes involved in the voice are high, Chion's account of cinema's vococentrism invites us to consider how the voice might raise the stakes of a film. In other words, since the voice is so fundamental to what a film "does" at the formal level, it makes sense that the voice might be fundamental to what a film "does" more broadly. Since the voice underpins the relationship between the individual and the social and physical spaces they occupy, it is no surprise that it plays a major role in the way films depict questions of subjectivity, sociality, and the relationship between the human and the nonhuman. This has been shown by several scholars including, recently, Tom Whittaker in *The Spanish Quinqui Film: Delinquency, Sound, Sensation* (2020). Whittaker (2020, 15) delves deeply into the role of sound and the voice in the *cine quinqui*, a group of low-budget Spanish films produced in the 1970s and 1980s that focus on the lives of juvenile delinquents. He conducts a detailed analysis of the way that sound and voice garner sociopolitical significance in these films and argues,

> The soundtrack of the films provided an authentic reflection of the auditory experience of delinquents and marginal young people on the outskirts of Barcelona and Madrid during this time. At the same time, their noise gave symbolic expression to the social location of the juvenile delinquency, a dissonance alerting us both to their deviance and their subsequent threat to the social fabric. The auditory experience of delinquency often illustrated the extent to which sound is uncontainable and elusive: it is able to move through walls and across borders. If the experience of delinquency in *cine quinqui* was one of walls, both geographical and metaphorical, their noise served to disrupt and transcend the oppressive geographies that contained them.

Whittaker makes a powerful case here for the historicizing potential of the cinematic voice. He is careful to connect the formal use of sound and voice in the films he studies to the broader sociocultural implications of sound in a Spain that was just emerging, with some turbulence, from the far-right dictatorship of Francisco Franco. For Whittaker, the voice is crucial to how the *cine quinqui* explores themes around social order, crime, and the sanctity of the home during this period. This is precisely because sound and voice frequently mediate (or impose) human social interactions and the relationships between individuals and wider groups and power structures. *The Spanish Quinqui Film* reveals the cinematic voice's potential to function as a wellspring of historicity: he stresses that to understand these films and their relationship to a Spain on the cusp of massive social change, we must listen to them.[11]

The voice's value as a historicizing tool for film scholars is also explored by studies into how the materiality of film sound intersects the historical context surrounding national cinematic traditions, particularly in Italy. Mark Betz's *Beyond the Subtitle: Remapping European Art Cinema* (2009) devotes a chapter to the debates sparked by art cinema regarding the use of subtitling and dubbing. He explains that art cinema gained prominence at a time when European integration was expanding and flows of international capital were creating an increasingly globalized world. During this period, "the voice/celebrity (of the actor, but also of the director) emerges in the coproduced European art film as a means towards imaginary nation building" (2009, 32). By drawing on thorough historical research, Betz (2009, 52) shows that the "dialogue tracks of art films are thus a rich site of contestation and are symptomatic of larger economic, political, and cultural forces in Europe in the 1960s and 1970s." Betz demonstrates that the materiality of the cinematic voice binds the film text to a range of much broader and historically pertinent issues. His book—which primarily discusses Italian and French cinema—is complemented by Antonella Sisto's *Film Sound in Italy: Listening to the Screen* (2014). Sisto's book is a polemic analysis of the continued and uncritical use of voice dubbing—a largely Fascist intervention into film practice—by the Italian film industry following the fall of Benito Mussolini's government. There were several pragmatic reasons why dubbing continued after Fascism, but for Sisto (2014, 9–10), its postwar persistence remains a "cultural and semiotic violence" that manifests "the sonicscape of the nation's fascist repressed unconscious" because it uncritically sustains the ghost of Fascism. Her argument offers a powerful account of how history is audible in the Italian film industry's use of the voice. Together, Betz and Sisto produce a critical perspective within which the voice in Italian cinema functions as a hot point where formal, industrial, and sociopolitical issues of past and present converge and begin to talk to each other.

Existing scholarship on the voice (in general and in film and media) reveals that the voice is an invaluable tool for understanding how films both register and participate in the historical moments that created them. The cinematic voice is both the cornerstone of a film's auditory form and a tangible product of industrial processes, both of which may be entangled in wider contextual currents. At both the thematic and material levels, the voice weaves context into text and makes history audible. Giallo scholarship's neglect of sound design is therefore both surprising and in need of correction if the historicity of these texts is to be comprehensively grasped. I aim to make this correction by scrutinizing the thematic and material complexity of the voice in giallo cinema by listening to the conversations these films stage between text and context.

AN ECHO FROM THE PAST: ITALY FROM POSTWAR TO POSTMODERN

Since *Sound and Horror in the Giallo Film* is interested in historicizing the giallo, some brief historical details about the period in which these films were made are needed. Italy's history from the mid-1940s to the 1980s is characterized, on the one hand, by the dramatic expansion of industrialized, consumption-driven modernity, and on the other, by social and geographical divergence in how this modernity was experienced. The Second World War left Italy physically damaged and socially divided. Allied bombing and the slow liberation of the peninsula had ensured the former, while the divide between Fascist and anti-Fascist factions persisted long after the fighting had ceased. The anti-Fascist partisan movement was instrumental in the eventual fall of Mussolini's government and the ultimate expulsion of Nazi forces, and it became legendary in the immediate aftermath of the war. Importantly, communist groups figured prominently in the partisan movement, and the *Partito Comunista Italiano* (PCI) did an effective job of claiming the partisan narrative as its own as the country moved into the postwar moment (other groups, including the Catholic Church, had also been instrumental). The PCI became one of Italy's three major postwar political parties and attracted a significant part of the country's working-class vote. The conservative *Democrazia Cristiana* party (DC) was their main competition (the *Partito Socialista Italiano* made up the third party). The PCI's and the DC's competing claims for power in Italy came to a head in 1948 with the country's first free elections after Fascism, and in the run-up to the election, the outcome appeared highly uncertain. Intervention from the United States proved decisive: shortly after the war, the country began channeling vast amounts of capital into Italy as part of the Marshall Plan for

European reconstruction, an attempt to shore up capitalist democracy across Western Europe and, more pragmatically, to kick-start the continent's ability to trade with the US. The US made it clear that aid would cease to flow to Italy in the case of a communist victory, and though the exact degree of influence this threat exerted is impossible to judge precisely, its goal was realized. The capitalist DC won the election and remained in power (often in coalitions of various forms) until the 1990s. The PCI, although largely excluded from the national government, remained powerful in many regions of the center and North of the country.

The 1948 election had significant economic as well as political consequences. In Paul Ginsborg's (1990, 210) words: "Italy in the mid-1950s was still, in many respects, an under-developed country.... Most Italians still earned their living, if they earned it at all ... in small, technologically backward, labour-intensive firms, in the public administration, in a great proliferation of small shops and trades, in agriculture." Italy's social and economic landscape soon experienced seismic change, however: "The years 1958–63 saw the beginning of a social revolution [in which] Italy ceased to be a peasant country and became one of the major industrial nations of the West" (1990, 212).[12] This period, known as the "economic miracle" or simply *il boom*, was the result of a complex interaction of domestic and international variables. The country's heavy industry infrastructure had been improving since the late 1940s thanks to American aid money, and industry was able to leverage its expanding resources thanks to relatively low labor costs, the removal of protectionism, and significant growth in international trade throughout the 1950s. Italy quickly became a leading player in heavy industry, petrochemicals, and the production of consumer goods (Fiat cars, Olivetti typewriters, and Smeg refrigerators are notable examples).

The rapid increase in Italy's national prosperity translated into a marked but uneven increase in standards of living. Most Italians experienced a significant increase in per capita income, which grew faster from 1950 to 1970 than in any other European country (Ginsborg 1990, 239). Expenditure on automobiles, household appliances, televisions, and leisure activities all increased as the horizon of consumption expanded beyond necessity to include luxury goods. Along with these material advances, social mores began to change as women and young people assumed more personal freedom and patriarchal family models came under threat. The social benefits of industrial-consumerist modernity were tempered by its inconsistencies, however. First, the state did not match its economic stimulus with significant investment in infrastructure, which meant that civic resources languished while personal consumption grew, and the result was an increasing atomization of Italian society. Second, "the 'miracle' heightened the already grave disequilibrium between [Italy's] North and South," the latter of which was still predominantly agricultural and still bore the traces of its feudal history (Ginsborg 1990, 216). Italy's industrial base was concentrated in the North of the country, and the benefits of the miracle mainly went to the workforce in those regions and in Rome. The South, though it, too, underwent an increase in industrial production, experienced a significantly attenuated version of the miracle's socioeconomic benefits. Consequently, there was massive internal migration from the South to the North of Italy in the late 1950s and 1960s as unemployed southern workers moved to cities like Milan, Turin, and Rome in search of work. The third point is connected to this internal migration: in the face of modernization, the Church's influence—including attendance at services and recruitment to the priesthood—declined significantly (1990, 245).

The "boom" was a socially transformative period in Italian history, one that opened the formerly insular country up to the wider world but also exposed latent domestic fault lines. Indeed, the legacy of the "miracle" was characterized by turbulence. The state's continued reluctance to match economic development with reform of its ailing schools and universities led, in part, to widespread unrest among students. In the late 1960s, this unrest spilled over into outright revolt as Italy became embroiled in the international 1968 protest movement.[13] Student protesters soon began to interact with factory workers, and by the "hot autumn" of 1969, the protests had expanded to include (often fractious) factory occupations. Unlike in other countries, the effects of the 1960s protests in Italy extended well into the 1970s (see Downing 2001, 267). Militant left-wing groups such as *Lotta Continua* (Continuous Struggle) and *Brigate Rosse* (Red Brigades) responded to the 1968 movement's failure to effect radical change by adopting violent methods. Factions on the extreme right were also adopting terror tactics at this time in an attempt to unsettle Italian society and pave the way for a return to fascism, and the distinction between left- and right-wing terror attacks was often unclear (see Glynn, Lombardi, and O'Leary 2012). Alan O'Leary (2010, 244) writes, "According to official Ministry for the Interior figures, over 14,000 terrorist attacks were committed in Italy in the years between 1969 and 1983, resulting in 374 deaths and more than 1170 injuries." The period has subsequently become known as the *anni di piombo* (the "years of lead"). Perhaps most iconic of this violence was the Red Brigades' kidnapping and murder of the DC prime minister Aldo Moro in 1978. National media outlets showed images of his incarceration as well as his lifeless body being retrieved from the trunk of a car in Rome.

The destruction and ultimate futility of the "long 1968" led many to abandon the project of collective action. The 1980s saw an increasing withdrawal of Italian life into the private sphere, a phenomenon known as the *riflusso* ("reflux"). This reflux coincided with a period of significant economic deregulation and ushered Italy toward a second socioeconomic watershed, which Ginsborg (2001, ix) argues was as significant as the economic miracle of 1958–63. The 1980s marked Italy's adoption of an individualistic, neoliberal socioeconomic paradigm, the benefits of which were again concentrated in the North of the country and served to exacerbate socioeconomic divisions and wealth inequality by concentrating opportunity in the hands of speculative entrepreneurs. The 1980s were also a period in which wholesale media deregulation flooded Italy with a chaotic mass of media products from around the world, causing an audiovisual maelstrom that revealed the country's role in globalization and the cultural schizophrenia of postmodernism. From the postwar moment to the postmodern moment, then, Italy's history is characterized by virtually continuous, often abrupt, and often uneven change. Suspended between optimism and fear, Italian society from the mid-1940s to the late 1980s presents a complex point of origin for the country's cultural output, including its cinema.[14]

Finally, a very brief account of Italy's postwar film industry is also necessary. Italian neorealism, which gained prominence immediately after the war, was characterized by documentary-style filming that used nonprofessional actors, location shooting in war-ravaged cities, and narratives that tended toward aimlessness and stasis. Neorealism urged audiences simply to witness Italy at a moment of flux and uncertainty and to carefully consider its options for the future. The form was also a break with the escapism and bombast of much Fascist filmmaking, though many neorealist directors had produced Fascist films, and the antecedents of neorealist form can be traced in those earlier works.[15] Neorealism was short-lived, and by the mid-1950s it had given rise to an art cinema movement that reflected on Italy's accelerating modernity with approaches ranging from the oneiric (Federico Fellini) to the existential (Michelangelo Antonioni), historical (Bernardo Bertolucci, Luchino Visconti), and allegorical-political (Pier Paolo Pasolini).[16] As mentioned above, from the 1950s until the 1980s, Italy was also an extremely prolific producer of filone cinema. Foreign films, particularly American, were also a constant presence on Italian cinema screens throughout this period (and remain so).

Italy's huge cinematic output was matched, at least initially, by its domestic consumption. In 1955, for example, the country had 10,570 operational cinemas, twice the number found in the UK (Forgacs and Gundle 2007, 147). In 1972, Italy recorded 553.6 million cinema admissions to the UK's 156.6 million (the two countries had similarly sized populations across this period [Thrower 2017, 110]). Not only did Italian consumption of cinema far outstrip that of other European countries, it initially outstripped other forms of cultural consumption within Italy. In 1960, Italians spent 120,987 billion lire on cinema admissions, compared to 8,191 billion lire on theater and 14,289 billion lire on sports (Gundle 1990, 201). From the mid-1970s, spending on television and radio increased at a far greater rate, and cinema attendance declined. Although cinema's revenues rose throughout the 1970s, ticket sales had been dropping steadily since 1955. In 1955, 819 million tickets had been sold. Ticket sales then fell to 662 million by 1965, and eventually 163 million by 1983 as television became a ubiquitous feature of the Italian household (1990, 203). Italian cinema must also be understood, then, in relation to a wider media landscape. In the second half of the twentieth century, Italian cinema was a dying leviathan, slowly but steadily descending from a state of plenty into a state of crisis as its sociocultural foundations shifted. At a very broad level, this trend shows that Italy's postwar film industry went through significant changes that were closely linked to the broader changes in Italian society. At many specific levels, the complex historical contingencies of Italy's postwar film industry and the wider sociocultural and economic trends that underlay them resonate profoundly in the giallo.

THE STRUCTURE OF *SOUND AND HORROR IN THE GIALLO FILM*

Sound and Horror in the Giallo Film traces the vocal historicity of the giallo over five chapters, each of which focuses on one or two case studies. The chapters proceed chronologically from the giallo's initial emergence (chap. 1) up to its final moments (chap. 5 and the conclusion), but they are also organized conceptually. Each chapter uses the voice to consider how the giallo film was intertwined with a different and specific form of context. *Context* is, of course, a broad term, and this arrangement of chapters helps us understand how the giallo staged active conversations with its historical moment(s) at a range of social, cultural, economic, and political levels (often simultaneously). By using this structure, I hope that *Sound and Horror in the Giallo Film* provides a nuanced account of the giallo's historicity and demonstrates the voice's profound and multivalent power as a means of historicizing films in general.

Notably, I do not dedicate a chapter to gender in this book. This does not mean that this important subject—one of much debate, activism, and change during the giallo's life cycle—is not explored here. Indeed, the giallo often displays an acute interest in liminal, fluid, and uncertain gender identities, and this interest is demonstrated by the use of distorted, disguised, and unrecognized voices. Many gialli feature such ambiguously gendered and acousmatic voices (voices without a visible, on-screen source [Chion (1982) 1999, 21–24]) that often enter the scene via phone calls, intercoms, or tape recordings. Typically, these are the voices of the killers, and they contribute to the "unconventional gender twists" around which the films' conclusions pivot (Mendik 2015, 110). The complex gendering of voices occasionally takes advantage of how these films were made. In Argento's *Deep Red* (*Profondo rosso*, 1975), for example, a minor character named Massimo Ricci (the lover of a more central character, Carlo) is presented as an androgynous man. He is played on-screen, however, by a woman in drag (Geraldine Hooper). Further, Hooper is dubbed by men in both the Italian and English versions of the film.[17] Ricci's uncertain gendering in the film exploits a pragmatic feature of the film's production; the visual and auditory performances that created his character were recorded separately and independently, allowing the filmmakers to align them in an unconventional way (I discuss the separation of image and sound recording in postwar Italian cinema in much more detail below). The combination of female body and male voice that constitute Ricci as a character means that his gender identity can never quite be classified. At both a representational level and a material level, the voice unseats the stability of gender categories in this example and, as the following chapters suggest, many others. While the instability of gender in the giallo has drawn quite a lot of critical attention, I aim to explore these concerns in their sonorous dimensions in a way that helps us grasp these films' wider historicity.[18]

The reasons for choosing the case studies discussed in *Sound and Horror in the Giallo Film* are worth noting. The following five chapters and the conclusion discuss eight principal case studies. Of these, three were directed by Dario Argento, two by Lucio Fulci, and one each by Sergio Martino, Aldo Lado, and Mario Bava (who also directed *Blood and Black Lace*, discussed above). To be sure, these directors' films are canonical gialli. This book is about the giallo broadly—a group of films numbering in the hundreds, many of which are lost and forgotten—so the question is how well the case studies reflect the filone overall. My answer is that the case studies are presented as far as possible as exemplary rather than exceptional. I make this argument in depth in relation to Argento in chapter 2, but none of the chapters are intended as auteur studies (i.e., celebrations of the unique style of a given director). Rather, the films are discussed as particularly salient and graspable examples of the giallo film, with references to other gialli throughout. Since these principal films are reasonably prominent examples of the giallo, there is a wealth of scholarly literature, fan response, and archival material (especially cast and crew interviews) available for each. The access to these resources allows, in turn, for sustained and nuanced research into both the films' textual qualities and their production histories, reducing the need for excessive speculation. I hope that my choice of case studies has allowed me to draw conclusions that might apply to giallo cinema more broadly while recognizing that a filone of such size, longevity, and generic fluidity can never be fully "summed up" and that more research will always be needed.

Chapter 1 considers the intertextual significance of the voice in the giallo, that is, how the voice may connect a single film to a wider collection of other films and texts. This is a useful framework for thinking through the emergence of the giallo film because it allows us to hear how the giallo developed in response to a range of cinematic and literary influences. The chapter focuses on Mario Bava's *The Girl Who Knew Too Much* (*La ragazza che sapeva troppo*, 1963), which is widely if tentatively regarded as the first giallo film. I argue that the sonority of the voice in this film serves as a complex and subtle intertextual gesture. The film features an anonymous male voice-over narrator, whose neutral tone emphasizes the importance of the written words he is reading and, in so doing, foregrounds the film's overt debt to crime and mystery literature. At times, he adopts tones reminiscent of American film noir narration and the voice-overs used in Italian television ads. In this way, the intertextual sonority of the narrator's voice draws together the various cultural influences—both Italian and foreign—that feed into the giallo's cinematic emergence. The increasing heterogeneity of Italy's postwar cultural landscape is consequently imprinted on the film's soundtrack, and the film testifies to the country's rising embrace of consumerism and internationalism. Furthermore, the erratic sonority of the protagonist's voice serves as the other side of this vocal coin, revealing how Rome's fragmentary modernization has rendered the city harder to perceive and talk about clearly. The chapter ends by considering the voice of singer Adriano Celentano, who recorded a song for the film's Italian soundtrack but whose voice was replaced when the film was adapted for Anglo-American release. The presence/absence of Celentano's voice in the different versions of *The Girl Who Knew Too Much* underscores the inseparability of the cinematic voice from the cultural contexts in which a film is produced and circulates.

Chapter 2 examines the role of the giallo director, suggesting that this role can be understood spatially—as establishing spatial relationships among the various elements that make up the film. I contend that the way the director arranges the characters' voices is crucial to this role because the voice always extends through space. The voice establishes spatial relationships between bodies and bodies, and between bodies and the physical environments they inhabit. As a result, the voice plays a vital role in underpinning the director's wider approach to a film's form and in the way a film may highlight certain historically specific themes. The chapter makes this argument through an examination of Dario Argento's directorial debut, *The Bird with the Crystal Plumage* (*L'uccello dalle piume di cristallo*, 1970). Argento's use of the voice in this film suggests that to possess the capacity for clear speech is to determine which sides of the film's many vague spatial borders constitute the "inside" and which constitute the "outside." This is similar to how a cinematic voice-over (which the film does not use directly) separates the inner diegetic world from the outer space of narration.[19] The voice becomes crucial to how the film spatially represents power relationships among different characters. The film further thematizes this issue by showing that the growing ubiquity of auditory technologies in a rapidly industrializing postwar Italy has made this audiospatial paradigm complicated and, for the individual, alienating. Throughout this chapter, I recognize that Argento's career is atypical of the giallo director and is perhaps more similar to that of the art house auteur. Thanks to powerful family connections in Italy's film industry, Argento appears to have been shielded from some of the pragmatic considerations that so often shaped the work and careers of the directors whose work he would end up influencing. *The Bird with the Crystal Plumage* is useful for this chapter because it provides a fruitful case study of a principle that may not be as noticeable in other films; that the director's approach to the voice underpins their approach to space and plays a pivotal role in their film's expression of theme.

Where chapter 2 is primarily concerned with the formal and thematic significance of the voice, chapter 3 concentrates on its industrial and material aspects, mainly the giallo's reliance on dubbing and the complex political implications brought about by the technique in the 1970s. Postwar Italian cinema generally depended on the practice of voice dubbing because the country relied on trans-European coproduction. Dubbing meant that international casts could be used and different soundtracks could be produced for each of a film's distribution markets (films were dubbed even in their Italian versions). Importantly, the increasing use of coproduction frameworks in the decades after the Second World War was part of a wider move toward the sociopolitical integration happening across Europe in this period (through the formation of the Common Market and the North Atlantic Treaty Organization, for example). The chapter argues that dubbing clearly leaves traces of an internationalist, integrationist ideology on the soundtracks of giallo films. However, dubbing's ideological significance in postwar Italian cinema has another layer. The ubiquity of the practice following the war was also a result of its normalization during Italy's Fascist period (1922–43), where it had served in part to facilitate censorship and bolster an ideology of cultural isolationism. This chapter explores the complex and contradictory ideological history of voice dubbing in Italy by taking Aldo Lado's *Short Night of Glass Dolls* (*La corta notte delle bambole di vetro*, 1971) as its case study. Lado's film offers a rich opening onto dubbing's ideological complexity because it uses a stylistic conceit that repeatedly foregrounds its use of the practice. Moreover, the film's narrative stresses that the voice plays a profound role in the political exercise of power. The film encourages us to consider dubbing's industrial basis from a political perspective and highlights that the cinematic voice reflects the ideology—or ideologies—that created it.

Chapter 4 examines the giallo's use of the voice in terms of these films' national context. It does this by shifting focus from the giallo's pronounced interest in the urban and instead examines two films set in rural Italy. Crucially, both films highlight vocal silence. Lucio Fulci's *Don't Torture a Duckling* (*Non si sevizia un paperino*, 1972) aligns the impoverished, rural Italian South with silence, in contrast to the excessively vocal and industrialized North. The film's blunt use of silence suggests that the southerner is somehow less human than the northerner; in this way, the film's use of sound builds on and continues discourses that had been widespread since the nineteenth century. These are views that the film seems to sensationalize for the sake of providing its audience with titillation and intrigue, and so the use of voice in *Don't Torture a Duckling* binds both the commercial imperatives of its production and wider social discourses into the form of its soundtrack. Sergio Martino's *Torso* (*I corpi presentano tracce di violenza carnale*, 1973) similarly casts the urban as a space of vocality and the rural as a space of silence, but the division is not absolute. Rather, the rural is placed in a tense relation to the urban, which always threatens to invade it. Likewise, silence in this film is always charged with the sense that it may suddenly be broken by the scream, and this is particularly clear during the film's long, climactic scene in which the killer hunts the sole survivor of his attacks around the villa in which she is trapped. *Torso*'s use of a rural setting thus serves its commercial need to provide suspense, and silence itself can be understood as a suspenseful resource the filmmakers extract from rural space. In this way, the film's production participates in the sort of extractive relationship that has been a part of the urban-rural dynamic in Italy since Roman times. This relationship is underscored by the film's use of the villa as its main location since the villa has historically served as a structure through which urbanites have occupied rural space and drawn on its resources. In both films, the voice serves to satisfy the giallo's need to provide intrigue and suspense, yet, in so doing, it speaks to very specific sociohistorical dynamics that had long been entrenched in Italy.

Chapter 5 moves from the national perspective to consider how the voice connects the giallo to its international context. The chapter approaches this international context in socioeconomic terms by taking two late and controversial gialli as its case studies: Dario Argento's *Tenebrae* (*Tenebre*, 1982) and Lucio Fulci's *The New York Ripper* (*Lo squartatore di New York*, 1982). These films illustrate how, by the early 1980s, the giallo had become implicated in Italy's entry into a neoliberal economic (and social) paradigm. This paradigm extended across national borders but was centered in the United States, and the fact that both films were set and shot in whole or in part in New York City emphasizes this. *Tenebrae* gives form to this moment in Italy's socioeconomic history by making a range of narrative and, most importantly, aesthetic gestures to commercial television, which exploded in Italy in the late 1970s and early 1980s thanks to the recent deregulation of Italian broadcasting. For much of the film, the camera remains trained on the "talking head" of a speaking character, a tendency that mimics the formal blueprint of television dramas of the period that relied on speech and dialogue to carry their narratives. During its violent set pieces, however, *Tenebrae* abandons this mimicry for a more impressionistic and visually led aesthetic. The film thus evidences the increasing ubiquity of foreign television in the deregulated Italian media landscape while also exploring cinema's persistent distinction from its small-screen cousin. *The New York Ripper* is less systematic in how it draws on the influence of other media. The film is notable for how its killer mimics the voice of Donald Duck during phone calls and while murdering his victims, and the film's repeated invocation of this internationally ubiquitous voice situates the film in a cacophonous and global media landscape. This voice, like several others in the film, can be understood as an aural version of the simulacrum, theorized by philosopher Jean Baudrillard ([1981] 1994) as the copy-without-original that characterizes postmodern cultural production—the signifier that refers to other signifiers rather than to a signified real. *The New York Ripper*'s use of vocal simulacra both demonstrates and participates in a postmodern moment in which the simulacrum had come to dominate media production and in which national borders were becoming increasingly blurry. As in *Tenebrae*, the formal use to which the voice is put in Fulci's film therefore speaks beyond the borders of the text and intimately connects the film to ongoing social, cultural, and economic developments that were global but were particularly noticeable in Italy.

Sound and Horror in the Giallo Film concludes with a meditation on the nature of the cinematic voice itself and a reflection on its value as an entry point into a film's historicity. It does so by briefly attending to one of the last giallo films, Dario Argento's *Opera* (1987), and by using the film to consider the similarities between the voice in opera and the giallo. Both engage in a pursuit of the voice in pure form; opera via the ecstatic high notes of the aria, the giallo via the scream. Both similarly exist between the artistic and the commercial, the avant-garde and the generic, the national and the international. The voice is crucial to how opera and the giallo negotiate these borders. The conclusion ultimately suggests that the voice in *any* audiovisual text operates as a mediator among a range of aesthetic, commercial, social, cultural, and economic imperatives. As it proceeds from one utterance to the next, shifting its sonorous qualities and its structural role in the text as it does so, the voice enacts an ongoing conversation between text and context(s), overlapping the two and staging the text's embeddedness in its historical moment. In the case of the giallo, this conversation reveals that, in various ways, these films both responded to and participated in Italy's complex postwar history. This is, however, one conversation among many. The relationships staged by the voice among other forms of horror cinema and their social, cultural, economic, and political contexts remain to be heard.

PICKING UP THE PHONE

Returning to *Blood and Black Lace*, what are we to make of the red phone, swinging by its cord in the film's final seconds? On the one hand, it points to the basic importance of sound in the film's narrative. All of the murders in *Blood and Black Lace* are about sound in a basic sense. They stem from the killers' need to keep the models quiet, to stop them from talking and revealing aloud incriminating details about the diary or the things they have seen. To a large extent, Massimo and Cristiana's violence is an exercise in sound management, and the phone mocks their film-long efforts to secure the silence of everyone in the atelier. On the other hand, the phone, as both an object and an infrastructure that mediates vocal relations, performs formal and thematic roles in the film and emphasizes the voice's importance to the industry that produced the film.

Telephony serves *Blood and Black Lace*'s narrative form quite straightforwardly. Several of the film's characters make phone calls that are often conducted in hushed voices and that establish alliances between some characters while keeping sensitive information out of the earshot of others. There are two plastic phones in the atelier: one that is entirely red and another with a red base and a black handset. These phones are contrasted to another in Peggy's home, which appears to be older and made at least partly of metal. Peggy answers this phone when Silvestri calls her, and the film cuts between the two as they talk so that we see both sides of their rather banal conversation. Three calls are conducted on the atelier's red phones: two between model Nicole and her partner Frank, in which they discuss their need to rifle through the diary and Frank asks Nicole to secure drugs for him. Frank remains unseen. The third is between Cristiana and Massimo where he informs her that he and the other men connected to the atelier have been arrested. The audience does not hear Massimo's half of the conversation in this instance, however, so they can never be sure exactly what information he (if it is him) is imparting. The interlocking and intersecting alliances that these calls layer on top of each other deepen the intrigue of the narrative and create fertile ground for suspicion and emotional investment on the part of the audience. The phone call also seems to ask more questions than it answers in the film. Since we often only hear (and see) half of the film's telephone conversations, the vocal relationships they support are vague. Who is really on the line? More importantly, where are they? Nearby? Far away? Where they say they are or somewhere else? The voice on the telephone gives little of this information away.[20] In part, this is because the telephone's microphone and speaker isolate the voice and detach it from the specificities of its spatial context. Rick Altman (1992, 24) describes the way in which the qualities of a sound (its volume, reverberation, timbre, and so forth) give us clues as to the space in which it has been created and through which it has traveled to reach our ears. He refers to these auditory clues as the sound's "spatial signature." The telephonic voice, in this sense, is unsigned. It is a voice displaced; we know that the person we are speaking to on the phone is elsewhere, but we rarely know their precise location. As such, the telephone adds "where" to "who" and "why" among the questions of suspense that propel *Blood and Black Lace*'s narrative. In the words of Marc Olivier (2020, 61), "Telephonic horror recovers the disorientation of telephony; it jostles the system and puts telephonic space simultaneously out of reach and too close for comfort." Like the camera that prowls around the atelier and like the killers' tendency to spring from the shadows or from the space beyond the frame, the frequent use of telephone calls in *Blood and Black Lace* means that we never quite have the film's spatial dynamics under control. Like the killer, the voice on the phone could be coming from anywhere. By existing in a sinister nowhere between near and far, the telephonic voice subtly contributes to the mood as much as the mechanics of the film's form.

Yet as well as supporting *Blood and Black Lace*'s generation of tension, the phone speaks to the film's thematic engagement with its historical moment. The red telephone on which *Blood and Black Lace*'s final shot fixates might symbolize Italy's economic miracle and its shift toward greater industrialization and consumerism. It is a bold object that could well be the product of the expansive growth in petrochemical engineering experienced by the country after the war, and the profusion of plastic goods that this industrial development led to.[21] This is an industrial-economic shift that is explored more concertedly in Michelangelo Antonioni's *Red Desert* (*Deserto rosso*), which was also released in 1964 and dwells on Italy's new factories as well as the plastic goods (and pollution) they produce. Putting this unlikely pair of films side by side demonstrates how broadly Italy's industrial changes were affecting Italian society at that time and reminds us that objects (including props in films) are often the tips of much bigger historical icebergs. The social effect of the telephone in *Blood and Black Lace* is unclear, however; it appears to both uphold and trouble the status quo. Silvestri uses the telephone to pursue his investigation and restore social order to the atelier (the reason the phone is hanging from its hook in the final shot is that Cristiana had attempted to call the police), yet elsewhere phone calls—particularly those made on the atelier's plastic phones—facilitate drug dealing and criminal action. The uncertain "moral" position of the telephone in the film thus supports Mikel Koven's (2006, 16) observation that if there is one "discourse that is common across the entire *giallo* cinema, it is that these films display a marked ambivalence toward modernity." If the phone and its usage reference Italy's changing social landscape, the handset's ultimate silence speaks volumes. The silence of the red phone can be read thematically as the sound of ambivalence, of a verdict not yet reached.

But who might we expect to hear on the other end of the line? Another character, presumably, which is to say an actor. Except it would not be an actor, exactly, but a voice actor. All we hear throughout the film are the voices of voice actors, who may or (more often) may not be the same as the actors we see on-screen. As mentioned in the summary of chapter 3, almost all films made in Italy in the 1960s were dubbed due to both historical habit and the practical considerations of coproduction. *Blood and Black Lace* is no exception. The film was an Italian/West German/Monegasque collaboration featuring Italian, German, American, French, and Hungarian-British actors, and it exists in multiple versions. The Italian, English, and German are still widely available, and all were dubbed in postproduction (only a guide track, in English, was recorded on set). Some actors dubbed themselves in their native tongues, but none would have dubbed themselves in every version.[22] In any case, every actor seen on-screen is, in truth, silent. Each is a puppet ventriloquized by a voice recorded at another time in a sound studio elsewhere. The silence of the swinging phone, therefore, emphasizes the necessary silence of every voice on set, the fact that nothing we see on-screen generates a sound that we can hear. Like the to-be-dubbed actor, it implies a voice that is yet to be added. Its silence, and the true silence of everything we see on-screen, ultimately allowed companies from three countries to cooperate and, in their small way, to strengthen the economic links that crossed their geopolitical borders. The phone swings silently, the actors perform lines on set that will never be heard, and, perhaps, the film industries of postwar Europe draw together a bit more tightly.

So, if the swinging phone that closes out *Blood and Black Lace* invites us to focus on the importance of sound to the film, it is with good reason. Alongside the dreamlike visuals that so easily attract or distract our attention when we watch the film, sound—especially the voice—propels its narrative, undergirds its form, and connects the film to its wider historical context both thematically and materially. Indeed, the voice in the film resonates at each of these levels simultaneously so that context is tangibly woven into text. Listening closely to the giallo is to eavesdrop on history, and while *Blood and Black Lace*'s final shot may be a joke or a throwaway callback to an earlier shot, it is also an invitation to start listening closely. *Sound and Horror in the Giallo Film* is an effort to accept that invitation.

NOTES

1. Although the term *filone* is still in use in contemporary Italian cinema, I focus here on what one might term the "golden age" of filone cinema, which ran from around 1950 until the late 1980s (see Tortaro 2011), at which point the explosion of commercial television in Italy rendered this type of filmmaking largely redundant.

2. All translations from Italian are my own unless otherwise stated.

3. This list is far from exhaustive (see Tortaro 2011).

4. See Kannas 2017 for an incisive discussion of the filone's relationship to both genre and notions of hybridity.

5. According to Cozzi (interview with author 2019), many producers would establish "fake" coproduction alliances with companies in other countries and collect subsidies from both without genuine collaboration taking place.

6. One might also add to this list fourth-run cinemas and parish cinemas operated by the Church.

7. Cozzi (interview with author 2019) was keen to stress that not *all* third-run cinemas fit this model, however.

8. It is important to note here that most technical and creative personnel in Italy's postwar film industry worked across both art and filone cinema in their careers.

9. Christopher Wagstaff (1992, 246) estimates that around 450 Westerns were produced by Italian companies between 1964 and 1978. Peter Bondanella (2009, 373) estimates that "several hundred" gialli were made in the 1960s and 1970s, and Danny Shipka (2011, 71) suggests it was "more than 250."

10. Though beyond the scope of this summary, on the influence of fumetti, see Hunt 2016. On the influence of the krimi, see Koven 2006, 5; Sanjek 1994.

11. See also Whittaker and Sarah Wright's edited volume, *Locating the Voice in Film: Critical Approaches and Global Perspectives* (2017) for a range of shorter investigations of this nature.

12. Due to internal demand, Italy's economy had actually been growing, though at a slower rate, since 1950 (Ginsborg 1990, 214).

13. Alongside their complaints about Italy's education system, many of the protesters were also hostile to the materialism and individualism that characterized the country's postboom society (Ginsborg 1990, 300).

14. Specific elements of this cursory outline will be elaborated on throughout the following chapters. For monograph-length studies of Italy's recent history, see Ginsborg 1990, 2001; Silveri 2019. For an extremely detailed study of the period from 1968 to 1980, see Lumley 1990.

15. For an in-depth account of the continuity between Fascist filmmaking and neorealism, see Leavitt 2020.

16. These illustrative labels are reductive; many of these directors experimented with multiple approaches to form and most had previously worked under the umbrella of neorealism. Further, the filmmakers noted here represent only some of Italy's most critically celebrated auteurs, and this list is by no means definitive.

17. Renato Cortesi provides the Italian track, and, while the English dubber is uncredited, I recognize his voice as that of prolific giallo voice actor Frank von Kuegelgen.

18. For more on gender in the giallo, see, for example, Hunt 1992; Knee 1996; Reich 2001; Mendik 2015; Lachetti 2017.

19. The "diegesis" of a film refers to the world of the narrative, the world "lived in" and "experienced" by a film's characters. Anything that pertains to this world may be described as diegetic, whereas elements of a film that are not part of that world (music that only the audience can hear or a voice-over, for example) may be described as nondiegetic.

20. The threatening undertone of the telephone call in *Blood and Black Lace* was previously explored by Bava in his film *Black Sabbath* (*I tre volti della paura*, 1963). This film is a three-part anthology of horror and thriller shorts, the first of which is a giallo-esque episode titled "The Telephone" ("Il telefono"), in which a call girl named Rosy is menaced by a series of threatening phone calls.

21. The film points to this phenomenon elsewhere too. When the killer steals Peggy's car, he is spotted by a garage engineer who is later interviewed

by Silvestri. In both scenes, the logo of the Italian oil company Eni is clearly visible on an illuminated sign and the engineer's uniform, which suggests that the presence of such industry was becoming omnipresent by the mid-1960s.

22. Most of the male voices in the English dub of the film were, in fact, provided by a single voice actor: Paul Frees.

ONE

INTERTEXTUAL VOICES

The Girl Who Knew Too Much

THE TRANSITION OF THE GIALLO from literature to film was a transition from the silence of the written word to the sonority of the spoken word. Mario Bava's *The Girl Who Knew Too Much* (*La ragazza che sapeva troppo*, 1963) is widely regarded as the first film to have successfully achieved this move, but not without a string of caveats. Strangely, it might have been both too late and too early to qualify as the first giallo film. The bleak criminality of Luchino Visconti's *Obsession* (*Ossessione*, 1943) seems to preempt it, and Leon Hunt (2022, 85) points out that Mario Camerini's comedy-thriller *Giallo* (1933) had used some of the tropes found in Bava's film thirty years earlier. However, the surreal and colorful visual aesthetic and prowling camerawork, not to mention explicit violence—which would soon be quintessential of this *filone*—did not appear until Bava's *Blood and Black Lace* in 1964 (see introduction) and Dario Argento's gialli of the early 1970s. Nonetheless, I have chosen to begin this book with *The Girl Who Knew Too Much* because of the film's effort to highlight its printed ancestors and expressly translate giallo literature into the realm of cinema. In Alexia Kannas's (2017, 185) words, "From its inception, [the] cinematic *giallo* engages reflexively with its roots in literary tales of mystery and crime, and with earlier and contemporaneous Italian and global cinema positioned across the spectrum of taste." Certainly, Bava's film is openly intertextual in the sense that it incorporates elements drawn from other texts and media. For example, its title refers to Alfred Hitchcock's two versions of *The Man Who Knew Too Much* (1934, 1956); its black-and-white cinematography seems to pay homage to Hitchcock's later *Psycho* (1960; Lucas 2007, 448); and its plot combines the setup of Billy Wilder's *Roman Holiday* (1953) with the criminal premise of Agatha Christie's Hercule Poirot whodunit (i.e., giallo) novel *The ABC Murders* ([1936] 2013).[1]

The Girl Who Knew Too Much was a three-way collaboration between American International Pictures and two Italian producers, Galatea and Coronet. Released in Italy in 1963 and the UK and US in 1964, it was significantly reworked for English-speaking audiences and retitled *The Evil Eye* (I discuss this in more detail at the end of this chapter). The plot of the Italian version—the one I am principally concerned with in this chapter—is a convoluted but ultimately rather simple murder mystery. Nora Davis (Letícia Román) is a young American and giallo novel obsessive who comes to Rome to visit a sick family friend, Ethel. Ethel dies soon after Nora's arrival, and Nora runs to fetch Marcello Bassi (John Saxon), the young attending doctor, but she is mugged on the Spanish Steps and passes out. She comes to a short while later to witness the murder of a young woman by an older man before passing out again. The next day, in the hospital, she is told that she hallucinated the murder, but she continues to believe that she saw it happen. Nora and Bassi investigate, develop a romantic relationship, and eventually team up with journalist Andrea Landini (Dante Di Paolo). It is ultimately revealed that the murder did indeed take place and was connected to a series of killings perpetrated years earlier by a murderer known as the Alphabet Killer. Landini had published articles on this first spate of killings and had helped to get the wrong man arrested, a down-and-out known as Straccianeve. This allowed the true killer, Laura Craven Torrani (Valentina Cortese)—Ethel's neighbor and Nora's friend—to go free. The woman Nora witnessed being murdered was Straccianeve's daughter, who had uncovered the truth and was blackmailing Laura; the older man was Laura's husband and seemingly enslaved assistant, who was disposing of the body. Laura is about to murder Nora for knowing too much before her husband shoots her through a closed door and Nora and Bassi escape to start a new life.

My contention in this chapter is that the film's use of voice—principally, its use of an anonymous voice-over—underpins specific intertextual gestures in *The Girl Who Knew Too Much*. It does so by functioning as an element of the film's form where the influence of crime literature intersects and merges with the cinematic influence of film noir as well as the less-obvious influence of Italy's boom-era television advertising. The term *text* is derived from the Latin "textus," meaning (among other things) "web" or "woven fabric." To turn this history into metaphor, if the multiple forms *The Girl Who Knew Too Much* draws on are strands woven together into a cinematic fabric, the voice is akin to a kind of textual loom. The sound of the voice-over shifts throughout the film and calls on different intertexts with each shift, binding them together and incorporating them into the fabric of the film.

The many intertextual gestures performed by the voice in Bava's film also emphasize the fact that *The Girl Who Knew Too Much* involved a broad and international collaboration of filmmaking professionals (typical of 1960s genre film production in Italy). The voice in *The Girl Who Knew Too Much* is marked by both the giallo's textual influences and the practical, economic realities of the giallo's emergence as a cinematic filone. Context is a concrete matter of form rather than (or as well as) a matter of content in Bava's film. The film thus reveals a broader truth about the cinematic voice: with any utterance, the voice may mimic, resemble, or otherwise resonate with voices found in other texts, whether because of conscious intention, shared convention, or common necessity. The voice infuses the film text with the echoes of other texts. In this way, the cinematic voice speaks to the sociocultural context that has brought those texts together.

THE SOUND OF THE VOICE AS AN INTERTEXTUAL ALLUSION

There is a long-standing philosophical distinction that can shed light (or, perhaps, turn up the volume) on how *The Girl Who Knew Too Much* uses the human voice. This is the distinction between logos (the word spoken) and phonos (the sound of the voice itself). Since antiquity, philosophical thought has been concerned with the stakes of the voice's ongoing negotiation of word and sound, and the potential conflict between the two. Italian philosopher Adriana Cavarero ([2003] 2005, 12–13) explains that the voice itself has been marginalized in dominant Western discourses. She writes that "outside speech, the voice is nothing but an insignificant leftover . . . logocentrism radically denies to the voice a meaning of its own that is not always already destined to speech." When Cavarero uses the word *voice* here, she is referring to phonos, the sound of the voice. According to Cavarero, the Western model of rationality prioritizes the word, which stands in for thought, universal reason, and intellect, and is gendered male. The sound of the voice, however, is aligned with emotion, irrationality, personal particularity, and the body and is gendered female. Logocentrism, in turn, is a philosophical tendency to favor words (and the thoughts they express) because words are universal and rational and can consequently provide access to truth. Personal trivialities like the sound of the voice are considered irrelevant and potentially distracting. The broader point that underpins Cavarero's analysis (which takes in examples from a wide range of cultural and philosophical contexts) is that the sound of the voice is independent of the words it utters, however mutually implicated the two may seem during an act of speech.

The vocal split between logos and phonos is vital to how Bava's film brings together the various intertexts on which it depends. The film's premise displays a strong interest in depersonalized, alphabetic logic. It is this logic that is used by the Alphabet Killer as she murders women by name to create a smokescreen for her true motives. Laura Craven Torrani murders an innocent woman whose surname begins with A, then another whose surname begins with B so that when she achieves her goal of murdering her sister (surname Craven), her true motives will be hidden by her fake alphabetic rationale. Cavarero ([2003] 2005, 82) argues that alphabetic writing is the logocentric schema par excellence because it "consists substantially in a muting of speech. Substituting the acoustic sphere with a visual map, the written sign translates sound and eliminates it." At the heart of this elimination of sound is, for Cavarero, a denial of the body in which the voice's sonority is rooted, and, indeed, the bodies of Laura's victims are eradicated by her plan, which is almost a caricature of logocentrism. Laura explains that her first victim "hadn't done me any harm, but I had no choice. Her name began with an 'A'!" Laura's elimination of her victims' bodies is the logical consequence of her ruthlessly rational, disembodying alphabetic ruse. What is more, Laura's frequent disembodying of her voice via anonymous phone calls and tape recordings separates her words from her body as if to grant each one maximum independence.

It is precisely in its otherness to alphabetic logic that the sound of the voice gains an insurgent potential in the film. Laura prepares to kill Nora, saying, "I know you won't say a word. I'm certain of it. When they find you, you won't be able to talk." With this comment, Laura recognizes that the voice can be dangerous because it is personal, potentially "irrational," and therefore uncontrollable. It cannot be tamed by the rigid logos of Laura's alphabetical scheme. Elsewhere in the film, Nora tells Bassi that he will know when she is ready to become romantically involved "by the sound of my voice," and it is the sound of Straccianeve's wails, as he is taken to jail, that ultimately convinces Landini of his innocence. In both cases, the *sound* of the voice fleetingly impedes the relentless march of logic. The embodied voice is eventually Laura's undoing when she is shot through a closed door by her dying husband as she finishes her final speech. The implication is that the sound of her voice has provided her husband with a clue as to the location of her body behind the door and has allowed him to aim correctly. The embodied sonority of Laura's voice at this moment undoes the disembodying effect of her earlier use of sound technology; it localizes her and leaves her vulnerable to mortal injury.

An interesting element of *The Girl Who Knew Too Much*, and so many of the films discussed in the following chapters, is how the manipulation of the voice at the narrative or thematic level echoes important work done by the voice at the level of the text's materiality (its nuts-and-bolts construction). The distinction between logos and phonos provides a framework through which the film collects and joins together the various cultural influences from which it draws. So much is clear from the opening scene when the camera looks down on the jetliner carrying Nora to Italy and a nondiegetic voice-over proclaims, "This is the story of a holiday." The voice is male, perhaps early middle age, level, and professionally upbeat. It is very similar to the style of voice-over that had become commonplace in Italy by 1963 via the Istituto Luce's state newsreel documentaries, which were often used to communicate information about the social and infrastructural developments made possible by the economic miracle. (This was a broad mode of filmmaking that Bava became familiar with during the Fascist period when he worked as a cameraman at the Istituto Luce and contributed to overtly propagandistic films [see Lucas 2007, 65–80].) Yet this voice-over carries something of the literary too. The narrator continues setting the scene as the camera tracks down the plane's cabin, toward Nora and the crime paperback she is reading. He states that Nora reads giallo novels to escape reality, but "this would be the last one." It is unclear whether the narrator is referring to the novel Nora is reading, the film the viewer is watching, or both, and so the distinction between film and book falters as soon as it is established. The voice-over at once stands as the narrator of a film and the narrator of a novel, while the film itself becomes a sort of hall of mirrors; Nora is at once reading a murder mystery novel and yet somehow folded into the novel's narrative.

Also important here is the narrator's relatively neutral tone. While his voice recalls the voice-overs used in newsreels, it is also literary in the way it prioritizes the words spoken. To return to Cavarero ([2003] 2005), the voice-over's evenness and lack of distracting emotion neatens the "insignificant leftover" of its actual sound; it clears a path for the words. In the opening moments of *The Girl Who Knew Too Much*, the voice is subordinated to logical information. It is as if the narrator is merely and transparently reading from the first page of Nora's novel. From his first utterance, the narrator has one foot in the cinematic and one in the literary, and he refashions the shot we see on screen as something like a page in a book. In general, the cinematic voice-over necessarily directs attention to written words; it exists purely to articulate words and address them to an audience. My contention regarding Bava's film, though, is that the figure of the literary narrator is folded directly into the film. The combination of the initial voice-over paired with shots of Nora's book and the narrator's neutral tone emphasizing *words* prompts the audience to understand the film in terms of the literary works that preceded it. In short, in its first manifestation, the voice-over serves as a condensation of the film's debt to literature.

As he announces "This is the story of a holiday," the narrator implies his mastery of the narrative we are about to witness. Like the third-person "Voice-of-God" narrator of a novel or documentary film, the voice-over hovers just beyond the limits of the narrative world. From this vantage point, the narrator suggests that he has an omniscient perspective on the story's events. This presumed authority is short-lived though, and its demise is central to how the film speaks to its wider textual and cultural context. First, the voice-over's utterances are unevenly distributed across the film: after the initial scene setting, the narrator falls mute until he offers a smattering of commentaries just before the midpoint. He then falls silent again until his final commentary shortly before the film's end. This intermittency suggests that the supposedly authorial voice has an unsteady control of the narrative, and this idea is supported by the changing nature of the voice itself. In the cluster of statements made toward the middle of the film, the voice-over no longer directs or controls what we see but repeats information given moments earlier by Laura's doorkeeper. He is led by the film's narrative rather than leading it. At one point, his words merge with Nora's internally voiced reading of some newspaper clippings that she finds during her investigation. Later, he vocalizes her inner thoughts: "It was useless for them [Bassi and a colleague] to comfort her." Here, the disembodied voice-over experiences a form of pseudoembodiment through its close alignment with Nora's interiority. In fact, the final voice-over of the film is an internal monologue by Nora, which suggests that by the end of the film, the narrator has been fully embodied by her. Finally, in the middle of the film, the *sound* of the voice-over becomes increasingly marked. He breathlessly rushes and yelps his words in line with Nora's state of tension, exclaiming, "That's right!" as she hatches a plan for foiling potential intruders using talcum powder. At other times, he whispers as if trying to avoid being heard by anyone lurking unseen in the scene (Sevastakis 2016, 17). The increasingly notable sonority of the narrator's speech shows that this voice-over is no longer separate from the diegesis in the style of an omniscient, third-person literary or cinematic narrator. Rather, the narrator is firmly and responsively involved in the narrative's events, spaces, and soundscape. The narrating voice has, in a sense, been pulled into the story.

The voice-over's shift from neutrality to emotional sonority marks a significant change in the film's overall tone. The narrator moves from a commanding third-person perspective to a fallible, quasi-first-person position. This is a shift from a model of narrator-as-author to one of narrator-as-character. It is also a shift of allusion from the literary to the cinematic. Specifically, the emotional voice-over alludes to film noir, an American style of filmmaking that originated in the 1940s and is distinguished by crime-driven plots and cynical social attitudes typically presented through shadowy, black-and-white photography. By 1963, film noir had long been popular in Italy. Mary Wood (2007, 239) explains that during Fascism, "American gangster films were freely imported into Italy on the basis that they showed the decadence of US society and values of rampant individualism foreign to the corporate fascist state." In both Visconti's *Obsession* and Michelangelo Antonioni's *Story of a Love Affair* (*Cronaca di un amore*, 1950), domestically produced Italian cinema incorporates elements of film noir's narrative and visual style (interestingly, both films draw on James Cain's crime novel *The Postman Always Rings Twice*). Wood (2007, 249–50) argues, however, that "for popular expressions of noir in the 1950s and 1960s, we have to go to mid- to low-budget genre films" and specifically gives those of Bava as an example. Certainly, the shadowy sets, canted (diagonally slanted) camera angles, cast of dubious characters, and plot full of murder and intrigue in *The Girl Who Knew Too Much* all clearly gesture to noir traditions. Against these visual allusions, the film's shift from a calm, controlled narrating voice to a frantic and subjective voice-over marks its most complex engagement with film noir. J. P. Telotte (1980, 15) argues that in film noir, the voice-over "suggest[s] an eruption of the subjective in a world that we initially see in a conventional, objective manner." For Joan Copjec (1993, 185), this subjectivity is signaled in "the grain or laboring of the voice-over as well as its periodic diegeticization [which is] proof of the faltering of the hero's knowledge, his inability to control or comprehend the image." The noir voice-over is infused with grain, a distinct sonority determined by the uniqueness of the speaker's body. The graininess of the noir voice-over is significant because it constantly reminds us that this voice stems from a single person, limited in their perception and subjective in their take on events.[2] The Italian dubs of American film noirs were careful to replicate the all-too-human sonority of their voice-over narration. In this way, the sudden increase in the sonority of the narrator's voice highlights film noir as a key influence on the film's textual constitution. The humanization and "diegeticization" of the voice-over—its being drawn into the story rather than remaining aloof from it—thus signals an entry into a new generic framework. With its shift to a more frantic phonos, in other words, the voice-over in *The Girl Who Knew Too Much* comes to resonate in a more complex intertextual network. The voice here straddles the border not only between the film and its literary precedents but also between the film and its cinematic near-contemporaries.

Film noir represented a set of cinematic tropes that *The Girl Who Knew Too Much* could tap into, engage, and activate alongside its references to mystery literature. In transitioning from a use of voice that references the author of written works to one that evokes the diegetic or semidiegetic narrator of film noir, the voice-over adds a layer of cinematic intertextual reference to its literary allusions. In so doing, it connects the film to a broader set of recognizable cultural references it seemingly wanted to capitalize on. That is, the voice-over and its aural mutability are central to what Valentina Vitali (2016, 60) characterizes as Bava's workmanlike "exploitation of well-tested sales points" in the film. Vitali (2016, 69) goes on to argue that reading Bava's work in terms of the challenges involved in Italian film production at the time "opens up his films to the actual constituents of the force field that the films can be seen to mediate." I argue that, in *The Girl Who Knew Too Much*, the voice-over drives this process of mediation. It collects and weaves together the various constituents of the cultural force field from which the film is emerging and to which it is very tangibly, and very audibly, still attached.

The connection between *The Girl Who Knew Too Much* and film noir is complicated by the fact that film noir was intimately linked to the same crime literature that the film draws on. The giallo literature Nora is obsessed with includes the hard-boiled American crime paperbacks that inspired film noir (it also includes English and German murder mysteries, as the narrator recognizes when he says that Nora has "appealed to Wallace, to Mickey Spillane, to Agatha Christie" when concocting a plan to defend herself). By sonorously replicating the voice-overs of film noir, *The Girl Who Knew Too Much* therefore refers to cinematic intertexts and redoubles its allusions to these books in the same breath. Speaking of the film's narration in general, Vitali (2016, 67) argues: "The narrator progresses as if suspended in a search for the most suitable means . . . to bring new layers out onto the already overloaded surface of the text." This process is driven specifically by changes in the sonority of the voice-over. By moving from calm and neutral to strained and frantic, the voice-over evokes the film's literary and cinematic influences, and it overlays and fuses the two. The voice-over emphasizes the mix of registers that characterizes both the film and filone filmmaking more widely.[3]

Curiously, *The Girl Who Knew Too Much* uses the voice-over in a way that sometimes complicates the very division between logos and phonos. The idea that the sound of the voice is entirely separate from the voice's power to signify never quite rings true in practice. Nina Sun Eidsheim (2019, 34) has questioned precisely this division regarding song, arguing that "singing is always made up of entrainment, style, and technique but is generally mistaken for essence." The very sound of the voice signifies in this sense; it is a performance that draws on technical and cultural convention to tell the listener something about the singer and then to disguise that "something" as an essential, natural, and inalienable aspect of the singer's identity. (Eidsheim's principal concern is with the vocal performance of racial or ethnic identity.) She continues: "The material voice manifests cultural and societal values and dynamics of power in its habituation of ligaments, muscles, and tendons, and sounds timbral identity categories accordingly" (2019). In other words, Eidsheim's view on phonos (which diverges from Cavarero's) is that it often invites logocentric signification in by the back door. In this sense, the intrusion of phonos into the narrator's voice is far from frivolous—it is an important act of signification by which the film stresses its intertextual constitution.

The voice-over narration of *The Girl Who Knew Too Much* points to the film's intertextual design, which plays to the wider emphasis on intertextuality that characterized the Mondadori publishing company's distribution of giallo literature. As Jane Dunnett (2010) has described, Mondadori's advertising of giallo paperbacks favored the interconnected collection of texts over the single work. The novels were consistently published with the yellow covers that gave the giallo its name and unified them into a singular collection. Dunnett (2010, 70) explains that "each book recorded, in capital letters, the number of 'Libri Gialli' published thus far, thereby seeking to assert and reinforce the popularity of the series." Bumper anthologies were also common (the cover design of the book Nora reads on the plane suggests that it contains two stories). So was intertextual advertising: "The books themselves served to promote the series by advertising other titles at the end of each volume and by giving details of how to take out a subscription to 'I Libri Gialli'" (2010, 69). Mondadori used these marketing strategies to establish giallo literature as a single intertextual network. A single text could be read and understood only in connection with the wider series it belonged in and referred to. The various references made by the voice-over narrator in *The Girl Who Knew Too Much* to other texts, genres, and media similarly serve to position the film within a broad intertextual network. The dynamic sonority of the voice-over functions like an audible extension of the yellow dustjacket, situating this cinematic prototype alongside other familiar cultural products.

THE TROUBLE WITH VOICING MODERNITY

For all its complexity, the voice-over is only one of several voices through which *The Girl Who Knew Too Much* establishes intertextual connections. The voice of Nora's friend Ethel serves a similar purpose during her death at the beginning of the film. Ethel sounds energetic and in reasonable health when the two women reunite in her bedroom, but as Nora starts to arrange her things in the next room, she hears the older woman desperately call her name. Ethel cries, "Nora!" as thunder crashes outside and the apartment's lights go out, leaving Nora in shadows with only a candle unevenly lighting the space around her. Ethel's call is strangled and barely human; it sounds like the ghostly note of a death rattle. When Nora runs to the bedroom, Ethel stammers briefly, on the border between speech and breath, before dying. The shift in Ethel's voice from the convivial to the ghoulish is as abrupt as the arrival of thunder and loss of electricity; it signals the film's first generic key change. The early emphasis on giallo literature is suddenly (but momentarily) replaced with the atmosphere of the gothic. Ethel's death cry coincides with the seeming reanimation of her body a moment later (it turns out to be her cat clawing at her duvet) and the flickering of the candles in the room to mark this generic shift. The scene of Ethel's death could have been staged differently of course, and different stagings would require different vocal performances. Even set against the same scene, a sigh or whimper instead of a cry could move the film toward melodrama; an exaggerated or prolonged gasping could move it toward slapstick comedy. Instead, the fatal tones of Ethel's last word recall the gothic horror film. Indeed, Bava had previously made *Black Sunday* (*La maschera del demonio*, 1960), a gothic horror loosely based on Nikolai Gogol's *The Viy* (1835), and that film is replete with the sort of bloodcurdling cries that Ethel utters as she dies.

Nora tries to call the hospital, but the man's voice on the phone is distorted; he cannot hear her. She then says, "I can't hear anything," before hanging up. At this point, it seems that all the voices around Nora occupy a slightly different astral plane from her, and she assumes the gothic bearing of the isolated woman alone in an unfamiliar, shadowy house. Indeed, as Keith Brown (2012, 184) notes, Nora's characterization as a naive, lost young woman struggling to comprehend her surroundings makes the film "a peculiarly Gothic *giallo* [perhaps even] an unconscious reworking of Jane Austen's gothic parody *Northanger Abbey*." As Brown recognizes, the critical distinction between the gothic and giallo only emerged retrospectively, after *The Girl Who Knew Too Much* was released. It is unlikely that either the filmmakers or the initial audiences noticed a clear division between Bava's gothic work and this less supernatural thriller. The gothic atmosphere of Ethel's death dissipates as the noirish concerns of a (seemingly) rational criminal investigation emerge. It reappears fleetingly, though, such as when Nora is drawn through an empty office block by the ghostly sound of Laura's disembodied voice. Again, the film is best seen as a mix of preexisting (and commercially viable) generic and formal models merging, cross-pollinating, and evolving. This evolution is audible, and the generic resonance of Ethel's strangled final cry illustrates how even very brief vocalizations can reach beyond a film and bring in specific aspects of other texts and genres. It also helps us understand how the different voices on a film's soundtrack might be used to map the complex generic terrain on which a film is building.

Following Ethel's death, Nora's attempts to communicate are often hindered by the sonority of her voice. The policeman who finds her on the Spanish Steps after the murder asks her what happened. Still dazed, she moans and cries. Mistaking him for the murderer, she pleads, "Let me go! I won't say a word!" Clear speech matters little here. In the following scene, a doctor explains to a group of medical students that Nora is an alcoholic, and her protests are shouted in an agitated tone of panic that markedly contrasts with the doctor's calm logocentric delivery. Nora's tendency toward sonorous screams and cries is consistent throughout the film, and her resulting estrangement from logos is connected to her inability to clearly perceive the spaces around her. As Cavarero ([2003] 2005, 35) explains, the voice as a conveyor of meaning is dependent on the eye because, through sight, one accesses the knowledge in which speech may be grounded.[4] To speak rationally, it is first necessary to see clearly. Clear vision eludes Nora throughout *The Girl Who Knew Too Much*, however. The mise-en-scène, lighting design, and camera placement during the murder scene on the Spanish Steps, for example, are all calculated to maximize the scene's obscurity: many shots are filmed at disorienting Dutch (slanted) angles; shadowy lighting and backlighting are used extensively to veil foreground details; a water screen (created by Bava) placed in front of the camera blurs midground and background details; and shots are often in hazy soft focus (fig. 1.1).[5] These visual choices initially seem to represent Nora's dazzled and confused perspective. As the assailant (later revealed to be Laura's husband and reluctant accomplice) retrieves a knife from the dead woman's body, Bava includes a long-shot of the act before cutting to a shot of Nora's bewildered reaction. The audience is led to believe that the long-shot was from her viewpoint. Nora then ducks behind a wall, but the next shot is the same hazy long-shot, revealing that its perspective and lack of visual clarity are *independent* of Nora's point of view. Perceptual confusion would soon become a central trope of giallo cinema. In *The Girl Who Knew Too Much*, as in so many gialli that followed, this confusion of perception impedes Nora's ability to rationally vocalize what she has witnessed.

The Girl Who Knew Too Much is particularly notable for how it ties the instability of perception to Rome's urban space. Unlike higher-profile contemporary works such as Federico Fellini's *La dolce vita* (1960), Bava's external scenes were shot on location. Arguably, the film engages with the "reality" of the city in a

Figure 1.1. Nora witnesses a murder in *The Girl Who Knew Too Much* (Mario Bava, 1963). The obscurity of the shot initially seems to be tied to Nora's perspective.

way that Fellini's work does not. *La dolce vita* makes extensive use of soundstages in Rome's huge and, by this point, world-famous Cinecittà studio to reconstruct the city's public spaces (budget differences would, of course, also underlie this difference). In Bava's film, the Trinità dei Monti church atop the Spanish Steps repeatedly draws the camera's gaze during the murder scene. The passage from the night of the murder to the following morning is conveyed by a shot of the church reflected upside down in a puddle disturbed by rain. It is as if the border is blurring between concrete urban Rome and its distorted secondhand image. In short, the "real" urban space of the city is heavily implicated in the perceptual difficulties that characterize the film's narrative.

Vitali (2016, 65) writes, "Like the best of Italy's films produced in the early 1960s, Bava's films engage in a search for new strategies to present 'the real' Italy of those years." For Rome, this new reality brought rapid changes to economic, societal, and cultural fronts thanks to the industrial boom and financial miracle that followed the large influx of foreign capital into Italy after the war (see the introduction and Ginsborg 1990, 210–53). For example, Rome Fiumicino airport, through which Nora enters the city, was opened in 1960 for the Rome Olympics. The airport symbolized a new Italian modernity characterized by international openness and the creation of an infrastructure that enabled the smooth exchange of people, goods, and capital between Rome and the rest of the world (Siegel 2011, 227). This opening location also establishes tourism as one of the film's guiding obsessions. The Piazza di Spagna, around which much of the film's action is set, carries overt connotations of tourism and had been a popular attraction since the Grand Tour era of the eighteenth century. But in the dawning jet age, this sort of sightseeing was no longer reserved for a tiny elite. Now even an unassuming young American like Nora could jump on a plane and be in Rome in a matter of hours. It is a running joke, once Nora arrives, that Bassi is obsessed with "selling" her Italy's beauty, great weather, and relaxed lifestyle. In one lighthearted montage sequence, he tries to take her mind off the murder by showing her around a series of tourist sites and pitching the restorative potential of the city. Bava's use of montage here is more than a cinematic time-saver. It depicts how the postboom repackaging of Rome as a commodity to be sold internationally on a new, mass scale has fragmented the city into a series of heterogeneous postcard-style sites that erase any sense of the city's overall connectedness. In a sense, the mass commodification of Rome has turned the city itself into one big urban montage. In Austin Fisher's (2019, 128) words, tourism in the giallo would come to be "framed as a tangible manifestation of the rapid changes that have visited Italian (and other European) cities and society in recent decades, and a symbol for how once familiar urban spaces have become corrupted and alienating." This process is evident in *The Girl Who Knew Too Much*. The tumultuous juxtaposition of Rome's key sites—a result, we are led to believe, of the postwar expansion of Rome's tourism sector—leads paradoxically to a decrease in actual perception. After Nora and Bassi return home from their trip, she tells him, "I swear that I'm so confused now, I couldn't tell the difference between the Colosseum and Via Veneto!" The hyperimaging of Rome, given form during the montage, only renders the city more obscure. Indeed, there are few establishing shots in the film so, like Nora, viewers struggle to orient themselves to the on-screen environment.

The film's commodified presentation of Rome leads it toward another intertextual reference point: television advertising and, particularly, Italy's long-running advertising show *Carosello* (1957–77). This thirty-minute-long program was screened daily by state broadcaster Radiotelevisione italiana in a prime-time slot immediately before the 9:00 p.m. news and featured a sequence of unconnected advertising "spots" each lasting one minute and forty-five seconds. The rules surrounding these spots were strict: the product being advertised could only be referred to directly for a total of thirty seconds at the beginning and/or end of the segment. The time in between was filled with short stories or sketches, either live-action or animated, that had at most a loose connection to the product itself. The show came at a time when television spectatorship was changing considerably in Italy: only eighty-eight thousand licenses were sold in 1954 when the medium was introduced to the country, but by 1965, half of Italian families owned a television (Ginsborg 1990, 240). Although people began watching television as a communal activity at bars and neighbors' houses, by 1960, viewers were also watching in their own homes, particularly in the North (Foot 1999, 380). That same year, *Carosello* became the most-watched television program in the country (Ginsborg 1990, 241).[6] It is important to note the very significant connection of *Carosello* to the wider sociocultural change being experienced by Italy at this time. Piero Dorfles (1998), in his history of *Carosello*, argues that the program's celebration of the commodity necessarily and inevitably arose from the conditions of the economic miracle. The show was at once a symptom and a driver of Italy's accelerating consumerist modernity. Children, for example, often went to bed "after *Carosello*," and its short-form, entertainment-driven, and often animated content greatly appealed to them. Through *Carosello*, children were "introduced in this familial, homely and seemingly innocuous way to the delights of consumerism" (Ginsborg 1990, 241).

According to Massimo Scaglioni (2013, 344), "The incumbent and heavy presence of the voice-over, typically male ... with an informative and generally paternalistic tone" was central to the *Carosello* advertisement. Even a cursory inspection of *Carosello* spots from the 1960s validates Scaglioni's observation. The use of the thirty- or forty-something male voice-over speaking evenly and clearly with an upbeat and enthusiastic yet professional tone is virtually ubiquitous whether the product in question is food, drink, clothing, or household appliances. Further, the voice-over in *Carosello* ads is largely reserved for the product or brand descriptions that bookend each segment, whereas the intervening sketches tend to play out with only diegetic sound and nondiegetic music. The paternalistic voice-over thus signals the presence of a commodity before it specifies that commodity. In other words, the primary purpose of the *Carosello* voice-over is to highlight the process of commodification per se.

Many *Carosello* narrators' voices are almost identical to the voice-over at the beginning of *The Girl Who Knew Too Much*, which we hear as Nora flies to Rome. Importantly, the film's voice-over reverts to this style—having shifted to that of film noir in the intervening period—during the montage in which Bassi takes Nora on their sightseeing tour. The fact that the narrator's voice should return to an even but upbeat tone when the film is most explicitly concerned with the abstraction and commodification of Rome suggests a link between the film's narrator and the ubiquitous narrator of the *Carosello* spot.[7] Moreover, several *Carosello* ads of the 1960s feature location shots filmed in Rome. Through the editing of these shots, the city is often cut up and rearranged into a montage of its "best bits," as it is during Nora and Bassi's day trip. For example, one spot for Esso (year unknown) shows a sculptor at work on a bust, superimposed over shots taken at Rome's key landmarks (the premise is that he is inspired by the chaos and beauty of Rome and that Esso petrol allows one to explore that chaos and beauty independently). Another ad for Alka Seltzer (1965) features dancers parading around the Trevi Fountain and across the Ponte Sant'Angelo bridge. A spot for Carpano Punt e Mes vermouth (year unknown) follows a woman as she drives her Mercedes around the Forum, the Colosseum, and into central Rome. Perhaps most comparable to the montage sequence in *The Girl Who Knew Too Much* is a spot for Agip petrol (1961) titled *La Straniera* (*The Foreign Woman*). The ad is part of a series in which Gabriele Ferzetti plays a driving instructor. In this ad, he is teaching a young blond American woman not unlike Nora Davis (played by Ivana King) who is interested only in visiting the Trevi Fountain. Unwilling to deviate so far from his plan, Ferzetti's character tricks her into viewing a much smaller fountain. These *Carosello* spots demonstrate that the rise of commodity consumerism *in* Rome and the commodification *of* Rome were becoming inseparable in the 1960s. Furthermore, the ads suggest that both forms of commodification were facilitated by the birth of television advertising in Italy at that time. These examples may be selling fuel, alcohol, or over-the-counter medicine, but they are also selling Rome.[8] Given this context, the intertextual resemblance of the voiced-over, touristic montage sequence in *The Girl Who Knew Too Much* to the *Carosello* spot seems less coincidental. At the very least, the sequence uses a series of formal tropes (including a paternalistic voice-over) that by that time both denoted and facilitated the widespread acceleration of consumerist modernity in Italy. This fragmented and potentially disorientating modernity was reconfiguring the urban space of Rome. By drawing on these formal models and participating in the reshaping of Rome that they facilitate, the film is necessarily complicit in the process it depicts. In other words, the montage sequence is not simply a reflection of how Rome was changing in the early 1960s; it is an active driver of that change by perpetuating a commodified and fragmented representation of the city.

Nora's seeming estrangement from logos—the sonority of her utterances and her inability to logically explain what she has experienced—stems from her unclear perception of the spaces that surround her, from modernizing Rome's perceptual impossibilities. Her voice is in dialogue with the voice-over in this regard. The narrator's voice signals the fragmentation of Rome in the era of growing consumer modernity; Nora's cries signal the mental blockages that such fragmentation might trigger. Owing to Rome's ongoing and very real modernization and commodification (effected both *in* and *by* the film), Nora's "journey generates a distinctly ambiguous experience of space and place" (Kannas 2020, 91). Nora the international traveler is in an unfamiliar and unreadable city, which can only be experienced impressionistically and, accordingly, can only be represented through the seemingly nonrational sonority that lies beyond logos. The voice in *The Girl Who Knew Too Much* not only straddles a series of borders within the intertextual network from which the film is emerging but also reverberates into the socioeconomic context that in turn surrounds and underpins that intertextual network. As the film's evocation of the *Carosello*-style advertisement suggests, the booming Rome of *The Girl Who Knew Too Much* had itself become a kind of fragmented text, accessible only through mediation/mediatization and therefore not accessible at all. The text of modern Rome is impossible for both the character and audience to read clearly or comprehensively. Again, this is a changing social and urban reality that the film's use of sound makes particularly tangible.

In the sonority of Nora's voice, *The Girl Who Knew Too Much* reveals another aspect of the cinematic voice in general: voices always interact with the spaces they occupy, and they always tell the audience something about those spaces. This is true of any voice. People tend to moderate their speech based on their surroundings. The same sentence uttered in a courtroom, a bar, a library, or a bedroom will probably sound very different in each space and will be further inflected by the sociocultural dynamics in those environments. In this way, the voice is vital to the cinematic representation of space. Bava's film shows that while camera movements and compositions are important in cinematic space, the voices we hear are just as essential. The voice responds to its spatial context in real time and registers even very subtle shifts in that context. By listening closely to the voices on a film's soundtrack, we might better understand how a film seeks to represent space. Furthermore, we might see how the representation of space in a film relates to people's experiences of space in the world beyond the film.

COLLABORATIVE VOICES

The fact that the voice in *The Girl Who Knew Too Much* orients the film to a range of textual and cultural reference points is most evident when one compares the Italian- and English-language versions of the film. First, as discussed in the introduction, it is important to note that Mario Bava celebrated the artisanal character of his career. In a 1979 *L'Espresso* interview, he told Dante Matelli: "I am just a craftsman, a romantic craftsman.... How could it be art, when there are 60 people working on a single film?" (quoted in Howarth 2014, 181, 184). Bava (quoted in Howarth 2014, 181) also repeatedly referred to his films as "bullshit" and "improvisations" and claimed that he could not remember the names of actors with whom he had worked (Howarth 2014, 173). Certainly, Bava was hugely prolific and worked in almost every popular film genre during his career, often due to financial necessity. Peter Hutchings (2016, 81) argues that Bava's career "brings with it ... a sense of some of the practicalities and contingencies of Italian popular film production from the 1950s through to the 1970s." In *The Girl Who Knew Too Much*, the voice is where the necessarily collaborative contingencies and practicalities of Bava's filmmaking, and filone film production more generally, are evidenced. The film's script, for example, was the result of collaboration by six writers (Lucas 2007, 458) and revised extensively midshoot. In Troy Howarth's (2014, 13) words, "The people who worked with Bava remarked of his love for adlibbing; for him, the script was little more than a blueprint." John Saxon (who plays Bassi) told Howarth that "working with Bava was like engaging in one long improvisation" (Howarth 2014, 13). The extensive reshoots after principal photography wrapped also suggest that significant changes to the script were made long into the film's production (Lucas 2007, 465). Lucas (2007, 452–53) suggests that each of the film's writers would have brought to the script their own textual influences and inspirations, which he identifies by carefully comparing each writer's prior work, their interests, and the final form of this film. If each contributor to the script added their own textual influences, then the narrator's voice marks both the film's intertextual allusions and its collaborative production, and it suggests a causal link between the two.[9]

This supposition is speculative, but the collaborative production of *The Girl Who Knew Too Much* is indicated by the voice in two more concrete ways. First, the film, like virtually all Italian cinema of the 1960s (and up until the mid-1980s), is dubbed in both its Italian and English versions. As discussed in detail in chapter 3, dubbing marks the intrusion of commercial pressures into the form of the cinematic text, and so the voice in *The Girl Who Knew Too Much* automatically "stages the socio-economic conditions of [the film's] production" (Vitali 2016, 158). *The Girl Who Knew Too Much* is remarkable, however, for the significant changes made to the film's voice-over when it was dubbed and reedited for Anglophone release under the title *The Evil Eye*. The English-language version is slightly longer than the Italian release because it contains extra scenes. It is also principally voiced over by Nora herself in the form of sections of her stream of consciousness. At times, *The Evil Eye* vocalizes the internal monologues of other characters too, such as the thoughts of Nora's fellow passengers as the camera tracks through her plane in the opening scene. In Lucas's (2007, 460) words, Nora's American voice-over (dubbed by Román) is characterized by a "giddy, girlish, 'Dear Diary' exuberance," which serves to align the audience more closely with Nora. This is notable given that, like its Italian counterparts, the film's American coproducer American International

Pictures (AIP) frequently sought to "capitalize on particular, perhaps short-lived trends" (Dickinson 2008, 59). Indeed, AIP was likely eager to use the film to exploit the relatively recent popularity of *Psycho* (Lucas 2007, 448; Balmain 2002). The replacement of the anonymous male voice-over with Nora's inner monologue recalls the audience's close and ultimately traumatic alignment with Marion Crane during the first half of *Psycho*, which in part relies on the audience hearing Marion's thoughts as she drives out of Phoenix. The major change of the voice-over in *The Girl Who Knew Too Much* adjusts the film's connections to other works according to its new cultural context. The American producers' commercial requirements led to a change in the form of the voice-over, and listening to the two voice-overs in parallel reveals the shifting commercial pressures that affected each stage of the film's international production and distribution. This comparison shows the diverse and significant changes made by various film industry players to the film's form, and these changes align with the wider cultural contexts in which those agents were operating.

Returning to the Italian version of the film, the recurrence of Adriano Celentano's singing voice is also revealing. Celentano was an up-and-coming singer in Italy in the early 1960s and had appeared in Fellini's *La dolce vita*. His music blended American-style rock and roll with Italian musical traditions, and he became a symbol of boom-era Italian culture in which the new and the international were mixing with the traditional and the national (see Gundle 2006). In a sense, Celentano's music engages in a similar cultural negotiation to Bava's film, and so it is perhaps fitting that his song "Furore" accompanies the opening shots of Nora's plane. In this version of the song, Celentano's words are clear and forceful. "Furore" is heard again, this time diegetically, when Nora moves into Laura's house and plays a record on the gramophone. After doing so, she moves to answer a knock at the door and Celentano's voice fades into background *sound*, his words hard to pick out. Finally, Nora searches for Landini in a deserted apartment and falls for a trap set by Laura when she walks toward a voice that is eventually revealed to come from a tape deck. She replays the tape, but, inexplicably, the only sound that comes out is the screech of a sped-up version of "Furore." At the beginning of the film, the clarity of Celentano's words pairs with the calm, literary voice-over; the sonorous screech of the final use of the song comes at the point in the film when the narrator's voice has become troubled by its increased sonority. Celentano's voice acts as a marker of the shift being experienced by the voice in general during the film.

Celentano's voice also held significant commercial value for the film's Italian producers. The inclusion of the singer's voice was, in large part, a marketing ploy; the track was used during the film's Italian promotion, and Bava was obliged to use it in the film (Lucas 2007, 464). Lucas (2007, 462) speculates that the song's distorted final rendition was Bava's way of getting revenge for this imposition, but he provides no evidence for this intriguing suggestion. Even if we discount the idea that Bava is manipulating Celentano's voice for his own purposes, the scene does present a moment at which the film's commercial necessities and thematic interests intersect. It is also another marker of how the voices on the film's soundtrack were changed when the film was tweaked for English-speaking audiences: "Furore" was replaced with music by Les Baxter for *The Evil Eye*, as Celentano's celebrity and Italian lyrics would mean little to audiences outside of Italy. Celentano's presence on the film's Italian soundtrack and absence from its English one is a microcosm of how the film's (or films') use of the voice was shaped and reshaped by the contexts in which the film was made and circulated. To put *The Girl Who Knew Too Much* and *The Evil Eye* together is to hear (in the changes made to the voice-over as well as to the musical soundtrack) how each version relies on the voice to align the film with specific and different intertextual and cultural contexts. By responding simultaneously to aesthetic, commercial, and sociocultural concerns, the voice in this early giallo sets a precedent by transcending the borders among these categories and weaving context firmly into the fabric of the text.

NOTES

1. Intertextuality has been theorized at length throughout the twentieth and twenty-first centuries. The term was coined by Julia Kristeva, building on the work of Mikhail Bakhtin, and was developed variously and extensively by Roland Barthes, Gérard Gennette, Paul Riffaterre, Harold Bloom, Elaine Showalter, and others (for overviews of intertextual theory, see Alfaro 1996; Orr 2003; Allen 2011). These writers' theorizations are based on the study of literature and represent complex and often schematic attempts to better understand the semiotic processes involved in reading and writing. I use the term *intertextuality* in this analysis of *The Girl Who Knew Too Much* in a less theoretical sense to designate the text's interaction—overt or subtle—with other texts through either its narrative content, form, or both. Although such a general and open definition of intertextuality is challenged by some of the previously mentioned writers, it will serve this chapter effectively "because it foregrounds notions of relationality, interconnectedness and interdependence in modern cultural life" (Allen 2011, 5).

2. The notion of "the grain of the voice" comes from an article of that name by Roland Barthes. In it, Barthes (1977, 188) writes that "the 'grain' is the body in the voice as it sings, the hand as it writes, the limb as it performs." For Barthes,

listening for grain allows for an embodied and therefore erotic relationship between listener and singer/performer.

3. The idea that *The Girl Who Knew Too Much* is a cinematic mix of its literary and cinematic pretexts is stressed further by the film's recurrent hints that Nora may be imagining or hallucinating her experiences (especially considering that the film's original working title was *L'incubo,* or *The Nightmare* [Lucas 2007, 453]). The film never relinquishes this possibility since it ends with Nora remembering that she smoked a cigarette on the plane that was given to her by a drug dealer. The sense that the film may be one long hallucination on Nora's part frames it as a composite of all the giallo texts she has consumed, with the noir-style narrator being one of their defining formal components.

4. Here it is important to go back to Cavarero's argument that Western thinking has long aligned woman with phonos and the body, and man with logos and the mind. In this sense, the film's representations of Nora's and Ethel's cries and wails, especially set against the supposedly rational speech of Bassi, Landini, and the film's male doctors and detectives, participate in this deep-rooted patriarchal prejudice.

5. *Mise-en-scène* can be translated into English as "put-on-stage." It refers to everything the audience can see on screen at a given point in a film and how those things are arranged to produce an effect or express an idea.

6. *Carosello* was later joined by several other programs of a similar format that broadcast at various times of the day (Dorfles 1998, 17).

7. It is noteworthy that Bava directed at least one *Carosello* spot himself, in 1970 (Hunt 2022, 10). His ad was titled *I Futuribili (People of the Future)* and promoted Mobil petrol. It depicts a science fiction–style world in which people live in a dome and wear tight jumpsuits and ends by suggesting that the future is already here in the form of Mobil's new petrol products (and in their flying saucer–like petrol stations). The spot also features a typical male voice-over very similar in timbre and tone to the voice-overs that overlay other *Carosello* ads and Nora and Bassi's trip around Rome. Since *The Girl Who Knew Too Much* was released seven years before the Mobil ad, it is hard to draw a direct and firm link between these two texts, but Bava's later spot indicates that a paternalistic mode of voice-over occasionally played an important role in his articulation of post-boom Italian consumerism.

8. Although beyond the scope of this book, it is noteworthy how frequently Rome is associated with the car in those ads. Clearly, the refashioning of Rome into a series of dislocated landmarks owes something also to the growth of the automotive and petrochemical industries in Italy in the 1950s and 1960s, which allowed increasing numbers of people to traverse the city at such a speed as to perceive it as a series of isolated landmarks.

9. See Hunt 2022 for an in-depth discussion of Bava's complex relationship to artisanship and authorship.

TWO

DIRECTORIAL VOICES

The Bird with the Crystal Plumage

FOLLOWING ITS BIRTH WITH MARIO Bava's *The Girl Who Knew Too Much*, the giallo's development into one of Italian cinema's most prolific postwar filoni was slow. Many gialli were made in the 1960s, including *Blood and Black Lace* (see the introduction), Romolo Guerrieri's *The Sweet Body of Deborah* (*Il dolce corpo di Deborah*, 1968), and Lucio Fulci's *One on Top of the Other* a.k.a. *Perversion Story* (*Una sull'altra*, 1969), but it was Dario Argento's *The Bird with the Crystal Plumage* (*L'uccello dalle piume di cristallo*, 1970) that marked an important turning point for the giallo and started a major cinematic cycle in Italy.

The Bird with the Crystal Plumage was Argento's directorial debut (he had worked as a screenwriter for other directors, including Sergio Leone), and it replicates many of the narrative tropes in *The Girl Who Knew Too Much*. Following Argento's rise to fame, these tropes quickly came to define the giallo film narrative. Sam Dalmas (Tony Musante) is, like Nora Davis, an American visiting Rome. A writer suffering from crippling writer's block, he has taken a job writing a textbook on the preservation of rare birds for an ornithological museum. One night, shortly before he is due to return to the United States with his British girlfriend Julia (Suzy Kendall), Sam passes an art gallery in Rome's EUR district and sees a man dressed in a black trench coat and hat attack a woman before fleeing.[1] Sam runs to help but is trapped between the gallery's two wall-to-wall glass doors and is left to watch as the woman writhes on the gallery floor. Eventually, the police arrive, take the woman—Monica Ranieri (Eva Renzi), one of the gallery's owners—into care, and question Sam repeatedly about what he saw. The detective in charge of the case, Inspector Morosini (Enrico Maria Salerno), confiscates Sam's passport in an effort to force his memory. The tactic fails, but Sam becomes obsessed with solving the case and remains in Italy even after his passport is returned. In the background of a threatening phone call he later receives (and records) from the killer is an unexplained sound, later revealed to be the cry of a rare bird held at the local zoo. Sam then realizes that the call came from the apartment next to the zoo, shared by Monica and her husband, fellow gallery owner Alberto (Umberto Raho). Sam rushes across the city to the Ranieris' apartment. In the ensuing fracas, Alberto falls out of a window and, in his dying moments, admits to being the black-coated killer in the gallery. Alberto's is a false confession, though; the real killer is Monica. A painting of a violent attack has released long-repressed traumatic memories of an attack she suffered in the past. With the return of these memories, Monica identified with the attacker rather than the victim and commenced her murderous rampage. She attacks Sam, but he is saved by the police officers who have followed him. He returns to America with Julia as the final credits roll.

The large number of gialli that followed *The Bird with the Crystal Plumage* and featured animal names in their titles highlights this film as the filone's main reference point. Indeed, among both fans and scholars, Argento represents something of a godfather figure to giallo cinema of the 1970s and 1980s (notwithstanding the lackluster nature of most of his post-1990 works). Leon Hunt (2022, 23) explains that this makes Argento an exceptional sort of filone director: "Rather like Sergio Leone, Argento initiated a *filone* but subsequently stood at a remove from *filone* cinema. However, if Argento was above formulas and trends—or at least encouraged audiences to see him as such—one of the factors in his later decline might have been the need to conform to his own authorial legend, to continue to make 'Dario Argento films,' rather than diversifying in the way that *filone* directors were forced to do." As Hunt suggests, Argento is often discussed in terms of his "authorship" of his films. This supports the idea that his work expresses a stylistic and thematic distinction that is identifiably "Argentian" in the same way a film may be described as, for example, "Felliniesque" (in the style of Federico Fellini) or "Bressonian" (in the style of Robert Bresson). In this way, Argento has often been elevated to the level of the auteur (author) in the way art house directors tend to be. Argento's ability to create and express a distinct style and exert so much personal control over his films and career trajectory, especially in its early stages, can be partly attributed to his powerful family connections within the Italian film industry. As a young filmmaker, these connections gave him an unusual degree of creative space within which he could pursue his artistic preoccupations. As Hunt notes, Argento's unique situation allowed him to work independently from the filone system, which typically restricted directors to commercially determined parameters and prevented them from focusing on the genres and themes that interested them the most. Argento's way of thinking of himself as an auteur is notable. Where Bava often insisted that he worked as a simple artisan, Argento once asked journalist Alan Jones (quoted in Jones 2016, 120), "Why shouldn't I use the same ideas all the time? . . . I am the same person writing all the stories—besides I like them . . . I have my own style and I don't want to change it. Why should I?" In his own view, then, Argento has enjoyed a level of creative autonomy that has allowed him to develop and refine a personal style and set of ideas. This freedom in turn rendered him both a leader and an outlier in relation to the wider giallo filone and the mode of production it typically entailed. Yet, as Hunt's book on Bava—*Mario Bava: The Artisan as Italian Horror Auteur*—suggests, the distinction between the journeyman director and the artist is not clear-cut (and is anyway largely determined by discourses among fans, critics, and film distributors). In this chapter, I argue that at a very basic level, all directors exert a degree of authorship over their texts because they orchestrate the coming together of the film's constituent parts, no matter how commercially determined those parts may be or how many different people work to create them. As such, Argento is actually more of a typical example of the controlling giallo director than an unusual one. His unique personal power and self-confidence as a director have allowed him to do more boldly what any director might do in the course of their work—organize the parts of a film into a coherent whole.

I briefly consider the history and usage of the term *auteur* before arguing that the director's role in a film's production is primarily one of creative organization. I argue that this is a fundamentally spatial task, as the formal arrangement of bodies, objects, lights, sounds, and camera involves establishing the spatial relationships among these things (and then, potentially, making those relationships more complex through montage). One way of identifying a director's authorship of a film might be to analyze the way space is represented and manipulated in a film because this reveals how the filmmaker has handled their task of synthesizing the parts of a film's form into a whole. This may in turn give rise to narrative propulsion and theme. Argento's debut is an instructive case study in this regard because it has a palpable and consistent interest in space at both the formal and the thematic levels. In analyzing this film, though, I want to go further and argue that the film's representation of space is anchored in the way the voice is used in the film. *The Bird with the Crystal Plumage* stages a profound awareness of the centrality of voice in defining and delineating space, and it does so in terms that are powerfully evocative of the act of cinematic voice-over narration (which this film does not employ directly, unlike *The Girl Who Knew Too Much*). In short, the film suggests that to possess the capacity for clear speech is to possess the power to determine which sides of the film's many vague spatial borders constitute the "inside" and which sides (typically those occupied by the speaker) constitute the "outside." This vocal-spatial dynamic replicates how the cinematic voice-over divides the inner diegetic world from an outer space that confers authority and control. After discussing the use of this principle in several scenes, I further explore the role the voice may play, both within and beyond cinema, in the human occupation of physical and social space. Finally, I consider how Argento's formal use of the voice in *The Bird with the Crystal Plumage* gives rise to some of the film's more historically specific themes. These revolve around the ability of voice technologies to grant the user the power to extend their voice's implication in space far beyond the limits of the body from which it originates, and this interest is in line with the increasing prominence of virtual space in postwar, postboom Italy.

DARIO ARGENTO: GIALLO AUTEUR?

The relationship between *The Bird with the Crystal Plumage* and *The Girl Who Knew Too Much* is ambiguous. Argento has stated that Bava's film convinced him that a murder mystery set in Rome could be effective (Argento 2014, 89) but has elsewhere entirely refuted the notion that he was influenced by Bava (Jones 2016, 19). In any case, intertextual influences are rife in *The Bird with the Crystal Plumage*, such as the casting of Reggie Nalder in the role of an assassin—Argento loved Nalder's performance in none other than Hitchcock's 1956 version of *The Man Who Knew Too Much* (Argento 2014, 99)—and the film's narrative debt to Fredric Brown's hard-boiled novel *The Screaming Mimi* ([1949] 1958). The film also references *Psycho* in the final "explanation" of events that is delivered by a police psychoanalyst. At the same time, Argento was not buffeted by commercial imperatives in quite the same way as Bava. He had singular control of the film's production: he wrote the script in total isolation and insisted on directing despite his lack of experience; he produced it through a company he started with his father Salvatore, a powerful producer in Italy at the time (the company was named Seda, from "Salvatore e Dario Argento"); he refused to use a more marketable English pseudonym; and, he also refused to hand over direction of the film when Goffredo Lombardo, head of Titanus and the film's distributor, was unimpressed with early footage (Argento 2014, 81–98). Notwithstanding Argento's esteem for his technical collaborators, such singular artistic control is in marked contrast to Bava's openly collaborative style and has contributed to what Hunt (above) terms Argento's "authorial legend" (a legend bought into by fans, critics, and scholars). Alberto Pezzotta (2008, 85) summarizes: "For Bava, style is probably a side effect and not intended as a signature.... For Argento, however, style is the means by which he builds his authorship and his modernism."

Argento's relative autonomy as a director seems to have been a privilege afforded to him by his father Salvatore's powerful position in the Italian film industry; the elder Argento was a producer and industry executive of some renown. Salvatore Argento helped his son acquire writing experience under the eye of producer Sergio Amidei, and Dario (with Bernardo Bertolucci) went on to write the script for *Once Upon a Time in the West* (*C'era una volta il West*, 1968) for Sergio Leone (see Argento 2014, 68–73). When Dario finished the script for *The Bird with the Crystal Plumage*, it was again his father who contributed money, acted as producer, and interceded to help the film find a major distributor (2014, 87–88). In the words of Manlio Gomarasca (2008, 246), "The production machine behind Argento's first film ... had an extremely familiar management, one that allowed the young Argento to be hands-on with all of the ongoing production processes." Argento's friend, archivist, and critic of his work Alan Jones (correspondence with author 2020) puts it even more bluntly: "You have to remember how powerful a figure Salvatore was in the industry. No one wanted to cross him or their export stream might suffer. Salvatore was not beyond using his clout for his son ... Dario was lucky to be born into such an esteemed family and he knows it."

Alongside the boldness of his style, Argento's control over his films and their unusual industrial preconditions have led people to call him an auteur. The way this concept has been used, challenged, and revised since the 1950s provides a useful starting point for understanding the director's role in the production of giallo cinema. The term began to gain currency after François Truffaut popularized it in an article titled "A Certain Tendency of the French Cinema," published in the French film journal *Cahiers du Cinema* in 1954. Truffaut argues that certain filmmakers—he mentions Jean Renoir, Max Ophüls, and Bresson, among others—stand apart from the metteurs en scène. He suggests that the latter group are competent technicians whose role amounts to adding pictures to the stories they are handed. The former group, the auteurs, exert more noticeable creative control over their work and are thus able to express bolder and more personal visions in their films (see Truffaut [1954] 2008). Truffaut argues that the artistry of auteur cinema should be celebrated, and his call was taken up by his colleagues at *Cahiers* (many of whom would go on to become directors of the French New Wave). Over the 1950s and 1960s, *Cahiers* became a bastion of auteurist criticism in which certain filmmakers were praised for the distinction of their personal style and the consistency with which a certain artistic vision was supposedly evident throughout their bodies of work. Perhaps surprisingly, the *Cahiers* critics often identified and championed auteurs who made seemingly throwaway genre films for studios in both America and Europe. They argued that these directors' personal styles were the more laudable for being expressed from within the strictures of generic models and studio organization. The respect shown to these directors led to an interpretive paradigm, often referred to as "auteur theory" in English but perhaps better referred to simply as "auteur criticism." This paradigm approached the "meaning" of a film as a matter of identifying and articulating the vision the auteur had implanted into their work by way of the unique approach they had taken to it (a method with a longer tradition in the study of literature).

The auteurist perspective came to be adopted outside of France, perhaps most notably by Andrew Sarris in the film criticism he wrote for the American magazine *The Village Voice*. Auteurism's central assumption that the director serves as the creative and expressive anchor of a film remains, to various degrees, central to much film scholarship and fandom today. The approach faced criticism early on, however. André Bazin ([1957] 1985, 256–57, original emphasis), one of *Cahiers du Cinema*'s leading contributors, appreciated the way that auteurist criticism—which he refers to as the *politique des auteurs*—valorized cinematic artistry on its own terms, but he also worried that the approach was ultimately too subjective to serve as anything more than an expression of the critic's personal preferences. As early as 1957, he cautioned that "the criteria of the *politique des auteurs* are very difficult to formulate, the whole thing becomes highly hazardous. It is significant that our finest writers on *Cahiers* have been practising it for three or four years now and have yet to produce the main corpus of its theory.... You can see the danger: an aesthetic personality cult." As Bazin states, and as many others have since underlined, auteur theory has never been a theory as such. Rather, it takes the form of a perspective in which the director is seen as the source for any "meaning" the text may contain. This position continued to come in for critique; the ascendancy of film and cultural criticism that had roots in poststructuralism, psychoanalysis, and ideological analysis in the 1960s and 1970s seriously called into question the notion of the author/auteur as a single, free, and coherent creative agent. To this broad shift, one can add the self-evident argument that films are not produced by individuals in the way that novels or paintings might be. As Mario Bava's comments in chapter 1 stress, films result from the collaboration of often huge groups of creative laborers. If a hundred people contribute to a film, can the director alone really be the only source of its meaning?

In 1973, Edward Buscombe ([1973] 2008, 82–83) acknowledged the advances that auteur critics had made in understanding film texts. He argued, however, that "what is needed now is a theory of the cinema that locates directors in a total situation, rather than one which assumes that their development has only an internal dynamic." Similarly, James Narremore (2014, 30–31) asserts that "critics need to understand the phenomenon of the author dialectically, with an awareness of the complicated, dynamic relationship between movie history, institutions, and artists, and with an appreciation of the aesthetic choices made by individual agents in particular circumstances." These views acknowledge both the director's considerable importance to the creative production of a film and the additional factors and agents that affect and shape their work. Such positions help us understand the director's role in giallo production. As I outlined in the introduction to this book, giallo directors often faced significant restrictions in available resources and time, and many seem to have been concerned with replicating relatively narrow (if always evolving) formulas. This has led to a polarization in the study of the giallo. On the one side are those who choose to study the giallo as a broad filone within which the importance of individual directors is diminished. On the other side are those critics and fans who strive, not unlike the early *Cahiers* critics, to identify the consistent stylistic signatures of certain directors despite the challenges those directors faced and the diversity of genres they often worked within. The cult status bestowed on filone directors like Bava, Lucio Fulci, Pupi Avati, and Sergio Martino demonstrates this mission.

If taken at face value, Bava's comments in chapter 1 suggest that he never thought of himself as an auteur in the way that Truffaut and his colleagues understood the term. Dario Argento, however, is another story. While always careful to recognize the talents of his collaborators, in interviews with scholars and journalists, Argento has often sought to explain the thematic and stylistic qualities of his films in terms of his artistic vision and creative approach to his material. Indeed, from 2022 to 2023, Italy's National Cinema Museum in Turin hosted "Dario Argento: The Exhibit," a detailed celebration of the director's career and work. The text panels that accompanied the exhibit's displays insistently presented Argento as a visionary artist who has carved a radical and personal path with his filmmaking (the words *auteur* and, in Italian, *autore* featured frequently). Quotes from filmmakers including Quentin Tarantino, William Friedkin, Guillermo del Toro, and Nicolas Winding Refn gave the same impression.[2] Moreover, many of the exhibition's annotations used Argento's own words to explain the form, content, and development of his films. The point was clear: Argento's films are *his* films, his visions and his creations.

Regarding the giallo, the most fundamental question raised by the emergence and evolution of auteurist criticism may not be whether certain directors can or should be labeled auteurs. Rather, and more basically, the auteurist approach to film criticism invites us to consider whether, how, and to what degree one can detect the unique specificity of the director-as-artist in the aesthetic, thematic, and narrative qualities of any film, including something as seemingly insignificant as a giallo. To answer this question, I refer to another response to the question of the auteur. In 1972, as reconsiderations of cinematic authorship (alongside, incidentally, giallo production) were accelerating, V. F. Perkins ([1972] 1993, 179) argued that the director's role was essentially one of creative organization: "The director is there to ensure that the details of performance and recording are related to the total design. It is through his control over detail that the director may become chiefly responsible for the effect and quality of the completed movie." Perkins treads a fine line between recognizing the limits the director-as-organizer model places on the potential for directorial artistry and claiming that the director's organization is creative expression in itself: "If the film's form embodies a viewpoint, explored in depth and with complexity, it is almost certain to be the director's. He is in control throughout the period in which virtually all the significant relationships are defined" ([1972] 1993, 184). More simply, for Perkins ([1972] 1993, 184), directorial expression is an issue of practical aesthetics: "Direction can determine which objects and actions are to be seen as foreground and which as background. By controlling the balance between the elements, by creating a coherence of emphasis, it can control the priorities of significance and so shape the movie's theme." Perkins's model can be accepted, refuted, or modified on a film-by-film basis, but his straightforward pragmatism is useful for considering how to identify the director's influence over a film. His consistent reference to the "director" helps bridge the notional division between the auteur and the artisan director or metteur en scène and stresses how both may necessarily engage in processes of organizational creativity. In his book on Bava, Hunt argues in great detail that the artisan/auteur distinction is a problematic one (2022; see also Hutchings 2016).

I aim to use Perkins's pragmatism to analyze Argento and the giallo, while also focusing on the unstated spatial implications of Perkins's argument. If the director is "in charge of relationships, of synthesis" of a film's constituent processes and parts (Perkins [1972] 1993, 184), then they are engaged in a fundamentally spatial exercise. To speak in broad terms, most film texts are ultimately spatial arrangements of bodies, objects, light, sound, and movement over time. A film's formal specificity—and perhaps also its narrative trajectory and themes—is determined not by the camera, actor, lighting, sound recording, or editing in isolation but by how those elements are connected with each other. Film form is not simply a matter of what is seen or heard but also how, from where, against and in relation to what, and for how long. At the most practical level, these are questions of space: where bodies and objects are placed, how and from where they are filmed, how and from where the sounds they emit are recorded (if at all), how the audience's perception of their spatial position is affected by lighting choices, and how editing clarifies or confuses these issues. I assert that the director's task is one of spatial creation.

Given Argento's relative insulation from the commercial pressures of the filone production system, this chapter has less to say about how the voice in the giallo is shaped by its industrial context than the rest of this book (although, in a tight doubling back, this fact shows the atypical industrial preconditions of *The Bird with the Crystal Plumage*). Instead, I focus here on the complex and nuanced role the voice may play in expressing theme in the giallo. Throughout his career, Argento has experimented with both camera placement and camera technology as a way to overtly manipulate space. He once mentioned this interest with a telling reference to another Italian director who is ubiquitously labeled an auteur: "My passion for architecture comes from Michelangelo Antonioni, a director who gave it primary importance . . . I've come to love the use of space in his films" (quoted in Mendik 2015, 123). Analyzing Argento for his films' interest in space rather than his unique family background helps to emphasize what Argento has in common with other giallo directors (a role as the organizational linchpin of a film and its form) rather than the ways in which he is exceptional. Consequently, Argento can be seen as exemplary rather than as an outlier. Much of his stylistic and thematic distinction comes down to questions of spaces—how they determine shot-by-shot aesthetics, how they are used to generate narrative propulsion, and how they explore wider conceptual issues. I contend that the incredibly precise ways in which the voice is used in *The Bird with the Crystal Plumage* are central to how the film represents and manipulates space. The voice is central to how Argento's directorial presence comes to be imprinted on the film and how the film expresses theme.

SPEECH AND SPACE

Space and speech are of prime, mutual importance in *The Bird with the Crystal Plumage*. Sam's textbook, "a manual on the preservation of rare birds," is literally a text designed to put things *in* cages. It is a way of using language to define which objects can be placed in internal spatial zones and how and is thus instrumental in defining as internal the spaces those objects come to occupy. This spatial operation is enforced and clarified by the mise-en-scène of the ornithological museum in which countless glass cages and display units are stuffed full of preserved birds. Each bird has a small descriptive label, and these labels perform the same sort of role as the book Sam has written. They construct logocentric walls that enforce the physical glass walls of the cages, screens of signification that define the birds they refer to and confer onto them fixed meanings just as the process of taxidermy has fixed their bodies. In this operation, logos itself encases the birds. The labels demarcate the sides of the glass panels occupied by the birds as the "inside" of the cases relative to the space "outside" the panels traversed by writers Sam and Carlo (Raf Valenti), a space that confers authority and the power to capture, collect, curate, and perhaps colonize (see Burke 2002). The fact that Sam and Carlo walk along narrow passages also hemmed in by glass surfaces as they navigate the labyrinthine museum further indicates that, within the museum, the inside/outside distinction is fragile. It is thus all the more important that this distinction is established and maintained through linguistic structures.

The Bird with the Crystal Plumage's overarching investment in spatiality has been incisively explored by Michael Siegel, who pays specific attention to the ubiquity of glass in the film. Siegel (2011, 212) notes that the gallery scene "emphasizes the transparency of glass, its subtle reflectivity, and its visual property of collapsing multiple planes of depth onto one surface [but also] its ability to demarcate and segment space by obstructing the passage of sound and bodies." Central for Siegel is the paradox underlining glass's separation of space since it enacts physical separation while allowing for the "optical interpenetration of space" (2011). As the glass cases in the museum illustrate, the spatial distinction that is threatened by this paradox may be supported by words that, in a sense, increase the *significance* of the glass surfaces to which they refer.

This operation is at the center of the crisis Sam faces in the gallery when he becomes trapped between two huge glass doors while trying to help Monica. On one side of Sam is a glass panel that keeps him separate but allows him to see Monica and several modernist sculptures in the gallery. On the other side is a glass panel separating him from the street. He is stuck in a narrow space, isolated in both directions and enclosed in glass like the museum's stuffed birds (a comparison that is invited by the abundance of bird-themed sculptures in the gallery [fig. 2.1]). Signaling Argento's characteristic concern with film form per se, this moment in the film is often interpreted as a metacinematic comment on spectatorship, in which Sam is both a trapped spectator and spectacle as the film condenses both sides of the voyeuristic act into one body (see McDonagh 2010, 49–50; Gracey 2010, 28).[3] This interpretation aligns with Argento's focus on the material aspects of cinema and the exploration of both film technology and perspective throughout his body of work. Regarding questions of voice,

Figure 2.1. Sam is trapped in a glass box between the gallery and the street as Monica lies stricken. The sculptures on the right and second from the left resemble the feet and talons of birds. *The Bird with the Crystal Plumage* (Dario Argento, 1970).

however, Sam's position between the glass doors also recalls a voice-over narrator (like the one used in *The Girl Who Knew Too Much*, but not in this film). Sam's liminal position between the "scene" of the gallery and the "real world" of the street closely replicates that of Bava's narrator, who hovers precariously and provisionally on the fringe between the diegetic world and the audience. Notably, Sam's characterization as a writer has already framed him as a narrator figure, even though he is, at this moment, a blocked one. Interestingly, Argento later recorded snatches of voice-over narration for the Italian dubs of his films *Suspiria* (1977), *Tenebrae* (1982), and *Phenomena* (1985). These vocal cameos underscore the general link, implied here, between scriptural authorship and voice-over narration within his cinematic paradigm.

Sam's struggle to narrate resonates in this scene as the glass doors almost totally dampen his voice. His shouted words cannot reach Monica in the gallery, and when he tells a passerby on the street to open the door or call for help, the man just points to his ear and shrugs as if to say, "I can't hear you." Unlike the cinematic narrator to whom he is visually compared, Sam's voice can neither command the "diegetic scene" played out in the gallery as Monica writhes on the floor nor reach and inform the "audience" on the street. Between the two doors, Sam is paradoxically both "locked in" and "locked out" of the gallery, and so his spatial status is uncertain. Mary Ann Doane (1980, 42, original emphasis) notes, "The voice-over commentary is necessarily presented as outside of that [diegetic] space. It is its radical *otherness* with respect to the diegesis which endows this voice with a certain authority. As a form of direct address, it speaks without mediation to the audience ... establishing a complicity between itself and the spectator—together they understand and thus *place* the image." Doane underlines the explicitly spatial dimension of the voice-over. That is, a narrator must vocally align themselves with listeners occupying an "outside" space to render the image an "inside" space—a "place"—*over* which their *voice* gains power. Sam's failure to tell the passerby to open the outer door is therefore significant. His failure to express himself verbally precipitates his inability to physically move from the space in which he is trapped and achieve, in Doane's terms, "radical otherness" to the "scene" in the gallery. The fact that Sam's voice cannot reach his audience on the street confirms the solidity of the gallery's outer door and with it Sam's spatial and discursive interiority. Sam's inability to speak and the confining space come together to render him powerless. The police eventually find him slumped silently on the floor, blending into the mise-en-scène of the gallery interior next to Monica, who lies among her sculptures.

The staging of the gallery scene relates to Kaja Silverman's (1988, 54, original emphasis) ideas about how the voice supports male pleasure in the cinema. Silverman argues,

> [In order] to sustain the male viewer/listener in an impossible identification with the phallus, classic cinema has elaborated a number of strategies for displacing the privileged attributes of the disembodied voice-over onto the *synchronized* male voice.... As a result of these mechanisms, interiority and exteriority are redefined as areas within the narrative rather than as indicators of the great divide separating the diegesis from the enunciation. "Inside" comes to designate a recessed space within the story, while "outside" refers to those elements of the story which seem in one way or another to frame that recessed space. Woman is confined to the former, and man to the latter. It is thus only through an endless series of *trompes l'oeil* that classic cinema's male viewing subject sustains what is a fundamentally impossible identification with authoritative vision, speech, and hearing.

Sam's failure to achieve vocal mastery over the action taking place in the gallery is precisely why he (and, perhaps, to follow Silverman, the male viewer) ends up uncomfortably contained with Monica in its feminized "inside." Silverman's model draws attention primarily to the gendered implications of scenes like this, but she devotes less time to considerations of the voice's centrality to the creation and demarcation of cinematic space per se. I focus here on the fact— which underpins Silverman's theorization around the gendering of voices and the voicing of gender—that vocalization is always to some degree involved in the drawing and redrawing of borders and spatial divisions. Indeed, the correlation between the ability to vocalize with authority and the mastery of space becomes one of the structuring tropes in *The Bird with the Crystal Plumage*. The spatial paradigm implicit in the commercial cinematic soundtrack (the fundamental division between diegetic/inner and nondiegetic/outer soundscapes) persists as the model according to which space is conceived and articulated—it forms a sort of micro-theme that the film repeatedly loops back to. Certainly, Sam is not the only figure in the film to suffer consignment to a space of powerlessness due to a failure or absence of voice. Hoping to help Sam remember the identity of the black-coated man, Inspector Morosini shows him a lineup of "perverts" who are each introduced by name and (sexual) criminal history (until, in a joke at the expense of forensic categorization, Morosini yells out that the last individual, who goes by the name Ursula Andress, "belongs with the transvestites, not the perverts"). The criminals are silent as a policeman's discursive speech classifies each like the labels in the birds' cages. Or, like a cinematic narrator; the policeman sits at the back of the darkened, studio-like room on a folding director's chair as if to explicitly tempt this comparison. Both mise-en-scène and sound design here push the silent, criminal group into a powerless interiority framed by the state power invoked by the police voice (apart from Andress, that is, who shouts back "I should hope so!" after Morosini's objection and walks off the stage and momentarily out of her recessed interiority). Similarly, Sam later visits a jail to speak to the pimp of one of the murderer's victims known as So Long in the English dub and Addio in the Italian (Gildo Di Marco). Their conversation is framed side-on as the two men sit on either side of a visiting booth in an almost totally symmetrical shot. They are separated by two low panels of glass in a direct replication of the "double-glazed" architecture of the gallery. As in the gallery, either side of the glass divide could be the "inside" or the "outside." So Long's interiority is, of course, determined again by the state power that operates through the prison. It is *signified*, however, by a stammer that interrupts his speech by fracturing his words and overwhelming them with the strained sonority of his attempts to form sentences (he is called "So Long" because he can only complete sentences by repeating the phrase "so long"). So Long's constricted voice forms a second cage within the wider container of the prison, as the bird museum's labels build secondary logocentric cages around the encased and stuffed animals.[4] Against the balanced and neutral framing of So Long's conversations with Sam, and even though as the interlocutor with the key information So Long should logically assume the role of "narrator," So Long's stammer extends and solidifies the glass panels between the two men to both confirm and perform his incarceration "inside" the prison. The voice, that is, *articulates* both the spatiality of the scene and the power dynamic entailed by that spatiality. Notably, Sam assumes an external position here, contrasting with his internalization in the gallery. Both cases demonstrate how, in *The Bird with the Crystal Plumage*, vocalization itself defines a person's/body's spatial status. This status is neither fixed nor a result of information asymmetry but is a quality constantly negotiated by the voice.

At a higher level, Sam's failure to exert vocal mastery over the unfolding scene in the gallery leaves him trapped in interiority at a national level. After Sam is released from the glass doors, Argento and editor Franco Fraticelli cut to a scene in Morosini's office where Sam tells the inspector, "We've been through the whole damn thing six times! Look, I've told you everything, everything!" Morosini replies, "Let's start over again, maybe there's a detail you've forgotten to mention?" Morosini is concerned by Sam's inability to convincingly describe the scene he witnessed. Sam's metacinematic characterization as a voice-over narrator who has "lost his voice" goes from implied to literal as the flashbacks through which he repeatedly recalls the scene are invariably wordless, literally lacking the explanatory voice-over he is unable to provide. Fittingly, Sam's passport—a written, logocentric text that directly grants one the ability to travel across spatial borders—is confiscated by Morosini in the hope that Sam will soon be able to tell his story more clearly. Just as Sam's failure to vocally explain his situation to the man on the street consigned him to the impotent interiority of the scene unfolding in the gallery, his inability to remember and share his memories of that scene has left him trapped within Italy's borders.

Sam's national entrapment is consequential given the film's jet-setting narrative: he is an American living in Rome, his girlfriend is British, and their friends are Italian. Whereas *The Girl Who Knew Too Much* begins with a scene of a TWA Boeing 707 flying into Fiumicino airport, *The Bird with the Crystal Plumage* ends with a shot of one flying out. The film portrays a time when globe-trotting subjects can travel across spatial borders at will, where anyone with enough money can become external to any location and ascend narrator-like to the very border of terrestrial space. Vitally, the film suggests that Sam's need to talk his way out of the scene in the gallery before he can physically leave Italy is self-enforcing. Even after his passport is returned, he decides to stay and keep investigating, and he continues to be haunted by silent, unnarrated flashbacks. It appears that, for Sam at least, attaining the spatial exteriority that is a benefit of his socioeconomic position is always contingent on discursive exteriority, the radical otherness of the voice-over narrator. *The Bird with the Crystal Plumage* uses the metacinematic paradigm of the voice-over to thematize the voice's importance not just in the demarcation of immediate or hyperlocal spaces, like the two sides of a glass wall, but in the organization of urban and national spaces too.

The previous examples of how voice and space are connected in *The Bird with the Crystal Plumage* are noteworthy for what they reveal about the voice's role in the representation—and creation—of space more generally, both in and beyond the film text. Chion's ([1982] 1999, 23, original emphasis) discussion of the *acousmêtre* is useful here because it reveals the importance of the voice to questions of cinematic space. Chion describes the acousmêtre as a voice without a visualized source, and he identifies this type of voice as a foundational possibility of sound cinema as an art and a medium. He bases this argument on the fact that, unlike an offstage voice in the theater that clearly comes from the wings next to the stage, the acousmatic voice comes from the same loudspeaker as a scene's visualized sounds. It thus creates an uncanny area between the spaces that are visually represented and those that are not. It is uniquely cinematic. Further, the acousmêtre is *"at once inside and outside, seeking a place to settle."* Conversely, the act of "de-acousmatization" is "the unveiling of an image and at the same time a *place*" ([1982] 1999, 28, original emphasis). Clearly, for Chion, the cinematic voice, which manifests in its most affecting form in the acousmêtre, always raises questions of space and its division. Once spoken, the voice fills space, giving substance to that which would otherwise seem empty. It connects the mouth and the ear, showing how they are both separate and linked. The acousmêtre is troubling precisely because the nature of these spatial relations (those between the utterer and others within the diegesis and those between the scene and the audience) are unclear. At a basic level, then, the acousmêtre shows how vocal sounds are mainly a spatial phenomenon, especially in a film.

In one sense, space can be understood in Euclidean terms (after Greek mathematician Euclid). In its simplest form, Euclidean space refers to the volume that results from the distance between a set of coordinates (normally framed in terms of height, depth, and width). As such, the Euclidean space of a room can be seen as that volume that results from the distance between the ceiling and floor, and the walls from each other. A person's voice can significantly alter or modify their occupation of this space. Steven Connor (2000, 5) has suggested that the voice is like a bodily projectile that extends the body's presence beyond its fleshy borders into the space around it. He writes, "The voice always requires and requisitions space, the distance that allows my voice to go from and return to myself." To give voice is to locate one's body *in* a space, to extend one's bodily presence *through* a space, and to put oneself into *relation* with that space. In the case of the character (or, for that matter, the documentary contributor) in a film, the use of the voice articulates the individual's relation to the physical space they occupy so that it may be perceived by the audience. This remains true, of course, when one is silent.

The involvement of the voice in the cinematic representation of Euclidean space is abundantly clear in the gallery scene discussed above. The image suggests a spatial continuity between the entrance to the gallery and the back wall against which Monica and the killer enter—and, thanks to the gallery's glass doors, this remains so even after Sam is trapped. But this visual continuity is challenged by the fact that Sam and Monica cannot verbally communicate, that the gallery contains two physically distinct spaces, each of which contains one body. In other words, the image misleadingly suggests that the gallery is a single space, but the scene's use of voice makes it clear that the action takes place across and between two separate spaces. This mismatch between these two representations of the gallery space generates the scene's narrative tension.

The gallery scene, however, also suggests that there is more to the voice's implication in space than the articulation of a Euclidean relationship between the body and its environment. As Sam and Monica's abortive conversation reveals, the voice is also intimately bound up in the creation of space in a social sense. Geographer Doreen Massey's *For Space* (2005) provides a detailed account of how social space is produced as a fluid and ongoing phenomenon through the interactions of diverse individuals at certain sites (which may be conceived at various orders of scale). For Massey (2005, 9), space is the social reality that is created and experienced in the coming together and crisscrossing of different people in certain locations at certain times. It is thus always provisional and always being (re)made. She opens her book by urging her readers to "recognise space as the product of interrelations; as constituted through interactions, from the immensity of the global to the intimately tiny.... Precisely because space on this reading is a product of relations-between, relations which are necessarily embedded material practices which have to be carried out, it is always in the process of being made." Massey does not focus on the voice when talking about space, but it is clear that, as a fulcrum of social interaction, the voice may play a major role in the creation of space as she understands it.[5] At the cinematic level, this is also clear in *The Bird with the Crystal Plumage*. The free man/prisoner dynamic that juxtaposes Sam and So Long in the prison is a creation of the contrast between Sam's clear voice and So Long's constricted, defensive stammer. Perhaps more clearly, when the silent suspects are "narrated" by the detective during the identity parade at the police station, the contrast between the policeman's commanding voice and the silence of the criminals shapes the social power dynamics of the dark room where the scene plays out. Both examples show how even subtle uses of the voice in a cinematic scene play a significant role in establishing and sustaining the social spaces depicted. Of course, a person's use of their voice very often signals the social nature of the space they occupy. One vocalizes very differently in a nightclub, at a funeral, in a job interview, and in an intimate setting with a partner. In this way, vocal performance often serves to flag the social connotations of the spaces represented in a film. *The Bird with the Crystal Plumage* seems to recognize this ironically; Sam's quieting in the gallery mimics the hush that is typically expected in such a space.

I have argued above that the director's role might be understood as one of spatial organization, of creating the spatiality of a film by arranging its various elements into a formal relationship. I hope I have shown that the voice is vital to a film's spatial organization at both the physical and social levels. At this point, the metaphor of the "authorial voice" seems particularly relevant, as does Bazin's ([1957] 1985, 255) suggestion, borrowed from Jacques Rivette, that "an auteur is someone who speaks in the first person." (Again, the fact that Argento has performed voice-over cameos in several of his films seems to flirt with this notion in literal terms.) Given the voice's potential importance in the organization of space in sound cinema, and given that the creative expression of the director might be best detected in a film's spatial characteristics, the commonplace notion that the director's creative distinction equates to their "voice" becomes almost literal. Perhaps it is in the combined vocal utterances of a film's characters/actors that the director's voice may be heard.

VOICE TECHNOLOGY AND SOCIAL CHANGE

Argento's thematization of the voice-space relationship in *The Bird with the Crystal Plumage* expands beyond the mechanics of its scenes to become a wider concern. The film explores the shifting spatial significance of vocalization in a historical period of accelerating technological change, and I focus on these aspects of the film for the rest of this chapter. Having established the centrality of the voice to reinforcing inside/outside distinctions at both the micro and macro levels, *The Bird with the Crystal Plumage* then deploys voice-mediating technology to turn this paradigm into a source of anxiety and tension. Monica and Alberto each make one threatening phone call, one to Morosini and one to Sam, both of which are recorded by their addressees. These audio recordings become the mystery's prime clues because a sound recorded in the background (the call of the titular rare bird kept at the local zoo) ultimately gives away the killers' identities. Aside from their overt threats of violence, Monica's and Alberto's anonymous calls are menacing because they isolate the callers' voices from identifiable and locatable bodies. Thus, according to Chion's ([1982] 1999, 24) seminal definition, these voices are rendered acousmatic and seem to gain the powers of omnipotence, omniscience, panopticism, and ubiquity. The first phone call to Morosini suggests that the anxiety introduced into the film via the acousmatic telephonic voices results particularly from their ubiquity, their ability to instantly be anywhere and everywhere. The telephone calls allow for an acoustic interpenetration of space where the glass effects, according to Siegel (2011, 212), the "optical interpenetration" of the spaces.

Siegel (2011, 227) builds on the work of Paul Virilio to argue that "the diminished importance of physical boundaries" characterizes *The Bird with the Crystal Plumage* and that "boundaries have been eroded by the new experiences of time and space produced by ever-advancing technologies of transport and telecommunications." Siegel focuses on the film's portrayal of air travel and television broadcasts as well as its cinematic depiction of Rome. He uses Virilio's analysis of television to suggest that this medium best represents the collapsing of space at work in the film. Because all of the film's diegetic television broadcasts originate in a studio (and at the compulsion of the police), however, it seems that the television cannot connect *any* two places. By contrast, the telephone allows virtually anyone in any place to duplicate their presence and occupy another place solely through their voice. Telephony is the most common and effective way to collapse space in *The Bird with the Crystal Plumage*, which explains the leading role it assumes in the structure of the film's mystery (in which sense, Argento's film echoes *Blood and Black Lace*; see the introduction). In contrast to the fleeting and narratively ineffectual television broadcasts made by Morosini and his psychoanalytical consultant, the killers' calls are replayed throughout the film as the investigating characters try to identify and localize the callers' voices. This is a struggle to solve a sort of audiospatial puzzle—who is talking, and from where—that is staged entirely through the manipulation of sound technology from which the television is merely a momentary distraction. It is a struggle to gain control over the sort of spatial compression that the film suggests is more clearly and significantly caused by telephony than by newer technologies. This is made particularly clear once the cry of the exotic bird in the zoo is identified and Sam rushes across Rome in a brief sequence of shots that ends at the Ranieri apartment. The solution to the riddle of the sound captured in the phone call helps one to understand and "decompress" the spatial aspects of the call so that they can be acted on (if somewhat ineffectually, given how Sam is subsequently misled by Alberto).

Importantly, the sleek science fiction aesthetic of the police lab in which the killers' calls are analyzed belies the fact that, historically speaking, much of the voice technology in the film had long been normalized. The telephone, to give the obvious example, had been invented nearly a hundred years earlier. Connor (2000, 410) writes, "The coming of the telephone and the phonograph meets with a puzzling lack of evidence for cultural trauma . . . the contemporary reaction to the coming of the telephone seems to have been 'about time, too.'" The telephone was, it seems, swiftly normalized. Furthermore, the tapping and secret recording of phone calls had been possible since the 1940s and was based on techniques originally designed to intercept telegram messages (Smith 2008, 167–69). The reel-to-reel tape deck used to record and analyze voices in the film had also existed, in essentially the same form, since before the Second World War. By 1970, this technology was increasingly overtaken by multitrack and then cassette-based formats. Even "voiceprinting" technology such as the oscilloscope monitor used by Morosini's technician to identify the killer's voice, although becoming more refined by the early 1970s, had existed since the 1940s (see Karpf 2006, 257–58).

The film seems to be less interested in the emergence of this technology than in its increasing ubiquity in everyday life. It explores both disembodied voices and the technologies that support this disembodiment, suggesting a broader social reality in which the displaced voice is now a given. The film's spatial logic reveals that internal/external spatial demarcation is an ongoing vocal negotiation while also suggesting that, in the social context beyond the film, voice technology has greatly expanded both the scale and the importance of that negotiation. As one of the killers tries to break into Julia's apartment, she grabs the telephone to call the police but panics when she finds that the line has been cut. This panic is a manifestation of the film's historical context, reflecting the disorientating and horrifying *unfamiliarity* of a scenario in which the voice *cannot* be disembodied and used to transcend space.[6] Crucially, it is only after the call fails that Julia tries to break out of a window. This suggests that, in the technologically developed society of the film, a trapped person's instinct is to use their voice to escape before or instead of their body. Julia's entrapment in her apartment is vocal before it is physical; the cut phone line is as constraining as the window she is unable to break through. The scene recalls Sam's entrapment in the gallery, with the cut telephone line replacing the glass wall. Like Sam, Julia is stuck behind a barrier in a single and isolated area where she cannot be heard and from which she cannot escape—in that order. In other words, the scene presents a technological interpretation of the film's exploration of the voice-space relationship, revealing the role played by voice technology in shifting the everyday experience of space in postboom Rome.

I hope to have shown that the voice is vital to the representation of space in *The Bird with the Crystal Plumage* at the thematic level as well as the formal. Of course, the two are linked; these thematic issues develop naturally from the way the film uses the complex spatial aspects of the voice to advance its individual scenes and overall narrative. The voice subtly supports the stylistic organization-in-space of much of the film and is therefore vital to how Argento synthesizes the parts of the film into a coherent whole. My assertion that the voice is often vital to the representation of space in a film and therefore to both directorial style and theme is meant to be neither definitive nor exhaustive. There are many ways directors leave traces of their authorship on their films. Such traces can be nebulous and, in the case of the giallo and similar types of filmmaking, they are often refracted through considerable commercial pressures and strictures. However, given the vital and very consequential role the voice plays in charting and creating cinematic space and thus mediating the relationships among a film's constituent parts, the voices in a film often have something to say about the approach and concerns of the director. In *The Bird with the Crystal Plumage*, it is the arrangement of diegetic voices that drives the film's tense manipulation of space and betrays the increasing and fraught complexity of Rome's spatiality at the end of the 1960s.

NOTES

1. EUR (Esposizione Universale Roma) is a district in Rome designed in a modernist, neoclassical style during the late 1930s and early 1940s. It was intended to host the (later canceled) 1942 World's Fair (which Mussolini's Fascists planned to use as a showcase for their achievements), and, after the war, it was the headquarters of many international corporations.
2. This text, as well as pieces by scholars and Argento's collaborators and hundreds of images, are collected in the three-hundred-page book produced alongside the exhibit. See De Gaetano and Garofalo 2022.
3. A concern he developed during his earlier career as a film critic at the newspaper *Paese Sera*.
4. Interestingly, Steven Connor (2014, 28) has noted historical links between stuttering and animality more widely.
5. I discuss this idea elsewhere in relation to the creation of political space during the 1977 Bologna riots. See Pollard 2021.
6. A similar scene opens Riccardo Freda's *The Iguana with the Tongue of Fire* (*L'iguana dalla lingua di fuoco*, 1971), and cut phone lines feature in *Torso* (see chap. 4). These parallels underscore how instinctively the giallo assumes and then manipulates the telephone's ability to control space.

THREE

IDEOLOGICAL VOICES

Short Night of Glass Dolls

ALDO LADO'S SHORT NIGHT OF GLASS DOLLS (*La corta notte delle bambole di vetro*, 1971) features a surprising paradox. The film shows the cinematic voice's great political significance, but it does so for the unlikely reason that its protagonist is mute, motionless, and glassy eyed throughout the entire story. The body of Gregory Moore (Jean Sorel)—an American journalist based in communist Prague—is discovered in a church garden before being taken to the city's morgue. It soon becomes apparent, however, that Gregory is not dead. He is paralyzed and unable to use any part of his body, including his voice, despite being fully conscious and aware of the world around him. While Gregory is trapped in this state, a voice-over provides the audience with access to his thoughts and unheard cries (the other characters in the morgue cannot hear them). The rest of the film alternates between Gregory's desperate and futile attempts to make the hospital staff aware that he is still alive (they suspect that something unusual is going on, as his body never achieves rigor mortis) and extended flashbacks through which he tries to piece together what has led him to this state. It is gradually revealed that Gregory has been trying to track down his Czech girlfriend Mira (Barbara Bach), who has disappeared. His search leads him to Club 99, a quasisatanic sex cult made up of Prague's elderly social elite, who go to great lengths to silence those who threaten their power. They have murdered Mira for her investigations into their operations and likewise consign Gregory to his paralytic living death in the final flashback scene before killing him as the end credits start to roll.

Giallo film production increased after the success of *The Bird with the Crystal Plumage* and Argento's second feature, *The Cat O'Nine Tails* (*Il gatto a nove code*), which was released later in 1970. Many of the films Argento inspired had titles that brazenly copied his preference for animals and numbers (see Argento 2014, 124); indeed, the working title of *Short Night of Glass Dolls* was *Short Night of the Butterflies* (*La corta notte delle farfalle*). It was changed before the film's release, however, to avoid confusion with Duccio Tessari's *The Bloodstained Butterfly* (*Una farfalla con le ali insanguinate*), which was released earlier in 1971. In any case, the openness with which gialli of the early 1970s exploited Argento's popularity indicates how giallo filmmaking embraced the typical filone production model during that time. A successful formula had been established by a small number of pioneer films, and it was copied many times. The premise of *Short Night of Glass Dolls* further demonstrates that the giallo gradually moved toward the oneiric (dreamlike) as it developed into a fully-fledged filone but that it also continued to draw on intertextual points of reference. The film recalls the story and style of the "Breakdown" episode of *Alfred Hitchcock Presents* (1955), in which a man paralyzed in a car accident is taken to the hospital and presumed dead. A voice-over conveys his thoughts to the audience as he tries to signal to hospital staff that he is alive. Gregory's voice-over also alludes to Billy Wilder's *Sunset Boulevard* (1950), an American noir in which the protagonist narrates the story of his death from beyond the grave. As in *The Girl Who Knew Too Much*, the giallo makes its debt to film noir audible here.

Chapters 1 and 2 showed how the human voice is used in two early gialli to invest the soundtracks with traces of the cultural contexts within which they were made. In this chapter, I consider the giallo's auditory connections to more diffuse and nebulous political concerns that circulated both in and beyond Italy in the postwar decades. I understand this political atmosphere as the giallo's ideological context, and I use the term *ideology* in a relatively broad sense to refer to the underlying principles, goals, and values that underpin the political actions taken by states and other national and international organizations at a given time. Using the term in this way, I draw attention to the fact that giallo cinema was caught up in political processes that extended far beyond the Italian film industry. Indeed, the notion of ideology recurs in the historical sources discussed in this chapter. The political forces that shaped the giallo's soundtracks (and, more subtly, those of both its filone and art house contemporaries) stemmed from some of the wider political, economic, and social trajectories Italy followed throughout the middle of the twentieth century. As I broaden the historical scope of my discussion, however, I also narrow my textual focus exclusively onto voice dubbing because this is the practice in which the giallo's ideological entanglements become most audible.

Short Night of Glass Dolls reveals the politics of the voice precisely because it is so interested in the removal and replacement of the voice. This is a complex issue in the film because, although Gregory is mute, he is not strictly silent; he talks extensively through the voice-over that articulates his inner speech for the audience's benefit. The film indicates that this voice-over represents a form of silent *voice* rather than (or as well as) *thought* in the repeated extreme close-ups of Gregory's unmoving mouth that accompany it in the first morgue scene. Gregory's mute cry "You! Listen to me! Look at me! Can't you hear me?... Don't leave me like this! Help me!" is also a plea for recognition, a desperate attempt to address the other characters in the morgue. Such is the pleasure of this scene. The audience's dual awareness of Gregory's urge to use his voice and his inability to do so generates the thrill of tension in a way that simply hearing his thoughts would not. More broadly, Gregory's muted voice reveals that silence, as Mladen Dolar (2006, 152) has argued, "always functions as the negative of the voice, its shadow, its reverse, and thus something which can evoke the voice in its pure form." By remapping Gregory's voice onto silence *Short Night of Glass Dolls* inverts the voice like a photographic negative inverts a visual image. As with a photographic negative, the silencing of the voice reveals details that would otherwise remain hidden.

In chapter 4 I explore the formal complexity of silence in the giallo in more depth. Here, I contend that the contrast between Gregory being muted and the film's cacophony of other voices thematically illustrates the great ideological importance the human voice may acquire as a political tool for both uniting and separating communities. The true significance of the voice in this film, however, lies in the striking parallels between its thematic role *within* the text and the political roles it plays *beyond* the limits of the text. Through its stylized use of voice-over, *Short Night of Glass Dolls* highlights the practice of voice dubbing, which the Italian film industry relied on for producing films' soundtracks. By doing this, the film creates a space where its thematic concerns with the voice's ideological power can interact with the material and ideological facets of voice dubbing. Like most gialli, *Short Night of Glass Dolls* was an international coproduction, that is, a collaboration among production companies in multiple countries. As mentioned briefly in the introduction, such deals were widespread in postwar European filmmaking because producers could receive state support from more than one country and share the financial risk of making a film. These coproductions (which I discuss in more detail below) used international casts; actors and crew members were brought in from each producer's home country, and those countries were also sometimes used as filming locations. *Short Night of Glass Dolls* was a coproduction involving producers from three countries and featuring actors of many nationalities. Dubbing was vital to a film like this because it removed the linguistic barriers among actors and enabled the creation of multiple language versions of the film, each ready for distribution in a different international market.

There was more than pragmatism involved in dubbing, however, because the coproduction of films was part of a wider ideological move toward economic and political integration in Europe—the formalization of the European Economic Community (EEC) in 1957 and the North Atlantic Treaty Organization (NATO) in the late 1940s, for example. The dubbed voices in coproduced films—including filone and art house varieties—were both symptomatic and enabling of this goal. But the use of dubbing in *Short Night of Glass Dolls*, and the giallo more broadly, also has roots in Italy's longer political history. Specifically, Gregory's voice-over hints at Italian dubbing's Fascist origins. This history shows that the technique may be used as a tool for *nationalism* as readily as *internationalism*. *Short Night of Glass Dolls* reveals this ideological contradiction and, in the process, the role played by the cinematic voice in making audible the political context (or contexts) within which a film is produced. In turn, the importance of dubbing to the giallo shows that these films cannot be labeled simply as apolitical entertainment. Rather, the way they were created tied them to social and political events that extended far beyond the cinema.

THE IDEOLOGY OF MONOTONY

The relationship between ideology and the voice in *Short Night of Glass Dolls* is striking. The film focuses on governmental politics, which shapes its setting. The search for exotic locations, newly accessible to both film crews and audiences in an age of rapidly increasing international mobility, is characteristic of the giallo, but *Short Night of Glass Dolls* is unique because it is set and partly shot behind the Iron Curtain (Ljubljana and Zagreb, as well as Prague, were used as locations [Bartolini 2017, 89–90]). The film was made in the wake of the Prague Spring, its brutal repression by Warsaw Pact countries, and the Soviet Union's imposition of a more hardline government in Czechoslovakia. *Short Night of Glass Dolls* confronts this political atmosphere indirectly but insistently, despite Lado's claim that Prague was chosen as an allusion to Franz Kafka (Lado 2012). In the first flashback scene, Gregory is reporting on the details of a Cold War standoff, and the film's dialogue often includes references to "the regime" and the "oppression of the party." Mira (whom Gregory is trying to expatriate to London with him) must also be "smuggled" out of the country, and Gregory's colleague Jessica (Ingrid Thulin) is politely asked to alter a recent article by a member of Prague's social elite.

The references made to the oppression of the Czechoslovakian-Soviet regime are supported by the omnipresence of Prague's police force. Plainclothes police officers begin spying on Gregory and are fronted by a belligerent commissar (Piero Vida) who wears a long black trench coat reminiscent of those worn by the Stasi in communist East Germany (as well as several villains in earlier gialli, including *The Bird with the Crystal Plumage* and *Blood and Back Lace*, thanks to which the commissar functions as a red herring for the film's killings). The film's politics get more surreal as the details of Club 99 are (literally) fleshed out and the geriatric, sex-crazed cultists are revealed to be the real seat of sociopolitical power in Prague. While the club members seem to be an isolated group operating with a power separate from that of the state, *Short Night of Glass Dolls* goes to some lengths to conflate the two. Even after Gregory realizes that Club 99 holds the key to Mira's disappearance, the commissar, a figure of *state* apparatus, continues to hound and impede his investigation as if he were a henchman of the cult itself. According to the film's sensational logic, the cult therefore becomes a microcosm of Czechoslovakia's totalitarian state. This link becomes clear when the cult leaders tell Gregory that "we will hold the reins of power in the world as long as there are people willing to be killed. . . . Our bitterest enemies are those who don't believe" and that they "must enslave the free to preserve our powers. We need the young to keep us alive. They must become like us, they must think as we do."[1]

The connection between the voice and power is clear. The cultists' explanations for their actions are delivered in a rapid series of surreal talking head shots in which their floating faces appear against a black background as they explain their malign intentions to a feverish Gregory. These *talking heads* suggest an authority that is centered purely on the voice; the cultists' bodies, seemingly irrelevant to the authority they wield and anyway shown to be withered and weak in the surrounding orgy scene, are excluded from the shots as if irrelevant. To drive the message home, this presentation inverts the image of the powerless young woman who writhes on an altar in the middle of the orgy, nude, fetishistically photographed, and notably voiceless. To stress this voice-powerful/silent-powerless dynamic, a leading cultist's mouth is shown in extreme close-up as he explains the truth about Club 99. This choice of shot suggests that the mouth is the linchpin of the cultists' power and forms a clear counterpoint to the extreme close-ups of Gregory's *unmoving* mouth in the morgue. The surrealism of the orgy scene makes the actual words spoken by Club 99's members seem irrelevant, pointing to Dolar's (2006, 114, original emphasis) claim that "all phenomena of totalitarianism tend to hinge overbearingly on the voice, which in a *quid pro quo* tends to replace the authority of the letter."[2] The words the cultists say matter far less than the voices that utter them.

Dolar makes a brief observation about Stalinist speeches that is enlightening here—and not simply because the ghost of Joseph Stalin hung heavily over post-1968 Czechoslovakia. Dolar (2006, 117–18) writes, "When the Stalinist leader makes a public speech, he reads in a monotonous voice.... The Stalinist ruler endeavors to efface himself and his voice; he is merely the executor of the text, just as he is the mere tool of the laws of history, not their creator." The voice, here, is a vessel for the pure power of historical inevitability. The Stalinist mode of voice seeks out an idealized form of sound, which either denies or transcends the contingencies of the time and place of an utterance. Although the example of Stalin is extreme, the idealization of sounds that are independent of the context in which they are produced is insidious. Nina Sun Eidsheim (2015, 2) writes, "The dynamic, multifaceted, and multisensorial phenomenon of sound is often reduced to something static, inflexible, limited, and monodimensional. Music, then, is most commonly experienced through . . . the *figure of sound*. With this term I attempt to capture the process of ossification, through which I argue that an ever-shifting, relationally dependent phenomenon comes to be perceived as a static object or incident" (original emphasis). For Eidsheim, the figure of sound verges on an aural ideology, one that understands sounds in terms of their fixed, abstract qualities (pitch, tone, timbre) and removes them from the "thick" (complex, subjective, contingent) events in which they are created and heard (2015). These thick events may be shaped by the medium in which the sound is created and heard, the acoustics of a given space, or the listener's affective response to what they hear. These events are unique and provisional. While Eidsheim is writing in the context of music and song, her argument harmonizes with Dolar's views on Stalin. Speaking their drawling words, the Soviet-style leader aspires to decontextualize their voice—there is little place in the totalitarian model for the provisional or the contingent. The Stalinist speech is not an unrepeatable event; it aspires to be "monodimensional"— an everlasting, universal, and stable text. Political ideology is underpinned by an ideology of voice. As they explain themselves to Gregory, the cultists—perverse proxies of the Soviet-backed regime at play in Czechoslovakia—share a sort of monotone Stalinist drawl. The cultists' acoustic oneness suggests that, like Stalin, they speak with one deindividualized voice that makes audible the immense and transcendental power they hold. The monotone as an ideological mode of sound/voice is significant here because, as Dolar and Eidsheim imply and the "mono" prefix makes clear, it presupposes singularity. Strangely, the cultists' singular voice echoes the orgy in which they indulge. Naked, elderly,

Figure 3.1. The cultists engage in a ritualistic orgy in *Short Night of Glass Dolls* (Aldo Lado, 1971). Their bodies seem to merge into one in the same way that they speak with a single monotonous voice.

and hazily photographed bodies surround Gregory in a writhing mix of flesh that challenges the separation of individuals and presents the cultists as a single body (fig. 3.1). They become the monobody that speaks the monotone. The cultists' shared corporeality and vocality point to an ideology that overwhelms the individual. Gregory's unheard voice-over, however, is typically frantic and animated, that is, polytonal. The contrast between Gregory's voice and the cultists' monotony shows his desire to break free, which is already clear in his plan to escape from Prague and smuggle Mira out with him. His voice sounds him out as a dissident. It therefore seems natural that the cult would remove this problematic noise by silencing his voice, first through paralysis and eventually through death.

Gregory's silencing can be interpreted as a form of monotony, and it destabilizes his identity. During the first scene in the morgue, a nurse (Franca Sciutto) tells the attending doctor (Daniele Dublino) what is known about the seemingly lifeless patient, gleaned from his passport: "He was an American... Gregory Moore, born in Springfield, Illinois, the sixth of December 1935." Dolar (2006, 14) writes, "We are social beings by the voice and through the voice.... Voices are the very texture of the social, as well as the intimate kernel of subjectivity," but Gregory's position in the "texture of the social" is constituted by and through the voice of another. In the following scene in the morgue, his voice-over is accompanied by a close-up of his face framed upside down, as if his now-voiceless body has become disoriented and disjointed.

Gregory's voiceless "corpse," unable to situate itself socially, undergoes a sort of "crisis of persona." The Latin origin of this term has roots in *per sonare*, or, roughly, "to sound through," and this etymology has theatrical overtones. In ancient theater, actors would project their voices through masks, and the word *persona* came to signify the face or character the actor presented to the audience (and then, more broadly, the character that any individual presents to the world around them). The voice is the specific type of breath one uses to bring a certain identity into existence. The giallo often seems to recall this aspect of theatrical history because so many of its killers wear literal masks or disguise their voices. In this way, the overt creation of a misleading, and often faintly inhuman, persona is often at the core of how the giallo's killers exert influence on their environments and how they generate both suspense and unease in the audience. The paralyzed and silenced Gregory, however, is denied this animating power and instead shifts identity erratically. For example, his enforced and passive silence naturally "deconstruct[s] the figure of the traditional male protagonist" (Olney 2013, 125); his state mirrors that of a silent and almost catatonically drugged woman (Michaela Martin) who is molested (with horrifying nonchalance) at a party during a flashback. Gregory's voiceless state also parallels those of the female victims in Paolo Cavara's contemporaneous giallo *The Black Belly of the Tarantula* (*La tarantola dal ventre nero*, 1971), who are paralyzed but left conscious by a killer who injects poison into their necks before murdering them, and of Sam in the gallery scene early in *The Bird with the Crystal Plumage* (see chap. 2). As in that scene, Gregory's inability to make himself heard clearly separates him from masculine subjectivity (like Sam, he is also a writer whose initial characterization is grounded in his presumed control of words). As if to emphasize Gregory's feminization, in the closing frames, his friend and former lover Jessica screams from the gallery as he is killed on the operating table and the film's credits begin to roll. Jessica lends Gregory her voice and provides him with his final cry, which stands at the other end of the auditory spectrum to silence but which, as pure sound, is just as removed from the masculinized territory of speech (see Chion [1982] 1999, 76–78; Brophy 1999, 53). Gregory acquires a feminine persona as he is penetrated by the scalpel: his silent body becomes the ventriloquist's dummy for another's voice and allows for a sort of gender performance by proxy.

Gregory's silencing exposes him to several other instances of identity performance by proxy, which extend beyond issues of gender. In the opening scene, as the church gardener (Joža Šeb) discovers Gregory's paralyzed body, Gregory is aligned with a passing amputee (uncredited) who propels himself around the churchyard on a skateboard and is also seemingly mute and ostracized from able-bodied society. At first, the audience is led to believe that the sound of the amputee driving himself forward using two pads attached to his hands that make a dull, rhythmic "bump-bump" sound is the sound of Gregory's heartbeat as the gardener presses his ear to Gregory's chest. In this way, the mute amputee invests Gregory's inert body with his own marginalized "kernel of subjectivity." Moments earlier, the gardener finds the body after being drawn to it by the crowing of a bird that also and more directly lends Gregory its voice to supply the cry that he cannot utter and align him with a sort of base, inhuman animality.[3] The silencing of Gregory Moore's voice has quite literally *unmoored* his body. Unable to give voice to a persona of his own, Gregory is cast adrift in a sea of social coordinates determined by the voices fleetingly lent to him. His challenge to Club 99's power is then resolved precisely through the incorporation of his voice into the monotone of ideology: the absolute, pure monotone of silence. His identity is now fully pliable, and, like the cultists, he does not speak in his own name. Unable to control his voice, Gregory cannot position himself in relation to others and is thus unable to maintain a position of resistance to the malign power of Club 99. Like *The Bird with the Crystal Plumage*, *Short Night of Glass Dolls* thematizes an equation of voice and power but at a more extreme scale and with a particular interest in the political implications of silence. The film proposes a sobering suggestion: Ideology is what you speak when you say nothing.

DUBBING AND THE IDEOLOGY OF EUROPEAN COPRODUCTION

The thematic concern for the politics of the voice in *Short Night of Glass Dolls* is particularly enlightening because it highlights the nondiegetic politics involved in creating the film's soundtrack. By overlaying Gregory's unheard voice onto the image of his motionless face, the film challenges one of the key norms of narrative filmmaking. This ploy frustrates the audience's expectation of what Chion (1994, 5) calls *synchresis*: "The forging of an immediate and necessary relationship between something one hears and something one sees." Synchresis occurs when a sound we hear seems to be "in sync" with something we see (the cause of the sound). For example, the sound of shattering glass and the image of a window being smashed or the sound of a voice and the image of a speaking mouth. This latter example is, of course, precisely what *Short Night of Glass Dolls* refuses to show us in the morgue scenes. The film highlights that in cinema, images and sounds are recorded separately by choosing not to make them perfectly synchronized in these moments. Rather, the film emphasizes that in cinema, the image and the sound are separately recorded (by a camera and a microphone, respectively) and separately reproduced when the film is watched (by a projector/screen and a loudspeaker, respectively). Rick Altman's (1980, 67) description of the image/sound relationship as a mechanism of cinematic ventriloquism is particularly apt: "The sound track is a ventriloquist who, by moving his dummy (the image) in time with the words he secretly speaks, creates the illusion that the words are produced by the dummy/image." The immobilized image of Gregory Moore (specifically, the repeated image of his unmoving mouth) is unable to fulfill its part in this bargain. Gregory is a broken puppet; his voice floats freely and the true separation of the film's soundtrack from its images is exposed.

The separation of the image/sound or mouth/voice is even more profound because Gregory's face and voice do not even come from the same actor. While we see French actor Jean Sorel on screen, Gregory's voice is provided by uncredited voice doubles (a North American voice actor in the English version of the film, and Giancarlo Maestri in the Italian). These voices were added to the film during postproduction long after Sorel filmed his part. In fact, up until the 1980s, the Italian film production system rarely recorded direct sound. For reasons of commercial necessity and historical habit (both discussed below), filmmakers shot silently, often with an international cast of actors speaking different languages in front of the camera. As the footage was edited, dubbing directors would select voice actors to dub the lines of each character. Typically, versions were made in several major European languages; the on-screen actors would sometimes dub themselves in their native language, but not always. The script would then be tweaked in each language so that the words recorded matched the movements of the lips on-screen (although Italian dubbing in the 1960s and 1970s was often quite lax in this regard). At the end of the process, several different dubs of the film would be ready for distribution. Notably, the Italian versions of giallo films had their dialogue recorded in this way too (I discuss this fact in more detail below).

Short Night of Glass Dolls takes the dubbing process to the point of absurdity. In the morgue scenes, the film repeatedly pairs one person's voice and the image of another's face without the vital pretense of lip-synching to "transfer the origin of the words, as perceived by the spectator/auditor, from sound 'track' and loudspeaker to a character within the film's diegesis" (Altman 1980, 69). The stylistic treatment of Gregory's silenced voice in the morgue scenes highlights the film's reliance on the practice of voice dubbing and so (presumably unwittingly) emphasizes the industrial preconditions of 1970s Italian film sound. Due to the looseness of dubbing synchronization in the film's other scenes, this awareness carries over into the whole film. The exposure of the voice dubbing process in *Short Night of Glass Dolls* reveals that Gregory's voice spans character, on-screen actor, and voice actor as well as narrative, set, and sound studio. The flat "spacelessness" of dubbed voices often betrays, in literal terms, the fact that such voices do not originate in the spaces that we see on-screen. Lado's film, however, makes it clear that Gregory Moore's voice comes from somewhere beyond the frame and beyond the text in a broader sense. Through the film's stylistic treatment of Gregory's voice, the practical concerns of Italy's filmmaking economy make themselves heard within the text. I discuss these conditions in the rest of this chapter.

By the time *Short Night of Glass Dolls* was produced, the use of dubbed voices in Italian cinema was mainly influenced by commercial factors that transcended national borders because dubbing was central to the transnational coproduction paradigm at the heart of the industry's economic viability. Avenues of cooperation and cross-pollination had existed among European film industries since the earliest days of cinema, but international collaboration was formalized through legal treaties in the immediate postwar years. During this period, American imports flooded into Europe (as they had done since the early years of cinema). The continent's small and weakened film industries were ill-equipped to fight back and risked economic ruin if the onslaught continued unabated (which came with the associated threat of a loss of European film culture/s in the face of Hollywood's dominance). Joining forces offered a possible solution for European producers, and this turned out to be remarkably successful. Europe's first formal and legally recognized coproduction treaty was signed in 1949 between Italy and France, following a series of experimental arrangements that had been in place since 1946. The treaty allowed filmmakers in Italy and France to collaborate on a film that would have national status in both countries. This meant that the producers could receive financial support through grants, loans, tax reliefs, and other incentives offered by both states. The treaty, and those that followed and copied it, also clearly outlined each producer's financial responsibilities (most agreements followed either a fifty-fifty or seventy-thirty split, at least initially), the producers' obligations to hire cast and crew from each participating country (see Romanelli 2016, 32), and the manner in which revenues from the various distribution markets would be divided among the parties.[4] The treaty proved effective in reinvigorating the film industries in both Italy and France; 230 Franco-Italian films had been made by 1957 (Jäckel 2003, 233), 711 by 1964 (Bergfelder 2006, 55), and 2000 by 1972 (Mitric 2018, 69). Perhaps unsurprisingly, Italy went on to sign coproduction treaties with countries across Europe in the following years, including West

Germany and Yugoslavia (where *Short Night of Glass Dolls* was filmed) in 1953 and 1957, respectively (Jäckel 2003, 238; Di Chiara 2013, 38). In the case of Lado's film, there were likely several different motivations behind these partnerships. By the early 1970s, West Germany was heavily involved in making coproduced genre films similar to those produced by Italian filmmakers, whereas Yugoslavian production companies appealed to producers in Western Europe because they could provide cheap labor and desirable locations (Di Chiara and Noto 2023).[5] In any case, Lado's film exemplifies a form of coproduction-facilitated transnationalism that became common in European cinema after the Second World War and that had come to dominate Italian filmmaking by the end of the 1960s. Barbara Corsi (2020, 86), for example, estimates that Italy was producing around 240 films per year between 1962 and 1968 and that 40 to 60 percent of these were made through some form of coproduction. These films included art films as well as filone fare; many of Michelangelo Antonioni's early films were Italo-French coproductions, for example. The giallo relied heavily on the coproduction system, however, as it played directly into the filone production model. Teaming up with a foreign partner guaranteed producers a considerable amount of financial incentive and protected their downside, meaning their films did not necessarily have to do well on the market to turn a quick profit.

Inevitably, the issue of determining a coproduced film's nationality is complicated because the cast, crew, and funding come from various countries, making it virtually impossible to classify the film as being "from" a single country. This is the case with *Short Night of Glass Dolls*, an Italian/West German/Yugoslavian collaboration that uses French, Italian, German, American, Swedish, and Yugoslavian actors to tell a story about an American in Czechoslovakia. Lado's nationality seems to be the only factor anchoring the film to Italy, but even this is problematic. Lado was born in Fiume (now Rijeka and part of Croatia), a town that was Italian at the time of his birth, Austro-Hungarian shortly before, Yugoslavian shortly after, and that was passed among British, French, Hungarian, and Croatian powers during the nineteenth century. Strictly speaking, *Short Night of Glass Dolls* is more accurately seen as a transnational film than a national one. Over the last twenty years, the terms *transnational* and *national* have been debated and productively complex terms in the study of cinema. The term *transnational* can be thought to describe texts that, in Andrew Higson's (2000, 61) words, originate from some "degree of cultural crossbreeding and interpenetration, not only across borders but also within them." The transnationalism that underlays the production and distribution of Lado's film and other gialli explains in large part why they were dubbed. The voice, of course, presents a serious stumbling block to transnational filmmaking of this kind because as the bearer of language, it does not always travel well. As an Italian-German-Yugoslavian text destined for exhibition in several language areas, Lado's film would have encountered linguistic obstacles during both production and distribution. In the latter case, several translations of the text's dialogue were required for each of its target markets. Dubbing multiple versions of the dialogue track solves this problem, although subtitling was also an option for markets where the audience deemed it acceptable. As mentioned briefly above, however, an international cast often could not perform together in a single language, so a "polyglot" film was shot, with each performer speaking in their native language in front of the camera (see Betz 2009, 83). Sergio Martino (2017, 114), a prolific producer and director of filone films including several gialli (see chap. 4), emphasizes the centrality of this system to filone production: "At that time, dubbing was a fundamental part of the films we made, above all adventure films, thrillers, and westerns. They were never shot with direct sound and they employed a wide array of actors of many nationalities." Dubbing these films in postproduction was the only way to manage the linguistic differences in the performers' voices. It also allowed a series of soundtracks to be produced efficiently, with each one calibrated to the needs of each distribution market and none being more authentic or original than the others (Betz 2009, 85). (The 88 Films 2016 UK DVD release of *Short Night of Glass Dolls* features both English and Italian versions, presenting them as a pair of interchangeable equivalents on the main menu.) In short, the dubbed voice is the technical solution to two industrial dilemmas, and through its use, the postwar economics of the Italian (and European) film industry significantly influence the film's aesthetics.

Coproduction and the voice dubbing that helped facilitate it were part of a bigger political picture, though. In the 1980s, filmmaker Jean-Marie Straub (Straub and Huillet 1985, 152–53) argued vehemently against the use of dubbing in this way and likened the technique to a sort of modern-day Esperanto with significant implications: "Only by accepting the dictatorship of dubbing can you use two or three stars from different countries in the same film. . . . The international aesthetic is an invention and weapon of the bourgeoisie. . . . Esperanto has always been the dream of the bourgeoisie." Straub's focus on a "bourgeois" aesthetic reveals its Marxist overtones and the emphasis it therefore places on the capitalist economic system that underpins postwar filmmaking. After all, dubbing served explicitly capitalist purposes by helping producers to both acquire financing and expand their distribution markets. Straub and Huillet (1985, 150) go on to claim that "dubbing is not only a technique, it's also an ideology," and this comment echoes the 1967 Amalfi Manifesto, signed by a group of Italian directors including Antonioni, Pier Paolo Pasolini, Bernardo Bertolucci, Francesco Rosi, and Vittorio De Seta. These filmmakers assert that dubbing and postsynchronized sound deprive films "of elements which should be integral to them, and at the same time they subject the film to maneuvers and mystifications on the part of producers and distributors, whose final effect has an ideological character" (quoted in Nowell-Smith 1968, 145). In their recurrent concern with ideology, the authors of these statements recognize that the stakes of voice dubbing in postwar European cinema are higher than mere commercial convenience. In the article in which he quotes the manifesto, Geoffrey Nowell-Smith (1968, 147) notes as much: "It has been going on for many years and is not unique to Italy. Events of the past few years have introduced a new and more sinister factor, which is the internationalisation of the European cinema industry, centred on [the Italian film studio] Cinecittà... which has led to the growth of co-production (and therefore parallel distribution) [between Italy and] other European countries, generally those of the Common Market, but also Yugoslavia and Spain." Nowell-Smith keenly observes a link between the integration of Europe's film industries and the wider move toward European political and economic integration that was happening at the same time. This process of integration was perhaps clearest in the signing of the Treaty of Rome in 1957 by six countries including Italy. The treaty marked the formation of the European Economic Community (EEC), which was designed to facilitate cross-border trade by ensuring compatibility of policy among member states and the removal of trade barriers (it would later evolve into the European Union). The Treaty of Rome had been preceded throughout the 1940s and 1950s by other economic treaties and agreements that had been narrower in scope (these included an extensive bilateral trade deal between Italy and Yugoslavia in 1948 that supported cross-border cultural exchange between the two countries, paving the way for the coproduction agreement that would underpin *Short Night of Glass Dolls* [Di Chiara and Noto 2023, 650–51]). This time also marked the formation of NATO, a military alliance that encompassed several European countries, also including Italy. The immediate postwar period witnessed a marked movement toward European integration at several levels and in various arenas. The coproduction of films was a concrete part of this process. In the words of Petar Mitric (2018, 69), "If one compares the content of the French-Italian co-production treaty with the provisions of the Treaty of Rome, one can see that they were implemented within the same political arena—with a shared goal to restore Europe as an economic power." Players in the Italian film industry validate this point. David Warbeck, a UK-based New Zealand actor who appeared in numerous Italian horror and thriller genre films of the 1970s and 1980s (and whose involvement was made possible thanks to dubbing), said in an early 1990s interview, "My own impression is that the Italian film world is gearing up to become the film center of Europe, the Common Market" (quoted in Palmerini and Mistretta 1996, 155). Warbeck's comment shows that by the early 1990s, the Italian film industry could no longer be understood in isolation. Even the agreement between Italy and Yugoslavia, which was not part of the EEC at this time, still "promoted the post-war internationalization of the Italian film industry and the strengthening of cultural and industrial ties with a neighbouring country" (Di Chiara and Noto 2023, 658). Coproduction meant that the Italian film industry was becoming a part of a wider European film industry, the emergence of which was inseparable from the broader cultural, political, and economic integration of Europe.

When *Short Night of Glass Dolls* was made, European coproductions were not directly controlled by the EEC or any other centralized body, but many producers hoped they would be. In the 1950s, some European producers (principally French and Italian) moved to create a European Union of Film that would serve as a centralized financing organization for European films and as a meeting place for European industry professionals. The initiative ultimately failed, but at a conceptual level, it shows how the wider ideological shift toward integration in Europe was infiltrating the continent's filmmaking infrastructure (see Corsi 1996 for a full history of this project). In fact, as the EEC evolved into the European Union in later years, its offshoots took on a more direct role in centrally coordinating European film production; the 1989 foundation of Eurimages as a support fund for trans-European filmmaking being one example. Nonetheless, the many disparate coproduction agreements that existed in Europe by the early 1970s show "that the period was not one of passive transition but one of intense cultural activity at a time of tremendous international economic and ideological changes" (Jäckel 2003, 240). It is this ideology that Straub rallies against, one that is rooted in capitalism and that promotes the transnational over the national. Straub suggests that this ideology risks negating European artistic diversity in favor of the sort of nonspecific, bureaucracy-driven cultural middle ground that elsewhere has been derided as "Euro-pudding." As Betz (2009, 33) summarizes, "Nationhood is a consistent and explicit concern in the economic history of postwar European film production.... The textual terrain on which this conflict was staged is the actor's body in (or out of) sync with her or his voice." The true ideological significance of the dubbed voice in the giallo becomes clear once one takes this history into account. The political significance of the voice is a thematic issue for *Short Night of Glass Dolls*, but the film's use of dubbing also makes it a *material* issue, one that is bound up in the very construction of the film. Because it facilitates these films' transnational production and distribution, the dubbed voice actively contributes to the wider political and sociopolitical changes happening in Italy and Europe at the time of their production. When we listen to the dubbed voice in *Short Night of Glass Dolls* and other gialli, we do not hear merely the result of commercial pragmatism. These voices introduce into the text the deeper political issues that support those commercial imperatives. In the dubbed voice, we hear the process of European integration in action, history made audible, and ideology made material.

DUBBING AND THE LEGACY OF FASCISM

For those unfamiliar with the technique, there is something uncanny about dubbing. This is usually attributed to the mildly surreal effect of loose lip synchronization, but in the final part of this chapter, I suggest that there is a deeper and more complex strangeness to the dubbed voice. Dubbing performs a neutralization of national difference, whereas the national *specificity* of each dub does the opposite. There is something unsettlingly paradoxical at work here. Geoffrey Nowell-Smith (1968, 146) references the uncanny in his discussion of the Amalfi Manifesto. He writes that in the dubbed film, "national difference, the specificities of social and cultural situations, are all ironed out.... The concrete becomes abstract; and then, in an effort to make the abstract concrete again, it is reduced to the homely and easily understood." There are distinct Freudian tones to Nowell-Smith's phrasing (presumably inadvertent but perhaps all the starker as a result). In his 1919 article "The Uncanny," Sigmund Freud explains that uncanniness results when one encounters an object or experience that is at once familiar and unfamiliar: an extremely lifelike mannequin, a near-identical double of oneself, or a new location that one is somehow sure they have visited before. In Freud's ([1919] 2001, 219, 245, original emphasis and parentheses) words, while the uncanny "is undoubtedly related to what is frightening," more specifically, "the uncanny [*unheimlich*] is something which is secretly familiar [*heimlich-heimisch*], which has undergone repression and then returned from it." *Heimlich* is usually translated into English as "homely," which brings us back to Nowell-Smith's comment. The dubbed voice renders the unhomely (Freud's *unheimlich*) strangely homely (*heimlich*), and vice versa. The dubbed voice uneasily attempts to reconcile the national and the foreign, the familiar and the unfamiliar, and, in this sense, it is uncanny. The dubbed voice represses national difference, but not fully. In more practical terms, the coproduced giallo's dubbed voices produce a logical contradiction. The national-linguistic specificity of the dubbed voice insists on the (repressed) national specificity of an audience as it also seeks to minimize Europe's cultural borders. The transnational ideology behind the coproduction of *Short Night of Glass Dolls* sought to present Europeans as a more singular community, but its reliance on the dubbed voice risked the opposite effect. Dubbing blocks intercultural interaction and strengthens rather than weakens national-linguistic borders. If Lado's film and other gialli are examples of Euro-pudding, then they are, perhaps, only half-baked and their reliance on dubbing reveals and reinforces the perseverance (for better or worse) of national distinctions.

The reasons for this paradox can be understood by considering the longer history of dubbing in Italy. If Club 99 stands in for the Soviet regime imposing itself on Czechoslovakia after the 1968 Prague Spring, the club members may also be seen as a caricature of the Italian Fascist Party that led Italy from 1922 to 1943. Like Club 99, Benito Mussolini's propaganda policies required that everyone in Italy "think as we do" and, as with Club 99, this often meant "speaking as we do." This equation is most evident in the Fascists' imposition of voice dubbing once sound films began to circulate in Italian cinemas (slowly and unevenly at first) in the late 1920s and early 1930s. During this period, Italy was already importing large numbers of foreign films, predominantly from the United States but also from other European countries; Carla Mereu Keating (2016, 81) writes that the ratio of foreign to Italian films screened in Italy in the 1930s was around nine to one. In the first instance, this presented the practical problem of translating these texts for Italian audiences. Subtitling offered a possible solution, but it relied on audiences having a high enough level of literacy to follow large amounts of fast-moving text, and in many parts of Italian society at the time, this was not the case. Notwithstanding its technical challenges, dubbing was a more viable technique, and it soon became the norm for translating imported films into Italian.[6] Dubbing also quite quickly came to serve important ideological purposes. Throughout the life of the regime, the Fascist Party was engaged in the task of cementing Italy's cultural unification (a concern that had also been a preoccupation of the preceding liberal government). The country at this point had been unified for barely fifty years and was still significantly divided along regional lines. Perhaps the most notable manifestation of these divisions was the widespread persistence across the country of multiple dialects and minority languages that were often not mutually intelligible. As Mereu Keating (2016, 76) explains, "It was necessary for the government to spread the use of Italian over the national territory in order to communicate successfully with the 'new Italians' and enhance mass consensus." While it may have begun as a practical solution to a technical problem, a side effect of dubbing was that it provided the Fascists with a valuable tool in the pursuit of this political goal. By insisting that foreign films be dubbed into standardized Italian (which had originally been the dialect spoken in and around Florence), the regime could educate the population in the use of that language and gradually move people away from dialect. Dubbing also helped to ensure that "impure" traces of foreign languages (English or French words, for example) did not enter the national lexicon (the Fascist state was broadly committed to a policy of economic and cultural isolation at this time). As Antonella Sisto (2014, 62) has argued, "Dubbing was never about art, it was about the protection and administration of *Italianicity* through the language itself and as a carrier of legitimated ideas" (original emphasis). Indeed, dubbing also allowed a convenient point of intervention for censors who could insist that alterations to undesirable characters or narrative details were made when the dialogue tracks were dubbed into Italian. Sisto (2014, 23) is unambiguous about the stakes involved in this process, stating that dubbing was "the result (and then cause) of a mix of fear, rejection, and ignorance of the other, in a process of linguistic, cultural, and vocal exorcism." Certainly, the history of Fascist dubbing in Italy is one of vocal nationalism. The dubbed voice acts like a cultural shield. In this sense, it relates to Roberto Esposito's political ideas of immunity, in which a community neutralizes threatening otherness by allowing a small amount of it within its borders. In Esposito's (2011, 8) words, "Evil must be thwarted, but not by keeping it at a distance from one's borders; rather, it is included inside them. The dialectical figure that thus emerges is that of exclusionary inclusion or exclusion by inclusion." Like medical vaccines, the immunological processes at work in the political or cultural spheres allow in just enough otherness for the community—the "body politic"—to build up defenses against it. Dubbing facilitates this sort of exclusionary inclusion. The threatening foreign other was allowed within Italy's cultural borders, but only in a deactivated form in which the dangerous aspects of their otherness—the articulation of a foreign language and the sense of there being a world of social and political difference beyond the Fascist state—are neutralized. The viewer of the dubbed film is exposed to just enough otherness to reject it, but not enough to be infected by a dangerous, alternative worldview. To use another metaphor, the dubbed voices of Fascism can be seen as aural equivalents of the fasces itself, the symbol of Fascist ideology that adorned much of the regime's visual culture. The icon consists of a group of straight lines (logs or sticks) bound into a uniform bundle often around an axe or spear. Fascist dubbing cut all voices to the same specification, bundling them together into a single consistent group that overrode the identity of the constituent part. Club 99's monotonous shared voice can also be considered a caricature of the insistence on vocal uniformity at play in Italy's recent political and cinematic history. The important fact revealed by Fascist dubbing is that unity can only be achieved in relation to difference; to unite is not so much to remove borders as to move them. The *Italianicity* of Fascist dubbing relied on the dissolution of regional, dialectical difference, but simultaneously insisted on uncrossable borders of national-linguistic difference. Translation through subtitling allows audiences to directly confront linguistic and cultural otherness and therefore offers a "porous" form of mediation. Dubbing always institutes absolute auditory boundaries between the audience and on-screen others.

The dubbed voice under Fascism was not limited to translated foreign films. As Mereu Keating (2016, 67) explains, "The dubbing of foreign-language films would soon be implemented on a large scale, and the Roman synchronization industry become one of the most enduring and profitable post-production practices in Italy." The size and sophistication of this subindustry meant that dubbing (and, relatedly, the postsynchronization of all the ambient sounds on the soundtrack) soon became the default method for adding sound to Italian films as well. Importantly, this remained the case after the fall of Fascism. Like a lifelong immune response, dubbing's prophylactic effect continued long after its original stimulus had passed, and so Italian film sound *after* Fascism remains influenced by an ideology of national insulation. In Sisto's (2014, 10) terms, the continuation of dubbing (which is still used to translate the majority of foreign films and television programs in Italy) "constitutes itself today as the sonicscape of the nation's fascist repressed unconscious." The nationalist implications of dubbing are persistent because the technique continued (and continues) to isolate audiences from vocal otherness. The dubbed voices of the postwar and post-Fascist giallo may have served to culturally integrate Europe, but they also continued to divide the continent along rigid linguistic lines and to hold otherness at arm's length. As under Fascism, in the dubbed, coproduced film, the other is integrated, but only through the neutralization of their otherness. The spectator is invited into an international narrative yet insulated from the international within a bubble of vocal familiarity made up of recognizable languages, accents, and exclamations. The goal of the dubbed voice seamlessly drawing the spectator into *Short Night of Glass Dolls*' transnational representation of Czechoslovakia is undermined because dubbing cannot help but insist on the rigidity of national or linguistic borders. In Freudian terms, the national specificity that dubbing seems to try to repress cannot help but return uncannily. Like the model of coproduction, in which *transnational* alliances are forged to protect *national* film industries, the dubbed voice in the coproduced giallo is paradoxically—uncannily—somehow both integrationist and nationalist. To take a wider perspective on these questions, the political and economic history behind the giallo's use of dubbing reveals the cinematic voice's capacity to make the broad, diffuse, and nebulous political context or contexts within which a film is made tangibly audible. And the dubbed voice tells us that these films were not simply entertainment; they were active components of major societal and political transformations.

Dubbing prioritizes the practical demands of film production and distribution over strict representational realism. It makes this trade-off so that funding may be acquired, production costs lowered, soundtrack production simplified, distribution markets expanded, and perhaps even political dogma advanced. The dubbed voice always foregrounds the contextual influences that are at play around the production of a film. More broadly, as the case of *Short Night of Glass Dolls* shows, the dubbed voice marks a point at which the political, economic, or social basis for those influences directly shapes the form of a film. It is useful to return to Altman here and his analogy of ventriloquist/dummy as a model for understanding the relationship between image and sound in film. *Short Night of Glass Dolls* makes it clear that the real ventriloquist at work is less the loudspeaker hidden behind the screen than the commercial, historical, and political forces that determine, unseen and easily unnoticed, the voices that come out of it. In the first instance, Gregory's unheard voice anchors the film's stylistic conceit and is a vital component of its form. But it also reveals both the economic imperatives that underpinned the film's production and the political forces—both contemporary and historical in origin—that shaped those economic imperatives. The voice links the textual with the contextual in this film, intertwining them. Lado's film uses voice dubbing to make its complex political context more substantial. In the words of Valentina Vitali (2016, 30), the film's use of dubbing "stages" the conditions under which it was produced. The use of the voice in *The Girl Who Knew Too Much* gives audible form to the rise of consumerism in (and the rising consumption of) Rome and so contributes to that process. Similarly, *Short Night of Glass Dolls*' use of dubbing contributes to the ideological project of European integration and sustains an unexpurgated Fascist practice. By understanding the voice as both a driver of theme and a material manifestation of industrial, social, economic, or political forces, we can appreciate the tangible—if unexpected and possibly indirect—involvement of films like *Short Night of Glass Dolls* in the political arena. In their use of sound, these films do not merely testify to the sociopolitical environments within which they are produced; they bolster and perpetuate them as well.

NOTES

1. *Short Night of Glass Dolls* has much in common with the very differently styled but contemporaneous Czech film *The Ear* (*Ucho*, Karel Kachyňa, 1970). In the latter, also set in Prague, a senior communist politician returns home from an official party with his wife and discovers that their house has been bugged. Taken together, the two films suggest that, for all the visual spectacle associated with totalitarian regimes (real or caricatured), it is the insidiousness of the acoustic that enables such states to monitor and control the individual.

2. The word *parliament* comes from the Old French *parler*, "to speak." With minor variations, the word *parliament* is used in many European languages, both Latinate and otherwise (the Italian term is *parlamento*). Seemingly, even in the most mundane of contexts, the exercise of political power is rooted in acts of voice.

3. It is hard not to interpret the crow as another glancing intertextual reference, here to Pier Paolo Pasolini's *Hawks and Sparrows* (*Uccellacci e uccellini*, 1966). In the film, the two (human) protagonists travel through the countryside on the fringes of modernizing Rome where they meet a talking crow. The crow continuously spouts Marxist philosophy, and so this allusion perhaps further frames Gregory's silencing/revoicing as a political act.

4. The full complexity of postwar coproduction treaties, which are still fundamental to European film production, is beyond the scope of this book, but for more, see Mitric 2018; Jäckel 2003; Romanelli 2016.

5. See Di Chiara and Noto 2023 for an in-depth account of the 1957 Italo-Yugoslavian coproduction treaty and its wider significance in the two countries' cultural, economic, and political relationship.

6. A third option known as the "multiple-language version" was also briefly used to facilitate the export of American films to multiple European countries in the early years of the sound film. According to this model, several versions of a film would be made using the same sets and often the same crew but different casts. Each cast would perform the script in one specific language, usually shooting each scene in the same session, one cast after the other. The process would result in several versions of a film being made in several languages with several sets of actors. The expensive and laborious nature of this form of filmmaking, as well as rapid improvements to dubbing and subtitling, meant that it had largely been abandoned by the mid-1930s.

FOUR

NATIONAL VOICES

Don't Torture a Duckling and *Torso*

AS *SHORT NIGHT OF GLASS DOLLS* makes clear, it is difficult to discuss the voice in the giallo without listening closely to silence. Silence carries an added urgency in giallo cinema because the silent presence of the corpse anchors the giallo's murder mystery plots and horrifying images. Perhaps even more than the scream, silence becomes a sort of siren call beckoning both characters and viewers toward inescapable confrontations with death. In the giallo, the silence of death haunts every voice and carries a significant formal weight. In Michel Chion's (1994, 5) terms, sound cinema is "vococentric" in that "it almost always privileges the voice." If sound cinema revolves around the voice, it makes sense that what I call "vocal silence"—the silencing of the voice (as opposed to the total absence of any sound on the soundtrack)—represents a distinct formal technique in such cinema. After all, silence is not simply the lack of audible sound. In *Silence: The Phenomenon and Its Ontological Significance*, Bernard Dauenhauer (1980, vii) claims that "silence is a complex, positive phenomenon. It is not the mere absence of something else." Similarly, Max Picard (1961, xix) writes, "Silence is an autonomous phenomenon. It is therefore not identical with the suspension of language . . . it is rather an independent whole, subsisting in and through itself."[1] Cinematic silence in the sound era is always an active component of form and part of wider processes of representation. The consequences of its use depend on its integration into wider representational structures, and like any element of film form, its uses and effects are multiple and malleable. In this chapter, I suggest that the use of vocal silence in the giallo is so significant that its consequences may extend beyond the film's soundtrack.

Certain gialli grant vocal silence a particularly prominent place in their sound designs. Notable among these are Lucio Fulci's *Don't Torture a Duckling*

(*Non si sevizia un paperino*, 1972) and Sergio Martino's *Torso* (*I corpi presentano tracce di violenza carnale*, 1973), both produced as the giallo's popularity grew in the wake of Argento's early films. Both Fulci and Martino were fairly typical filone directors, as they shifted among generic models based on commercial dictates.[2] Fulci's film features a cave-dwelling witch who lives outside the southern Italian village where the story takes place. She is silent for most of her time on screen. The final third of Martino's film is dedicated to a tense cat-and-mouse sequence in which the protagonist, Jane, tries to escape from a villa that has been invaded by a killer who does not know she is there. This final sequence takes place in almost total vocal silence, as Jane desperately tries to avoid discovery. Importantly, these films are also both set in rural locations: *Don't Torture a Duckling* takes place in the fictional village of Accendura in a remote but unspecified part of the Italian South (or *Mezzogiorno*), and *Torso*'s villa is situated in the countryside surrounding the town of Tagliacozzo in the region of Abruzzo. The films form part of a small subset of rural gialli that also includes Mario Bava's *Bay of Blood* (*Reazione a catena/Ecologia del delitto*, 1971) and Pupi Avati's *The House with Laughing Windows* (*La casa dalle finestre che ridono*, 1976). This group of films eschews the giallo's typical preoccupation with cosmopolitan, urban space and the international modernity the city often showcases. Rather, the rural giallo focuses on issues of a more domestically Italian nature. Austin Fisher (2016, 161) argues that rural gialli "gaze inwardly to invest in a set of discourses surrounding the nation's past, and thereby offer symptomatic insights into the preoccupations of their own era." These films pay close attention to specifically Italian geographical and social spaces. Tomas Milian, who plays Andrea Martelli, the protagonist of *Don't Torture a Duckling*, said at the time of the film's release, "My favorite thing about the film is its deep Italianicity [*Italianità*]. Enough with gialli set in London . . . or even in undetermined, vague cities . . . I believe that its setting, so typical and real, is one of the film's principal merits" (quoted in Albiero and Cacciatore 2015, 162).

The rural giallo reveals the filone's involvement in specifically Italian social, cultural, and economic concerns, and this chapter explores how the voice gives form to the domestic dynamics that persisted alongside Italy's international modernization. In *Don't Torture a Duckling*, the voice and its silences intersect representational discourses that date back to Italy's preunification history. These are representational models in which the spaces and inhabitants of rural zones, especially those of the Italian South, are presented as picturesque—and, crucially, silent—spectacles. This film shows that the voice in giallo cinema played into a diverse network of social conversations and did, at times, support elements of sociocultural continuity against the backdrop of wider socioeconomic modernization. *Torso* is set in Italy's central belt and is unconcerned with the country's North-South divide, but it similarly sets up a complex opposition between the urban and the rural. Like Fulci's film, *Torso* casts the urban as a space of vocality and the rural as a space of vocal silence as well as emptiness. The film also explores the interpenetration of spaces, however; the emptiness of the rural is constantly open to invasion from beyond, and its silence is charged with the possibility that it may be broken, at any point, by a scream. The silence of *Torso*'s rural setting thus reinforces the film's generation of suspense, and silence becomes a resource the film "extracts" from rural space. I also suggest that the film's use of the villa as a site from which it may extract this resource from rural space perpetuates the ways villas have been used by some Italian urbanites for centuries. In both *Don't Torture a Duckling* and *Torso*, then, the vocal silence of the rural intersects discourses and trends that, while still current at the time of the films' production, have a long history in Italy.

DON'T TORTURE A DUCKLING AND THE SILENCE OF THE DOLLS

Don't Torture a Duckling opens with panoramic shots of the Mezzogiorno countryside that quickly gravitate toward the gray line of an elevated highway (autostrada) cutting through the landscape. Following this establishing sequence, a woman (Florinda Bolkan) known only as Maciara (a generic term denoting a rural witch in some southern Italian folklore) exhumes the skeleton of her dead child from the roadside earth with her bare hands (figs. 4.1 and 4.2). She accuses a trio of boys from the nearby village of Accendura of disturbing her child's grave and later, in the cave where she lives, she makes three anthropoid clay models before piercing each through the throat with a needle. Sure enough, one by one, the boys are found dead, and a scrum of police and media descend on the village. This group includes Milanese journalist Andrea Martelli (Tomas Milian), who discusses the case with the chief inspector, and the young local priest, Don Alberto (Marc Porel). Martelli forms a friendship with a young socialite, also from Milan, called Patrizia (Barbara Bouchet). Following a drug scandal back in Milan, Patrizia is lying low at a modernist home on the outskirts of Accendura that is owned by her father, a wealthy businessman originally from the village. Maciara is suspected and cleared of the crimes, but the villagers' fear and distrust of her lead a group of men to trap and brutally beat her to death. The real killer is eventually revealed to be Don Alberto, who has murdered the boys to save them from the impurities of their imminent sexual

Figures 4.1 and 4.2. Maciara exhumes her dead child's skeleton in *Don't Torture a Duckling* (Lucio Fulci, 1972). Her macabre act is set against the encroachment of the highway into the countryside of the Italian South. This contrast establishes the film's juxtaposition of a modern North and a supposedly archaic, superstitious South.

awakening. While trying to kill another child atop a nearby cliff, Don Alberto is apprehended by Martelli and, in the ensuing scuffle, falls to his death.

The opening shots of *Don't Torture a Duckling* make a spectacle of Italy's postwar infrastructural development. Angelo Restivo (2002, 46) argues that following the economic paradigm shift of the 1958–63 boom, "the road becomes not only a new reality in the physical landscape of Italy, but also a central trope in the construction of a new Italy based on a culture of consumption." Certainly, Fulci's film uses its opening shots to establish the narrative's economic-political landscape as well as its geographical setting. As Restivo (2002) points out, this "social transformation ... was directed from the North," and by opening *Don't Torture a Duckling* with images of a newly built highway overlaying the rural southern landscape, Fulci uses the highway to show not just Italy's changing economy but also the economic disparity between the North and South of the country. This disparity goes back to the Risorgimento (Italy's nineteenth-century unification, which was driven largely by the efforts of northern states to their own benefit) and was exacerbated by the northern-centric nature of recent economic changes (Ginsborg 1990, 216–17, 229–33). Furthermore, by setting the film in the fictional and regionally unidentified Accendura, Fulci allows the village and the rural landscape around it to stand in for the Italian South in a way that sidesteps the immense regional variety present in the South at social, cultural, and economic levels. Whether its implications are benevolent or malign, the modernity of the highway is set against the archaic rural southern landscape. *Don't Torture a Duckling* frames its story in terms of a blunt sociogeographic polarity between the modern, urban North and the premodern, rural South. The film, particularly through its manipulations of the voice, dwells extensively on this distinction (see Fisher 2016, 168).

The film's northern characters, Martelli and Patrizia, are consistently associated with both the automobile and the disembodied voice. Being Milanese, the two are framed in terms of their urban origins and mobility; they presumably traveled from the city to Accendura via the new highway, and both are shown driving. Martelli arrives at the initial crime scene in a car, and Patrizia is seen driving at various points on the highway and around the village. The villagers mostly traverse Accendura on foot (in one case, a man named Giuseppe uses a small moped). Even Maciara's murderers are shown emerging from their Fiat 500 only after it has been parked, disassociating the car (and its occupants) from images of movement. At the same time, Martelli uses telephones repeatedly to dictate his reports to colleagues in Milan, and he and Patrizia make and receive phone calls related to the case from her house. In contrast, although the family of one murdered boy does have a phone at home, a small shop in the village center has a public telephone sign above its door. This implies that many villagers have limited access to a private telephone. In other words, the film's northern characters seem to have easy access to space-transcending vocal technology as they do to space-transcending automotive technology. The disembodied voice is, in this sense, the voice of urban (and northern) modernity.[3]

The connection between a northern, urban modernity and the disembodied voice is reflected in the film's portrayal of Maciara, who, by contrast, is constructed as an incarnation of the rural landscape. The film merges Maciara with the rural space she occupies through her behavior and physicality. In the first instance, her exhumation and reburial of her child's skeleton and her voodoo-style ceremonies embed her (maternal) body in images of superstition that, in Italian culture (particularly in the North), are frequently associated with the rural South (see Saunders 1998; Fisher 2016, 168). This connection blurs the distinction between Maciara's body and the landscape it occupies. The association is made clear by her intense physical bond with the earth: she lives in a cave and frequently emerges into view from behind shrubbery or trees as if sprouting from the landscape. She digs up her child's skeleton with bare hands caked in a mixture of blood and earth, and she has the feral appearance of an animal.[4] Further, she is almost totally silent; she makes virtually no vocal sound other than during her brief scolding of the three boys, her police interrogation, and her murder (though she is quickly returned to silence by her wounds).[5] film theorist Béla Balázs ([1952] 1970, 206) writes, "Sound differentiates visible things, silence brings them closer to each other and makes them less dissimilar." Maciara's disheveled appearance and silence as she walks through the village's rural areas make it difficult to distinguish her from the landscape; she no longer seems to stand apart from it. (This has the opposite effect of the highway, which not only contrasts with the fields and valleys geometrically but stands apart from them atop concrete pillars.) As the disembodied voice identifies Martelli and Patrizia as modern outsiders, Maciara's silence blends her into the rural landscape. It becomes a sort of auditory equivalent of the cave where she lives.

Naturally, the combination of Maciara's silence, her feral appearance, and her intense connection to the landscape also suggest connotations of animality, indicating that her estrangement from audible vocality in part complicates her classification as human. Maciara's characterization intersects that of Don Alberto's six-year-old deaf and dumb sister. Patrizia tries to speak to the girl when she finds her walking through the village, but Martelli stops her and explains that "she can't understand you . . . the girl is sub-normal, retarded."[6] *Don't Torture a Duckling* suggests that vocal silence may somehow characterize the rural South, and the film heightens the importance of this idea by also implying that to be estranged from vocal interaction is to risk becoming somehow estranged from normative models of humanity—an animal or "retarded." This equation resonates with a political statement made shortly before the film's production. At a conference held in 1967, prominent Italian economist (and soon-to-be senator) Manlio Rossi-Doria said that the migration of southern labor from the countryside was a cause for celebration. He explained that the "exodus" of southerners to northern Italy and Europe "means that finally the men of the South will find a way of living worthy of human beings, and not of non-humans as they were in the past" (quoted in Ginsborg 1990, 231–32). Rossi-Doria, who had long advocated for improving the conditions faced by rural Italians, is here celebrating the new possibilities open to southerners. To be clear, his use of a human/nonhuman binary describes the living conditions *faced* by southerners and not southerners themselves (as it may seem at first glance). Nonetheless, by framing his argument in these terms, he recalls exactly the sort of dehumanizing rhetoric that had long been present in discussions of the South's estrangement from the rest of Italy's commercial and industrial development. Forty years earlier, Sardinian Marxist theorist Antonio Gramsci ([1926] 2000, 173) wrote, "It is well known what kind of ideology has been disseminated in myriad ways among the masses in the North, by the propagandists of the bourgeoisie: the South is the ball and chain which prevents the social development of Italy from progressing more rapidly; the Southerners are biologically inferior beings, semi-barbarians or total barbarians, by natural destiny . . . Southerners are lazy, incapable, criminal and barbaric." Gramsci describes a discourse taking place since "the end of the nineteenth century, [by which] Southern Italians were represented in Italy as racial or cultural others whose differences from northerners were intrinsic and for all time" (Schneider 1998, 12). In 1967, Rossi-Doria described southerners' difference from northerners as one of circumstance and not biology. He is, however, describing their otherness *in terms of* humanity. The process he is interested in is how southerners' circumstances can be altered to bring them back into the fold of the human. By suggesting that the current state of the rurally dwelling southern Italian is one of inhumanity, Rossi-Doria's comment flirts uncomfortably with established, dehumanizing rhetoric and intersects *Don't Torture a Duckling*'s equation of silence with both the rural South and the inhuman. If postwar Italy's wider political-economic paradigm might (still) somehow place the rural southern Italian on the border of the human, then Fulci's film uses the voice to trace that border. This is shown most clearly by those silent characters who, unable to use their voice to overcome a border, seem to slip across it with no hope of return. A paranoid urgency may be heard running through the vocality that accompanies the film's northern characters, an urgency to constantly (re)state a northern humanity from within the potentially inhuman spaces of the South. In a moment of frustration, Patrizia tells, or perhaps reassures, fellow Milanese Martelli that he is "the only civilized human being in this lousy place." If, following Balázs, sound differentiates visible things, then the production of vocal sound by the urban North in *Don't Torture a Duckling* is a constant act of differentiation, maintained to keep at arm's length the southern, rural, and potentially less-than-human other. The voice connects film form and national context by organizing the film's sound design in ways that reflect its much wider social and political discourse. In this way, the film's equation of silence and the rural South is both a thematic pursuit and a material consequence of its recourse to long-running national discourses.

According to Gabriella Gribaudi (1997), the South has long been discussed in terms of the northern qualities it lacks, such as individualism, solidarity, and an entrepreneurial class. *Don't Torture a Duckling* reinforces this idea when the chief of police responds to the villagers' vigilante attack on Maciara by criticizing their backwardness. He explains, "We can build highways but we're a long way from modernizing people like this." He also criticizes the villagers for observing a code of omertà and remaining silent when questioned about the crime. Throughout Fulci's film, adherence to the rural South's (supposed) cultural codes and the adoption of vocal silence signal the lack of the urban North's modern humanity. The distinction between voice and vocal silence is a key way the film shapes and highlights a particularly stark boundary between Italy's North and South, pointing to the division of the human and inhuman that supposedly haunts that border. In *Don't Torture a Duckling*, vocal silence is defined simply as the absence of voice, as the rural South is defined through the absence of the North's modern, humanistic values. The film precludes the possibility of silence acquiring a positive definition of its own and the possibility of the South acquiring a cultural identity that is not defined through critical comparison with the North.

Unsurprisingly, *Don't Torture a Duckling* has often been understood as a "critical message aimed at a bigoted and provincial society" (Chianese and Lupi 2010, 105), an interpretation that led to Fulci being attacked as a bigot for his portrayal of the South. To fully understand these polarities—North/South, urban/rural, human/inhuman, voice/vocal silence—however (both separately and together), they must be considered in terms of the film's industrial construction as well as its diegetic themes. This understanding allows us to focus on elements of the film that are banal but, for that reason, reveal the sociocultural forces underpinning the text. It is important to clarify that *Don't Torture a Duckling* is not a *southern film* but a film *about the South*. Tellingly, Fulci had originally wanted to set the film among a group of southern migrant workers in Fiat's Turin factory, where he claimed to have seen voodoo ceremonies being performed in the courtyards (Palmerini and Mistretta 1996, 59). The film was initially conceived within an overtly northern frame, its story rooted in the insertion of imagined southern superstition into a wider urban/northern industrial modernity. According to Fisher (2019, 142), this aspect of the film's development shows that "the anachronistic incongruity of what were perceived to be southern cultural mores in contemporary Italy was, therefore, the driving theme behind this film's production from the start."

Although Fulci's producers insisted that the film be relocated to the South (Palmerini and Mistretta 1996, 59), the narrative structure retains a fundamentally northern perspective. The two protagonists, whose actions and gathering of clues and information drive the film's plot, are both Milanese, and the film follows their perspectives. As such, a northern point of view frames the film's representation of the South. In the end, *Don't Torture a Duckling* may have been set in Accendura rather than Turin, but it still sees and hears the society and geography of the South with northern eyes and ears. Despite his original plans, Fulci commented that "the story could not have taken place anywhere but in Italy, in the South of Italy, in a village far from the big cities and lines of communication, where ancient customs, beliefs, and superstitions still live" (quoted in Albiero and Cacciatore 2015, 171). Fulci's comment brings the film's take on its setting into sharper focus. Fulci views the South not as a complex and dynamic society but rather in terms of its exoticism. In so doing, he follows long-standing cultural precedent.

By focusing a northern gaze on the rural spaces of the South, the film engages with the tradition of the picturesque. Rosalind Galt (2011, 134) explains that, in the eighteenth century, "the picturesque emerged as a specific aesthetic category, akin to the beautiful and the sublime, but it also described a practice of looking in which members of the landowning class engaged both the created views of their landscaped gardens and the natural scenery of wild tourist destinations such as Sicily." The picturesque is a way of looking at the rural (and its inhabitants) that celebrates the beauty of nature but by doing so indulges the predilections and preconceptions of the privileged classes whom these artworks were created by and for. Galt (2011, 139) goes on to explain that the picturesque therefore engenders a certain model of "looking relations" in that it encodes "the power dynamics of looking at and being in a landscape, underwritten by questions of which Europeans get to look/own and which are framed as exotic displays." John Dickie (1997, 135) notes that northern Italian culture has long looked on the South of the country through just such a picturesque frame, one that seizes on wild elements of the South and "aestheticizes and patronizingly celebrates the South's anomalous position between Italy and the Orient, between the world of civilized progress and the spheres of either rusticity or barbarism." Fulci's film presents Accendura broadly in these terms.[7] Transposing the picturesque onto the stylistic conventions of the giallo, *Don't Torture a Duckling* constructs a sort of nightmare-picturesque representational frame. Maciara's ceremonies with her clay dolls and her child's skeleton provide the fetishistic intrigue of the giallo by drawing upon stereotypical associations of the Italian South and magic (see Saunders 1998). The film makes no clear effort to understand how, why, or to what extent such practices might persist, if at all, in the South; the scene works purely as an unsettling spectacle. Further, neither the background nor the social significance of the villagers' refusal to break their silence around Maciara's murder is explored in the film; the villagers are simply written off by the police chief (and the film) as backward. Consequently, any cultural insight that might lie behind the film's use of silence quickly disappears. Instead, the film's focus on titillation prevents it from having concerted political or social value. Contemporary commentators noted as much. A reviewer for the newspaper *La Stampa* wrote, "At moments, director Lucio Fulci seems to have been tempted into bitter sociological analysis, but immediately falls back under the laws of commercial production" (quoted in Albiero and Cacciatore 2015, 172). Another critic, writing in *l'Unità*, made a similar argument: "In this movie there is no trace of any socio-ideological analysis. . . . Instead one finds only irritatingly over-simplified attitudes . . . *Don't Torture a Duckling* clearly and fully reveals its commercial intent rather than its social engagement" (quoted in Thrower 2017, 140).

Maciara's silence, then, reveals the one-way conversation between Italy's postwar film industry and the country's outlying regions. In a very literal sense, the figure of the rural southerner is denied a voice in the film. To approach the issue at its most practical level, it is important to note that Maciara is silent for much of the film because her picturesque estrangement from the core narrative means that she rarely engages with other characters. As a folkloric spectacle who functions to provide creepy titillation for the audience, Maciara has no substantial place in the conversations that propel the film's investigative drive. Instead, and as Troy Howarth (2015, 148) suggests when he describes her as "not a main part, *per se*" (original emphasis), Maciara is situated on the story's edge throughout the film. From this position, she can add macabre cutaways to the text without substantively affecting the film's investigative thrust (her consideration as a suspect by the police and Martelli is brief and quickly dismissed). Bolkan has underlined how profound her character's narrative isolation was: "The amazing thing is that I never met any other [principal] actors during the shooting of my scenes" (quoted in Howarth 2015, 150). Maciara's silence is the banal but revealing consequence of the film's indulgence in a nightmarish form of the picturesque that casts her as a picture—or perhaps as a sort of human prop, similar in her silence and her instrumental function to the dolls she makes and the absurdly unrealistic model of Don Alberto that is torn apart, in slow motion, by the cliff face when the priest is finally thrown to his death. As a sort of pictorial window-dressing, Maciara is meant to be part of the landscape, part of the exotic setting for a northern story that touches her without pausing to engage her, as the elevated highway crosses the equally spectacular countryside she lives in without touching it.

The technologically mediated voices of the northern (urban) characters in *Don't Torture a Duckling* restate the association, explored in previous chapters, of such voices and urban modernity. The film's insistence on the vocal silence of the rural South strengthens the cultural estrangement of those regions from modernization, suspending them in a picturesque Neverland. With a conservatism not often seen in the giallo's more urban texts, Fulci's film uses the power of vocal silence to connect with depictions of rural southern space and society that date back to at least the nineteenth century. Again, the voices (and silences) on the film's soundtrack mediate its engagement with much broader sociocultural trends and phenomena. By spanning text and context, the voice interweaves the two. In *Don't Torture a Duckling*, the voice is an aesthetic component that captures the (long-standing) contextual discourses within which the film was produced. As indicated by the hostile press reviews, the voice also shapes these discussions into a tangible form and keeps them alive.

TORSO AND SILENCE AS A RESOURCE

Sergio Martino's *Torso* was released a year after *Don't Torture a Duckling* in 1973 and follows an international group of female students who are studying at the University of Perugia. A series of murders begins when a young couple are killed in their car (another Fiat 500 parked under another rural highway overpass). The group heads to a rural villa on a mountainside overlooking the town of Tagliacozzo (unnamed in the film), owned by the family of Dani (Tina Aumont). Jane (Suzy Kendall) is late to arrive, having gone on a date with the group's art history lecturer Franz (John Richardson) after which her car broke down. In the countryside, the women are subjected to leering attention from the local men and visited by a Peeping Tom from the town. They also encounter Stefano (Roberto Bisacco), a spurned suitor of Dani's who has followed the group from Perugia. The murders continue in Perugia and Tagliacozzo; meanwhile, Jane sprains her ankle after falling at the villa. After taking the pills prescribed by the local doctor (Luc Merenda) with champagne, Jane wakes up to find that the killer has broken into the house and killed all three of her friends (as well as Stefano). Unaware that she is upstairs, the killer is now dismembering the bodies. The final third of the film features a silent cat-and-mouse sequence in which the injured Jane tries to escape without giving away her presence. The killer is Franz, who has been inspired to kill women by a traumatic childhood memory of his brother falling to his death while trying to retrieve a female friend's doll. Franz eventually finds Jane, but she is saved by the return of the doctor.

Unlike *Don't Torture a Duckling*, Martino's film avoids overt engagement with Italy's domestic division of North from South. Instead, the film opens by expressing a "duality of Italianness/otherness which, for an Italian audience, is easily recognizable in the location of Perugia, which with its popular university for foreigners, always merged its provinciality with a global horizon" (Baschiera and Di Chiara 2010, 116). Where *Don't Torture a Duckling* opposes North and South, *Torso* homogenizes (or, perhaps, unifies) Italy in blunt opposition to the non-Italian.[8] In so doing, it also homogenizes the foreigners. Dani is presumably Italian given that her family owns the villa, but Jane is American (and, like Patrizia in Fulci's film, drives a car with a number plate—from Chicago—that flags her status as an outsider). Ursula (Carla Brait) and Katia (Angela Covello), the other two women in the group of four, have indeterminate national identities. (Ursula is Black and, in the English dub, speaks with a non-English accent, which flags her status as an outsider.) The result is that regional divisions in Italy are eclipsed by the film's focus on the country's border with the rest of the world. This is not to say that *Torso* lacks regional specificity; the settings in the film display a marked attentiveness toward the nuances of location. The locations in Martino's film, however, are much more liminal than those in *Don't Torture a Duckling*. For instance, Perugia is in Umbria in Italy's central belt. Sometimes referred to as the "Third Italy," this segment of the country is neither fully northern nor fully southern, and, during the boom, it developed a specific regional economy. This economy was "characterized by small firms employing less than fifty people—and often less than twenty. These firms flourished in traditional sectors like clothing, shoe-making, furniture production, ceramics and leather goods" (Ginsborg 1990, 234). So, in the postboom years, central Italy was not only geographically liminal but also economically liminal, occupying an artisanal middle ground between the industrial North and the agricultural South. Even the very topography of central Italy garnered a degree of liminality as the categories of urban and rural became more complex. Ginsborg (1990) notes, "The terms 'diffused industrialization' (*industrializzazione diffusa*) and the 'urbanized countryside' (*la campagna urbanizzata*) became widely employed to describe this model of economic growth" (original emphases). The binaries that govern *Don't Torture a Duckling* do not translate well to the Umbrian context.

Tagliacozzo, the unnamed town next to the villa where the second half of *Torso* is set, is not in Umbria but in the region of Abruzzo and thus in the South (Abruzzo is generally considered Italy's northernmost southern region). The fact that the town is unnamed, however, continues to obscure questions of North versus South. The film is more interested in the border between the urban and the rural more generally, and especially in how permeable that border might be. As in *Don't Torture a Duckling*, the urban is cast as a space of vocality in *Torso*. The audience enters Perugia by way of Franz's art history lecture on hagiographic painting, a vocal performance that gives life to the values of education and enlightenment that the university suggests. The police also address the university students about the murders from within the lecture hall, which suggests that the authoritative voice underpins social order in the city as well. Furthermore, a minor red herring is introduced when Jane overhears Dani's uncle breaking off an affair with Carol (another friend) shortly before Carol is murdered. In Perugia, even "unofficial" social structures are rooted in vocal acts and accidents. However, and again like *Don't Torture a Duckling*, rural space is suffused with vocal silence. The women sunbathe noiselessly after they arrive, indicating that the relaxed atmosphere in this recreational area makes vocal silence the norm. It is also in the villa that Ursula and Katia are shown to be having a sexual relationship, and doing so in total silence (their relationship appears to be a secret). When framed together, they communicate with lingering looks and light touches but say nothing (even a sex scene of the two in bed features no diegetic sound). At one point, Dani remarks on their vocal reticence, joking, "You two make wonderful company" as the couple gaze into each other's eyes. It seems that it is the silence of the rural villa which allows their silent relationship to burgeon.[9] This sex scene (like the sex scene that opens the film) is clearly an effort by the producers to borrow from the sensational appeal of contemporary soft-core pornography and sexploitation movies. The silent lovers are framed here as tantalizing spectacles that appeal on a visual basis. They are similar to Maciara in *Don't Torture a Duckling*, but their appeal is erotic rather than macabre.

The Peeping Tom who approaches the villa is mute. He is shown briefly in the piazza as the women leave, taunted by men who jeer, "If you could only speak to them, how they'd love it." The attraction of a mute character to the villa strengthens the link between rural space and vocal silence. The villa and its surroundings are framed in several instances through carefully composed long-shots that emphasize the aged rusticity of the villa, the idyllic beauty of the land around it, or both. Such shots signal that the film, like *Don't Torture a Duckling*, draws on the picturesque tradition in its representation of rural Italy. The rural exists as a picture in the film, a visual rather than audible space. In fact, rural space seems to have an almost asphyxiating power to silence the voice in *Torso*. When a delivery boy arrives to discover the sunbathing women, he pants, gulps, and gasps as if robbed of his voice. Even once he enters the house moments after Jane sprains her ankle, he stands dumbstruck until the women tell him to get a doctor. At other points, the killer and Stefano both gaze silently at the house from the surrounding bushes, as if the space itself stills the voice. Notably, the villa and its lush grounds are where three of the women, the Peeping Tom, Stefano, and Franz are all killed and consigned to silence in its most profound and irrevocable form.

The silence that surrounds the villa and the rural space around it peaks during *Torso*'s final thirty minutes. The suspenseful sequence begins with Jane waking up to discover that Franz is in the villa and has murdered her friends (whose bodies he is now sawing into pieces). Stifling the urge to scream and struggling with her sprained ankle, she tries to escape and alert people in the town to her situation. She moves carefully and quietly around the villa, desperately trying to evade Franz. At one point, after seeing her friends' bodies, she holds her mouth shut with her hands to suppress a cry. Franz begins to suspect that he has missed someone in his murderous spree and also begins to move silently through the villa, hoping to find them. The vocal silence that has characterized the villa and surrounding space throughout the film seems to expand during this drawn-out cat-and-mouse climax. In Alain Corbin's (2018, 5) words, "There are houses that breathe silence, where it seems to permeate the walls." As *Torso* draws to its conclusion, the very silence of the voice becomes palpable, as if the villa is holding its breath. Silence becomes less a feature of the building than the thick atmosphere that surrounds and permeates it, as total, inescapable, and vital as the air itself.

At this point, it is helpful to take a more nondiegetic look at the giallo and consider the commercial basis for its use of vocal silence, which is closely tied to how the filone often uses empty space to create narrative tension. According to Baschiera and Di Chiara (2010, 118), *Torso* "gives us all the spatial information and the coordinates that we need to be placed in that cinematic/physical space. We know exactly the location of the villa in relation to the village." *Torso* highlights the villa's spatial position by repeatedly—almost fetishistically—outlining the volume of empty space that separates the villa from the town in the repeated zoom-pans between the two places. In doing so, the film (presumably inadvertently) participates in an Italian artistic tradition going back to the fifteenth century. Andrea Mantegna's fresco *Camera degli sposi* (1465–74), for example, features in its background a castle perched on a clifftop above a town. Art historian Martin Warnke (1994, 42) notes that, in such representations, "castles have hardly any contact with the earth: only remote, torturous paths lead up the mountainsides." The women's villa, repeatedly shot from the town below, also appears to be at the very edge of the earth, surrounded by clear air. Through these shots, the villa almost seems to float above the town, and rural space is further associated with empty space.

The material basis for the film's emphasis on supposedly empty space is clear; in the giallo, as in horror cinema more broadly, empty space is generative of suspense. In a 1997 interview, Martino (2016) explains this in relation to the formulaic nature of filone film production: "In genre films the stories are often very mechanical and the characters are moved not by true reactions to the situation, but by the necessities of moving the story along. For example—why, in giallo films, do so many beautiful and vulnerable girls sleep alone in sinister, isolated castles instead of comfortable and secure hotels in the towns nearby? Because otherwise, it would not be possible to generate any suspense." In terms that apply directly to *Torso*, Martino finds suspense—the beating heart of the giallo narrative—in the empty rural space that might surround an "isolated" building but that is filled up in the crowded town nearby. The mechanism by which empty space drives cinematic suspense is simple enough: empty space is suspenseful because at any moment, it could stop being empty. Karl Schoonover (2018, 346) writes that the void in horror cinema is "a genre-specific device for generating an anticipation of horror to come ... vacancy is established in relation to the contents of the frame, in tension with those parameters" (2018, 346). Schoonover suggests that the void cultivates narrative potential. It is the space where, at any moment, something unknown (and invariably threatening) may appear within the frame, a possibility that challenges the reassuring integrity of the frame itself. *Torso* is explicit in representing the empty space that surrounds the rural villa as threatening. After gazing out the living room window, Ursula comments on the security bars that crisscross the glass: "With all the windows barred, it seems like a prison." Dani replies, "There's no one here most of the year. It was a paradise for thieves so we put up the bars to discourage them." The empty space around the villa, emphasized so pointedly and repetitively by cinematographer Giancarlo Ferrando's camera, is a space of thieves, bandits, and threats to both property and life. Later, Dani looks out into the scrubland beyond the river as the group relaxes and seems to see Stefano lurking behind a tree; a momentary realization of the threat that always seems to fill the rural. Similarly, early in the film, two lovers are killed in a rural spot under the highway overpass, and Carol is killed in the woodland outside a building where she had been attending a party. So it is not just the space around the villa but all rural space in *Torso* that promises the appearance of a sudden threat.

The way *Torso* uses empty space to generate fear is key to the film's final scene and that scene's use of silence. Through the prism of the giallo, *Torso*'s escape the city in a villa but perhaps will never forget it. In other words, the city is always nearby, in terms of both the villa's typical location just beyond a city's border and its socioeconomic underpinnings. It is this border haunting that seems to have attracted Martino to the villa used in *Torso*. As mentioned above, he has claimed that suspense can only be generated in isolated buildings when there are "towns nearby" (2016). Tagliacozzo cannot be considered a city, but it represents the closest group of people, buildings, and businesses to the villa. Further, since the town is unnamed in the film and Jane appears to arrive there soon after her date with Franz (despite her car breaking down), it would seem that Perugia is close by. In terms of the film's visual schema, Tagliacozzo provides a counterbalance to the villa's isolation and stands in for a denser, more urban form of space (even if this "casting" may be slightly at odds with the true nature of the town). Both the villa's proximity to and its separation from more densely populated space are extensively emphasized by the film via the several extreme long-shots that begin on the villa before zooming and panning to end on the town, or vice versa. The women also frequently look down on the town from their bedroom windows, Jane is told that she will need to walk up the hill from the town to the villa after her car breaks down, and the doctor comments on the state of the hillside road when he arrives to treat Jane's ankle. The villa's paradoxical proximity to and separation from the nearby town is one reason the villa functions in the film (as it does in *The Lonely Villa*) to create suspense. It occupies a precarious position on the front line between two opposed sets of, in Ackerman's words, "values and accommodations" and is constantly threatened by an otherness that comes from somewhere else. The empty space around it is threatened by the possible sudden appearance of people coming from more developed areas; the Peeping Tom who comes from the town; or Stefano and Franz, who come from Perugia. The silence of that space is in turn threatened by the potential screams that might be caused by the appearance of those people. Yet at the same time, the villa is too *far* from more populated areas to offer the security of nearby help. As Jane tries to attract the attention of people in the piazza as she hides from Franz, she reflects the light of the sun toward the piazza using a hand mirror (fig. 4.3). She fails to alert anyone, though, and the town appears both close and agonizingly far away. The villa, which returns the film to its focus on liminality, sits on a border that the film alternately casts and recasts as permeable and absolute. As suggested, the tense silence of the villa also threatens to become permanent through the murder of its inhabitants. The spaces the villa occupies—physical and auditory—are therefore suffused with anxiety, and the villa's borderline position subtly upholds the tense mood of the film.

Figure 4.3. Jane tries to attract the attention of the town's residents in *Torso* (Sergio Martino, 1973). The shot emphasizes the liminal space the villa occupies, at once close to and far from the town below.

There is, perhaps, an extractive quality in the film's use of the villa and the rural space it occupies. Ackerman's description of the villa as an economic "satellite" of the city is notable for its colonial implications. It is a structure where urbanites can retreat and enjoy "the benefits of villa life [such as] the practical advantages of farming, the healthfulness provided by the air and exercise—particularly hunting—relaxation in reading, conversation with virtuous friends and contemplation, and delightful views of the landscape" (Ackerman 1990, 14). The villa allows urbanites to easily venture into the countryside and "expropriate rural land" so that they may extract resources from it. These resources might be physical, like crops, or less tangible values like personal rest and recuperation (1990, 10).[12] The four women in *Torso* travel from Perugia to the villa in pursuit of the latter, of course. Similarly, it is implied that Patrizia's father in *Don't Torture a Duckling* has built his villa in Accendura as a holiday retreat but continues to live in Milan. The villa represents a sort of microcolony, an extractive settlement built in the countryside by the rich city dwellers so that valuables—both tangible and intangible—can be extracted and carried back to the city. The villa may be in a rural area, but it serves the city it is connected to. This is, of course, how the villa is used by Martino and the producers of *Torso*. They were based in Rome and leveraged the villa's long history of exploiting the surrounding countryside.[13] If, as I have suggested above, rural space is aligned with silence in *Torso*—as it is in many other representational forms—then silence can be seen as a sort of resource found in this rural space. It is a resource that serves the film because it generates narrative tension. The makers of *Torso*, like the villa's inhabitants during the production of the film, used the building to occupy rural space and extract the resource of silence from it, as earlier residents might have stayed at the villa to extract crops or personal edification.[14] To be clear, my interest here is not in making or implying moral judgments around the way the film's production is "using" rural Italy. Rather, I am interested in how the urban and the rural have long participated in relationships based on the flow of resources between them and how the villa has helped mediate this flow. The use of silence in *Don't Torture a Duckling* ties that film to Italy's wider cultural history by drawing, bluntly and uncritically, on long-standing domestic discussions and stereotypes. The silences on *Torso*'s soundtrack cut across Italy's national history in a more circumspect but perhaps more complex way. Even though Martino and his collaborators may not have considered the villa's long history when making the film, their use of it still connects to how these buildings have been used in Italy for centuries.

Postwar, postboom Italy was in many ways a place of radical internationalization, modernization, and social change. As the other chapters of this book suggest, the giallo and its use of sound can often be understood as both a symptom and a component of that change. The giallo's use of sound was complex and worked differently in different cases, however. The soundtracks of *Don't Torture a Duckling* and *Torso* demonstrate how long-running discourses and trends around the relationship between the urban and the rural, and the North and the South, persisted in Italy despite the country's headline transformations. These films' use of vocal silence speaks volumes about the persistence of these discourses.

NOTES

1. Notable in this regard is John Cage's musical composition 4′33″ (1952), in which the performing musicians do not play their instruments for four minutes and thirty-three seconds. Cage's work provides space for the audience to consider silence as an auditory phenomenon that can be encountered and experienced. The inevitable presence of incidental sounds originating from the audience and performance space (shuffling, coughs, distant doors closing, and so forth) also highlights how silence is often experienced alongside and in relation to sound. The incidental sounds of the performance space, in a way, trace the edges of the silent performance and emphasize its silence.

2. Fulci's turbulent professional and personal history has been chronicled in Simone Scafidi's semifictionalized documentary *Fulci for Fake* (2019).

3. As this chapter shows, *Don't Torture a Duckling* leans heavily on stereotypes and simplifications, of which the mutual equation of urban, northern, and modern is one. By no means did all northerners live in cities, of course, and by no means were they all affluent beneficiaries of the economic miracle. It would be equally preposterous to claim that all southerners were wedded to archaic practices.

4. In her cave dwelling, Maciara perhaps also suggests the Palaeolithic cave settlements of the Sassi di Matera in the southern region of Basilicata, which puts a greater distance between her character and notions of urban society.

5. Maciara does speak in the police station when she confesses to the boys' murders because she thinks that the spell she has cast via her dolls is the cause of their deaths. She soon becomes manic and collapses back into mute unconsciousness, however, frothing at the mouth like a rabid animal as if her body is fundamentally unable to sustain vocal utterance.

6. These are the words spoken in the film's English dub.

7. Fulci was from Rome, and Medusa Distribuzione (the film's producer) was also based there. Rome is ambivalently placed between the North and the South of Italy and belongs fully to neither. However, Rome is north of the historic Kingdom of the Two Sicilies, the borders of which are still considered to define the Italian South. The city's rapid, urban modernization following the war further aligned Rome with the North from the 1950s onward. Consequently, Fulci's film may be considered a northern cultural product for the purposes of this analysis (the fact that its narrative revolves around two Milanese characters further encourages this reading).

8. Martino (2017, 112) has said that he chose Perugia for the film's opening because its connotations of internationalism would make the commercially mandated use of foreign actresses more credible.

9. Here, the film (surely inadvertently) glances off contemporary discourses of *lesbofeminismo*, an Italian lesbian-feminist movement that argued that female sexuality should be understood separately from male sexuality. Such arguments also pointed to silence as a potential tool of feminist resistance to male hegemony as expressed through language (see Rafaella [1983] 1991). As lesbianism proffers models of sexuality that are not determined by male desire, perhaps *in some form*, female silence could offer resistance to cinematic soundscapes determined by and in relation to male voices.

10. To be completely clear, Jane does (m)utter a handful of words under her breath at two points during the film's finale and stifles a slight yelp when she falls (again) on the stairs. Such isolated moments of strained audible vocality, however, seem to exist only to ensure that her vocal silence throughout the scene is not overlooked.

11. Vocal silence need not, literally, always anticipate a scream. The broader point is that vocal silence may be thought of as an anticipation of the audible. The idea that the scream, specifically, exerts a sort of narrative gravity is also expressed by Chion ([1982] 1999, 75–79) in his discussion of "the screaming point."

12. It might seem odd to discuss crops and personal rest as similar resources because taking personal rest does not change the landscape or deplete the countryside like the extraction of physical resources. However, Ackerman (1990, 10) stresses that the leisurely activity enjoyed by the villa's occupiers requires "the care of a laboring class or of slaves," and so there is still a very human cost to this form of extraction.

13. *Torso* was not a coproduction. It was produced solely by the Rome-based Compagnia Cinematografica Champion (Fisher 2019, 145).

14. Of course, the idea that *Torso* extracts silence from rural space is complicated by the fact that the film's soundtrack was dubbed and postsynchronized (see chap. 3). The fact that the silences on the film's soundtrack were not "recorded" in situ does not change the role played by the villa in determining the film's use of sound, though. The villa's close association with silence determines the soundtrack of the scenes filmed in and around it. As such, it still underpins the film's use of silence even though the film's ambient sound was not literally recorded on set.

FIVE

ECONOMIC VOICES

The New York Ripper and *Tenebrae*

LUCIO FULCI'S THE NEW YORK RIPPER (*Lo squartatore di New York*, 1982) is a gruesome film. It opens with a man walking his dog and discovering a decomposing human hand beneath the Manhattan Bridge. We learn that the hand belongs to a missing sex worker named Ann-Lynne, whose landlady tells Fred Williams (Jack Hedley), the burned-out police detective assigned to the case, that shortly before Ann-Lynne disappeared, a man had called her and spoken with a duck-like voice. This murder is followed by a string of similarly gruesome killings of women by an unseen killer who mimics the voice of Disney's Donald Duck. Williams recruits psychiatrist Paul Davis (Paolo Malco) to his team, but their conclusion that the killer is a sex worker named Mickey Scellenda (Howard Ross) is proven wrong when Scellenda is found dead shortly after being implicated in the attempted murder of another woman named Fay (Almanta Keller). Having escaped the attack, Fay recuperates with the help of her boyfriend Peter (Andrea Occhipinti), who, in a twist ending, is revealed to be the killer. Peter has a daughter named Susy (Chiara Ferrari) who is suffering from a rare illness and must live inside a protective plastic bubble in a hospital room. Peter began using the duck voice when talking to his daughter over the phone and has been killing sexually active women in revenge for the feminine sexuality that he thinks has been denied to Susy. His final attempt to murder Fay is interrupted by Williams, who shoots him dead. The film's end credits roll over an aerial shot of New York that begins on a patch of derelict buildings and squalid vacant lots before tilting up to show the Manhattan skyline in the distance (fig. 5.1).

More than ten years after *The Bird with the Crystal Plumage* was released, giallo production was in decline and Italy's popular cinema industry was

Figure 5.1. The final impression of New York featured in *The New York Ripper* (Lucio Fulci, 1982). Throughout the film, the city is depicted as a derelict, hopeless, and violent place.

suffering "a seemingly disordered proliferation of highly derivative, very low-budget films" as moviegoing in the country started to wane (Baschiera 2016, 47). The extent of the crisis facing Italy's film industry in the 1980s was significant. In 1975, 513 million cinema admissions were recorded in the country. By 1980, the number had fallen to 241.9 million; by 1989, the total was 94.8 million (Gundle 1990, 203; Ciofalo 2011, 21). *The New York Ripper* reflects a somewhat desperate time in Italy's film history. The film blends elements of the giallo and the neighboring poliziottesco, a filone which shares the giallo's interest in crime but in which killers are typically pursued and apprehended by police officers rather than amateur detectives.[1] Fulci's film features many of the giallo's stylistic hallmarks: violent set-piece murders, an unknown killer, and bold camerawork, for example, but its protagonist is a jaded police detective working (loosely) within a legal system, rather than an outsider.[2] Moreover, the film is sensationally violent and features a degree of sadistic gore that is striking even for the giallo, especially because so much of that violence is inflicted on nude or seminude women—the film was banned in the United Kingdom until 2002.[3] *The New York Ripper* is part of a general rise in violence seen in many Italian horror films of the late 1970s and early 1980s—the emerging zombie and cannibal filoni being good examples. As Italian moviegoers drifted away from cinemas, the use of graphic violence became a way to lure them back.

The New York Ripper was released in the same year as another notoriously bloody giallo, Dario Argento's *Tenebrae* (*Tenebre*, 1982), which was also initially banned in the UK as a "video nasty." (Fans and critics point out, though, that *Tenebrae* is not significantly more violent than Argento's earlier films.) Like

Fulci's film, *Tenebrae* features police officers, but, true to the giallo formula, they are largely ineffectual. The film opens with American crime novelist Peter Neal (Anthony Franciosa) cycling through New York City to John F. Kennedy Airport. There, he boards a plane to Rome where he is due to intensively promote his new novel, *Tenebre*. (The book is advertised in Rome as "The giallo of the decade," which shows that the filone's literary roots had not been forgotten two decades after *The Girl Who Knew Too Much*.) Peter is greeted by his Italian agent Bullmer (John Saxon, another link to Bava's film) and a team that includes his assistant Anne (Daria Nicolodi). Peter begins a packed schedule of press and TV interviews but soon learns that a murderer has been killing women around Rome and stuffing pages of his novel into their mouths. He joins forces with Detective Germani (Giuliano Gemma) to investigate as the murders continue. Throughout the film, the narrative is periodically interrupted by shadowy images of a groaning man reaching for pills, and hazy flashbacks to a scene on a beach in which a young woman (Eva Robin's [sic]) performs sex acts on a group of men. In one flashback, the woman humiliates one unseen man after he slaps her in disgust, and he later returns to murder her. In the narrative present, the killings continue until almost no characters are left alive. In an ending full of twists, it is revealed that there are actually two killers. The initial murders were committed by a moralizing television presenter named Christiano Berti (John Steiner) in a crusade to rid the world of "filthy, slimy perverts." His actions triggered a repressed madness in Neal, who is also the humiliated murderer in the flashbacks. After killing Berti, Neal continues his spree and murders all of the film's remaining characters except Anne. The film ends in a sleek, modern villa where he is about to kill Anne but he slips and impales himself on a sculpture. Anne screams, and the screen fades to black.

Tenebrae returns to the giallo formula that Argento had established and refined in the 1970s. In the meantime, he had explored slightly more gothic territory with *Suspiria* (1977) and *Inferno* (1980). This return shows how, unlike the genre-hopping Fulci, Argento was relatively free to choose his career path and did not have to cater to changing audience tastes. Nevertheless, *The New York Ripper* and *Tenebrae* share important similarities. Most notably, both bring the giallo to the United States, specifically New York City. Although *Tenebrae* only shows the location for about two minutes, the film's treatment of New York gives important insight into the film's connection to its historical context. Fulci's film, of course, features the city more overtly: the opening shot across the East River is taken up by the Manhattan skyline and emphasizes the city's centrality to the film. Claudio Bartolini (2017, 271) describes the city as the film's "main character," and the fact that Fulci's team filmed guerrilla-style without permits or permission highlights the film's raw engagement with New York's streets and spaces (Albiero and Cacciatore 2015, 305, 307). Importantly, the New York City in both films is a city at a poignant and powerful point in history, a time when neoliberalism was rising to prominence as the West's leading economic model.

The voice, again, profoundly connects both films to their settings. Each film shows, in very different ways, how the voice evidences the giallo's increasing entanglement with other forms of media and, more broadly, the increasing neoliberal globalization of the Italian economic, social, and media landscapes in the early 1980s. *Tenebrae* explores this interest by referencing the formal templates of commercial television that rapidly developed in Italy in the early 1980s. The film presents the television interview as both a key part of its story and an aesthetic model that dictates the image-sound—or, camera-voice—relationship throughout the entire film. Argento, however, uses the film's violent set pieces to invoke a different image-sound relationship, and in so doing, he not only explores television's aesthetic specificity but also insists on the continued distinction of the cinematic from the televisual. The influence of other media is more insidious in *The New York Ripper*. By using the voice of Donald Duck, the film repeatedly references a ubiquitous voice in an ever-more-global media landscape. This voice and others in the film can be best understood as aural forms of the simulacrum, theorized by philosopher Jean Baudrillard ([1981] 1994) as the copy-without-original that characterizes postmodern cultural production—the signifier that refers to other signifiers rather than to a signified "real." The voice in *The New York Ripper* reflects a historical time when the simulacrum dominated media production—a time that was marked by economic and cultural shifts, especially in Italy.

NEW YORK, NEO-YORK

Like the booming Rome of *The Girl Who Knew Too Much* and the post–Spring Prague of *Short Night of Glass Dolls*, the New York depicted in *The New York Ripper* and *Tenebrae* is a city undergoing a profound transformation. According to geographer David Harvey (2005, 1), the years from 1978 to 1980 were "a revolutionary turning-point in the world's social and economic history" in that they marked the explosion, around the world, of neoliberal economics. Neoliberalism is closely associated with the economic policies of US president Ronald Reagan, British prime minister Margaret Thatcher, and Chilean dictator Augusto Pinochet. It valorizes a laissez-faire political attitude to the free market, minimal regulation, individualism, short-termism, speculation, and a shift toward services and intangible commodities, especially financial services (which is why it is sometimes referred to as *postindustrial* capitalism). Harvey identifies New York as the epicenter of this revolution and explains that its social effects had already begun in the 1970s: "Capitalist restructuring and deindustrialization ... and rapid suburbanization had left much of the central city impoverished" (2005, 45). Italian media activist Franco Berardi (2018, 70), who visited New York at the end of the 1970s, observed as much firsthand: "When I arrived in New York, its urban decay was impressive: wide swathes of the city looked like abandoned cemeteries, full of deserted factories and empty stores." At the social level, neoliberalism led to significant wealth inequality in those countries where it took root. According to Harvey (2005, 34), "The opening up of entrepreneurial opportunities as well as new structures in trading relations, have allowed substantially new processes of class formation to emerge." Michael Siegel (2014, 7), in a discussion of *Tenebrae*, explains how neoliberalism "adds a key dynamic to the spirit of capitalism: namely, the care for the self, the notion that individual fulfilment is a physically, spiritually, and socially healthful endeavor, one that is not contrary to but fundamental to the structures of capitalism." Neoliberalism made some people rich and equated wealth with personal fulfillment. Meanwhile, the segments of society less able to seize the new opportunities of the 1980s fell increasingly toward destitution. Life for those in New York's lower socioeconomic strata became grueling as the restructuring of the economy around financial services—dominated by a small portion of the city's population—meant that "redistribution through criminal violence became one of the few serious options for the poor" (Harvey 2005, 48).[4]

Harvey's suggestion that the inequality of neoliberalism had reshaped New York's urban space is a useful guide to understanding the opening and closing images that bookend *The New York Ripper*, and *Tenebrae*'s early shots of Neal cycling to John F. Kennedy Airport. In the former, Manhattan's financial district is shot across the East River from a vacant space between the Brooklyn and Manhattan Bridges. The dilapidated, rubble-covered, and weed-strewn space between the bridges is an obvious contrast to the shimmering forms of the World Trade Center and neighboring towers (icons of globalized financial services), and the sense of a rich/poor divide is redoubled by the East River. The river represents a sort of moat, a forbidding physical separation between the spaces inhabited by those who have profited from economic restructuring and those who have been dispossessed by it. The bridges, framed high above the weary man who walks his dog on the Brooklyn side, seem literally unreachable. The transition between the two spaces (physically and socially) seems like a virtually unattainable promise. The film ends with an aerial wide-shot of Manhattan. In the foreground is a mix of vacant, squalid lots (Berardi's "abandoned cemeteries"); dilapidated postindustrial buildings; and housing projects, while in the background, the shot freezes on the financial district. The skyscrapers are veiled by a layer of haze—serendipitous for its effect of walling off the city's neoliberal core from the wider metropolis. The film's urban aesthetic is therefore governed by the social and physical separation of distinct socioeconomic groups.

The New York Ripper is one of six films that Fulci shot, in full or in part, in New York between 1979 and 1984, and it represents his most in-depth engagement with the city. Revealing the urban reality of New York at this time was one of Fulci's prime intentions for the film: "I wanted to show the real New York and not make a postcard-film" (quoted in Albiero and Cacciatore 2015, 305). Cinematographer Luigi Kuveiller claims that, without official permits, "we shot internal and external locations that were very degraded, squalid . . . the police didn't have the courage to go where we filmed!" (quoted in 2015, 308). The squalor of its mise-en-scène gives the film an unsurprisingly cynical stance toward the city, and many of the critics reviewing the film have noted that hopelessness characterizes the depiction of New York. Albiero and Cacciatore describe it as "a metropolis that kills off the souls of its inhabitants and establishes the grounds for their destruction" (2015, 310). Critics Gordiano Lupi and As Chianese (2010, 161) similarly claim that "New York as a city symbolizes human loneliness and collective fear," whereas for others, the city is simply "cold, barbarous and full of hate" (Thrower 2017, 289) or "a damned and degraded hell on earth" (Bruschini and Tentori 2013, 113).

Fulci's wider comments suggest that the isolation, loneliness, and fear that saturate *The New York Ripper* stem from his take on neoliberal America's wider social attitudes. On various occasions, and regarding this film specifically, Fulci has described America as operating according to a "cult of success" (quoted in Albiero and Cacciatore 2015, 305) in which "being a winner is compulsory" and failure to succeed on an individual level may literally drive a person mad (quoted in Palmerini and Mistretta 1996, 62). When Williams approaches Davis in the hope of recruiting him to the investigation, Davis asks, "Who's paying? It's a fine art hedging. I'm quite busy and the time I'd dedicate to you I'd have to take away from my other work." Williams promises that the police will be able to meet his fee. Davis asks, "Any idea what a genius costs per hour?" Williams does not know: "I just know what's in my paycheck." The quick exchange shows the extent to which neoliberalism and the manic pursuit of individual success criticized by Fulci are rooted in the world that the film represents. On the one hand, Davis's reference to hedging demonstrates how the language of financial services has come to model all human activities in the neoliberal city. On the other, his suggestion that his own genius exists to be monetized shows how the individual fits into a service-based economy, as does his concern that his time might be used unproductively.

Like the opening shot of *The New York Ripper*, *Tenebrae*'s first scene emphasizes the bridges connecting New York City's various boroughs.[5] On his way to the airport, Neal cycles out of Manhattan over the 59th Street Bridge, a short distance north of the industrial wasteland where Fulci's unnamed character walks his dog. In the background are the office buildings that now make up New York's economic engine room, and it looks like Neal is a product being exported from this zone. Neal—healthy, wealthy, and full of neoliberal optimism (Bullmer later tells him that *Tenebre* has been on Italy's bestseller list for weeks)—enjoys an entirely different relationship to New York City's urban space than Fulci's disheveled man.[6] Where Fulci's character dawdles on the shore of the East River, far below the bridges that span it, Neal cycles over one of those bridges. The two are social opposites: Neal represents the "haves," while the dog-walker is one of the "have-nots." Not only does Neal have access to the roads that seem out of reach for the man below, he also has plenty of freedom to move around: he cycles to get on a plane, while his chauffeur follows with his luggage. New York City in *Tenebrae* appears to be as socially stratified as it is in *The New York Ripper*, but Neal is distinct from Fulci's characters in his financially secure ability to master and transcend that space, which he soon does when he leaves for Rome.

It is important to note that while Peter Neal may depart from New York City, the neoliberal ethos travels with him. Although Italy did not form an international economic hub in the style of the United States (or its main European counterpart, the United Kingdom), the country in the early 1980s was an enthusiastic participant in the global neoliberal revolution. In a detailed sociocultural history of Italy in the 1980s, Giovanni Ciofalo (2011, 18) refers to the decade as Italy's "second boom." Paul Ginsborg (2001, ix) interprets the period in similar terms: "Over the last twenty years [1980 to 2000] Italy has witnessed a socioeconomic transformation as dramatic as that of the 'economic miracle' of the 50s and 60s, but strikingly different from it in both content and consequences." The magnitude of this claim should not be underestimated. Ginsborg bases his argument on the rapid expansion of the Italian services sector, particularly financial services, which benefited from advances in telecommunications and not only reaped huge profits but also changed the fabric of the Italian cityscape as increasingly redundant industrial plants were replaced by skyscrapers (2001, 7–8). He also highlights the social ramifications of this economic metamorphosis: as in New York, while some got richer, many got poorer in relative terms, and so wealth inequality increased markedly (2001, 34). Yuppies (young, upwardly mobile professionals) and a new elite of moguls also proliferated in Italy as they did in the Anglophone countries: "The new bourgeoisie was wedded to efficiency, lower taxes, and the absolute freedom of the markets; it hated cumbersome bureaucracy, the rigidity of Keynesian labour markets, the restrictive control of trade unions. It was as international as the old bourgeoisie had been national" (2001, 48). As in *The New York Ripper*, *Tenebrae*'s early shots establish the film's entire socioeconomic context. The sequence depicts Neal's neoliberal privilege and highlights the international orientation of neoliberal economics.

TENEBRAE AND THE "NEOLIBERALIZATION" OF ITALIAN MEDIA

Ginsborg (2001, 84) identifies television as the way Italy's economic transformation became social transformation during the 1980s and describes the television set itself as "a passport to modern Italy." Certainly, the history of *commercial* television in Italy is central to the country's experience of neoliberalism since it was both a symptom and a driver of that project. Up until 1974, the Italian state broadcaster Radiotelevisione italiana (RAI) held a monopoly on the country's television and radio broadcasting. Two constitutional court rulings in 1974 and 1976, however, allowed private stations to begin broadcasting at a local level. Local television suddenly became an open, and totally unregulated, field for the operations of opportunistic entrepreneurs, and the scale at which this opportunity was seized is astonishing: Ciofalo (2011, 107) notes that there were over 250 local television stations operating in Italy by 1978 and that this number exceeded 600 by 1980. Key among these new media entrepreneurs was property developer (and future prime minister) Silvio Berlusconi. Berlusconi's first foray into television was the TeleMilano station he had started as a support service for his Milano 2 housing development, but following the court ruling, he quickly acquired local stations across Italy. In a move typical of his commercial cunning, Berlusconi instructed his stations to broadcast the same material simultaneously across the country using videotapes sent from his headquarters. This allowed him to circumvent the ban on nationwide commercial broadcasting and create a national, private channel that he named Canale 5 in 1980 (Balbi and Prario 2010, 401). Following further acquisitions, his Fininvest holding company added two more national stations over the next four years—Italia

1 (1982) and Rete 4 (1984)—and opened a production company and a highly successful advertising sales company named Publitalia. By the mid-1980s, RAI and Fininvest (later via its subsidiary Mediaset) held a duopoly over national broadcasting, with three channels each.[7] The rise of commercial television in Italy, of which Berlusconi's Fininvest is just one paradigmatic example, was a direct result of neoliberal economics. Commercial television fed on market deregulation and speculation, it offered almost limitless potential for profit growth, and it made individual entrepreneurs fantastically rich through the exchange of intangible, service-based products (principally on-screen advertising space). Through television, neoliberalism entered Italy emphatically. Pierre Sorlin (1996, 145) writes, "Broadcasting deregulation extended to most developed countries in the 1980s but nowhere was it as rapid and unsupervised as Italy." Berardi (2009, 12–13) goes further and argues (with Marco Jacquemet and Gianfranco Vitali) that "neoliberal policy burst onto the Italian scene in the 1970s under the banner of [media] 'deregulation,'" which handed control of public opinion to a "tiny minority of mega-capitalists." Italian commercial television was not a neutral medium; it was suffused with profound socioeconomic significance before one even sat down to watch it.

Television audiences had been growing rapidly in Italy since the early 1960s (see chap. 1), and thanks to deregulation, this trend continued apace in the 1980s. Ciofalo (2011, 21) calculates that between 1980 and 1989, the amount of money Italians spent on television increased by 32.1 percent. The explosion of television in Italy was a major factor in the concurrent collapse in cinema attendance in the country. He writes that "television consolidated its position as the dominant medium [in Italy] thanks to an offering that was always getting bigger and was almost always free, and it transformed Italians into a nation of 'tele-spectators'" (2011, 56). This transformation added further impetus to the neoliberal project in three ways: First, commercial television accelerated neoliberalism's drive toward globalization. Milly Buonanno (2012, 40) explains that because television operated twenty-four hours a day on several channels, new audiences emerged (such as late-night viewers) that advertisers could target and that required new streams of content. She writes, "The commercial networks, which were to start producing a modest quantity of TV drama only in the second half of the 1980s, went ahead with massive imports; and the stimulus of competition induced public television to do the same, thus breaking its own 20-year-old tradition of resolute self-sufficiency. At the beginning of the 1980s the Italian television market had the dubious honour of being the biggest European importer of foreign programmes: primarily from the United States, as well as from Brazil and Japan." Buonanno (2012, 7–8) writes, in summary, that "the reshaping of the Italian televisual system . . . was accompanied by a process of internationalization, more specifically of Americanization" (see also Barra 2013). In particular, American police dramas were imported into Italy in vast numbers in the late 1970s and the 1980s. Once Italian audiences grew accustomed to American television, Italian production began to copy American formulas and styles, which included daytime formats like talk and quiz shows as well as dramas and soap operas. Italian detective programs eventually merged American and Italian elements in a process of hybridization too (Buonanno 2005). Through neoliberal business practices and telecommunications and video technology, the world (America, especially) came to Italy as a spectacle to be consumed within the home, and foreign models were eventually integrated into the country's "domestic" media landscape.[8]

Second, commercial television perpetuated neoliberal economics by aggressively promoting the purchasing of consumer goods. Ginsborg (2001, 86) points out that the skill of the entrepreneur in this sector was not in developing programming but in developing audiences that could be sold to advertisers. He also states that by 1984, Italian television was screening around fifteen hundred ads per day: "Italian commercial television advertisements in the 1980s were a noisy, endlessly repetitive, frontal attack." The television advertising statistics in Italy at this time were striking: the total amount spent on television advertising in the country was 105.2 billion lire in 1977, but by 1980, this had risen over threefold to 332.6 billion (Ciofalo 2011, 178). The carefully marshaled ads of RAI's boom-era *Carosello* (see chap. 1) were set free in an explosion and celebration of consumerism for its own sake, and this drove new patterns of consumption.

Third, commercial television accelerated the move toward individualism and private living that was already becoming apparent at the end of the 1970s as the post-1968 social movements died off: "Television of this sort [commercial] took hold of its viewers and rooted them to the home" (Ginsborg 2001, 110; see also Ciofalo 2011, 15, 29). The development of Italy's commercial television sector is thus best understood as both a cause and an effect of neoliberalism and its attendant social transformations; it provided an insidious and fertile cultural ground on which neoliberalism could grow and which neoliberalism nourished in turn.

The histories of neoliberalism and Italian commercial television are more than just interesting backgrounds to *Tenebrae*'s production history; they are also important keys to unlocking the film's formal logic.[9] Argento has claimed that the film is "hysterical" and "consumerist"; typical of the time when yuppies were replacing Italy's political activists (quoted in Costantini and Dal

Bosco 1997, 143–44). It is also highly indebted to the aesthetics of television. Domenico Monetti (2008, 300) describes the film as "apocalyptically televisual," and it is worth noting that Argento had previously made programs for television. Following the success of his initial "Animal Trilogy," Argento was commissioned by RAI to produce *The Door into Darkness* (*La porta sul buio*, 1973), a four-part giallo anthology series made up of one-hour episodes, two of which, "The Tram" ("Il tram") and "Eyewitness" ("Testimone oculare"), he directed himself. (Argento would return to television in the mid-2000s, making two episodes for the American mini-series *Masters of Horror* [2005].) Although *The Door into Darkness* appeared before the rise of commercial television, the episodes directed by Argento demonstrate a marked sensitivity to the aesthetic specificity of the medium and its formal distinction from cinema. "The Tram" is a helpful guide for understanding *Tenebrae*'s engagement with its televisual context, and I discuss it further below.

Televisions as objects figure prominently in *Tenebrae*'s mise-en-scène. As the first victim, a shoplifter who has stolen a copy of Neal's book (Ania Pieroni), enters her apartment, her television set is highlighted by Luciano Tovoli's camera. Bullmer also has a video screen on his desk with which he can see his secretary when she calls his office, and stacks of monitors are wheeled through the television studio as Neal and Berti discuss their upcoming interview. The diegetic presence of the television screen is also reflected by Tovoli's framing: Berti is often positioned within internal frames created by windows and doorways, which gives the impression that he is always "on screen." Neal, too, is shot through windows several times to similar effect, and when one of Berti's victims escapes from a maddened dog by running into his basement, the dog reappears on the other side of a tiled glass wall that displays the spectacle of the animal's anger as if it were being broadcast to a wall of monitors in a studio or electronics store. *Tenebrae*'s Rome is a city in which both space and the people within it have become inescapably televisual.

The 1980s were a decade when cinema developed an obsession with television, both in Italy and around the world. Umberto Lenzi's zombie sci-fi *Nightmare City* (*Incubo sulla città contaminata*, 1980) takes place largely in a television studio, and Fulci's dance-giallo *Murder-Rock* (*Murderock uccide a passo di danza*, 1984) starts with a group of young dance students competing to secure television gigs. Ruggero Deodato has also discussed his *Cannibal Holocaust* (1980) as, in part, a critique of television journalism's increasingly graphic depictions of violence (see Dickinson 2008, 150). In the art cinema tradition, Federico Fellini's *Ginger and Fred* (*Ginger e Fred*, 1986) tells the story of two retired dancers teaming up for a one-off television performance, and Maurizio

Nichetti's *The Icicle Thief* (*Ladri di saponette*, 1989) revolves around a film director's outrage at the bastardization of his film during a television broadcast. In terms of Anglophone horror cinema, David Cronenberg's *Videodrome* (1983) and Paul Michael Glaser's *The Running Man* (1987) both contemplate the growing ubiquity of cable television. The diegetic treatment of television was a global trend but one to which Italian cinema (and Italian horror cinema specifically) had become particularly attuned at the time when commercial television was exploding in the country.

Argento is clear about the influence of imported television on *Tenebrae*'s bright, sleek aesthetic: "We started from American television series like *Columbo* and *Charlie's Angels* in defining a realistic manner of lighting.... a very precise aesthetic, produced in all these shows by the quick shooting schedules and the cathode light. This economically imposed standard and the conditions of projection are embedded in the style" (quoted in McDonagh 2010, 166–67).[10]

As I have argued, the arrival of shows like *Columbo* and *Charlie's Angels* in Italy was both a symptom and a driving force of the country's neoliberal development. Argento frames these programs in terms of their "economically imposed" style; these are products manufactured according to the strictures and priorities of the market economy, and this can be seen in their "very precise aesthetic." As a result, by giving television such a powerful presence in *Tenebrae*—both thematically and aesthetically—Argento and his collaborators directly build the neoliberalization (and the Americanization) of Italy into the form of the film.[11] Further, the film's diegetic and stylistic references to television work in tandem and reference each other. Umberto Eco (1984) labels the Americanized, light entertainment that populated Italian screens in the 1980s "neo-TV" and compares it to the more arcane "paleo-TV" delivered during the RAI monopoly. He specifically argues that where boom mikes and cameras were kept out of shot at all costs during the paleo-TV era, they are incessantly highlighted by neo-TV as a sign of veracity: "Television no longer hides artifice, rather, the presence of the boom-mike [and the camera] assures (even when it's not the case) that the transmission is live" (1984, 25). Argento and Tovoli mimic this convention by framing Neal and Berti amid several television cameras as they sit down for their interview; by foregrounding the apparatus of television, the film does not merely take it as a theme. By activating the reflexive connotations that Eco identifies, the film uses the television cameras to confer on itself the aura of a televisual broadcast. In other words, by holding the apparatus of the television studio in its gaze, *Tenebrae* does not keep the medium at a distance but rather identifies with it.

As Argento's comments suggest, the film's mimicry of television is pervasive. Crucially, the talk show interview between Neal and Berti is never shown and therefore never contained. The format of the talk show interview instead seems to spill out into the entire film. Siegel (2010, 205) notes that the shot-reverse-shot technique is frequently used "to banalize and normalize Peter—and therefore to persuade us not to suspect him—by depicting him within such a familiar, television-friendly discursive register." This method not only distracts the audience from suspecting Neal but also, along with the film's frequent use of the two-shot, makes every conversation feel like part of an endless string of talk show interviews. The importance of the voice to the film's interaction with the televisual aesthetic becomes clear. Tovoli's camera displays an almost total loyalty to the speaking voice (though that "almost" is vital, as discussed below). The extensive use of the shot-reverse-shot and two-shot techniques means that the film's visual center of gravity is almost always the face of the speaker. This loyalty of image to voice lies at the heart of the televisual aesthetic. Chion (1994, 157) explains, "The difference between cinema and television lies not so much in the visual specificity of their images, as in the different roles of sound in each.... Television is illustrated radio. The point here is that sound, mainly the sound of speech, is always foremost in television."[12] For example, Argento's televisual debut "The Tram," although intricately and engagingly plotted, is a static and dialogue-heavy piece in which the talking head is always present and sets a precedent for many of *Tenebrae*'s shot setups. *Tenebrae* is most profoundly televisual in its invocation of an image-sound—or, more specifically, camera-voice—relationship by which the former is obsessively tied to the latter. It is this relationship that defines the televisual. The rapid growth of import-dependent commercial television played a major role in Italy's neoliberal economic (r)evolution, and *Tenebrae*'s use of this aesthetic model strongly reflects the neoliberalization of the country's media landscape. Tovoli's camera turns instinctively to the voice and so displays its televisual, neoliberal training. *Tenebrae*'s use of a televisual aesthetic is *not quite* total, however. Like the dog that chases one of Berti's victims into a basement, Argento's/Tovoli's camera shows moments of madness where it refuses to be tamed by the voice. In these moments, when the film rejects television's version of the image-sound relationship, *Tenebrae* sets the cinematic apart from the televisual, creating a formal contrast between the two.

Television shows, as presented in Argento's film, are characterized by order. Neal's appearance on Berti's show is scheduled precisely, the background and lighting as he arrives is carefully arranged. Berti tells Neal that he has only two slots per year for such interviews, and he wants to talk about their conversation ahead of time (leading to a revealing dialogue between the two about sexuality, murder, and deviance). In terms of style and content, nothing is left to chance. The film's dialogue-driven shot-reverse-shot and two-shot setups—its visual loyalty to the speaking voice—also copies television's need for "coverage," for all available content to be accounted for so that no story elements are missing. Understanding *Tenebrae* only as a televisual film might limit its broader significance, though. The film's televisual veneer is pierced by moments organized according to another logic, one perhaps more cinematic in nature. For instance, Monetti (2008, 300) claims that "the frequent flashbacks do not merely interrupt the story like publicity spots, but shine with the aesthetic of a perfume advert." But the interruptions created by these interludes are perhaps less a shift between televisual registers than a shift away from the televisual altogether. The surreal and hazy scenes on the beach, with no diegetic sound and guided by dreamlike, affective logic, betray an expressionistic subjectivity that is more reminiscent of the midcentury art film. The scenes' location in time and space is ambiguous. So, too, are the identities, motivations, and histories of those involved, and, together with the impressionistic nature of their images, these scenes ask the sorts of narrative questions typically suggested by the work of Michelangelo Antonioni, Jean-Luc Godard, or Fellini. These sorts of vague, implied questions, to which the film offers only the sketchiest of answers, run counter to the mechanical, televisual order of the main thrust of the film, as does the aesthetic scheme through which they are asked.

The televisual aesthetic favors sound—and speech—above all else. The cinematic, it would seem, implies the opposite, and many of cinema's early critics and theorists explicitly take this position. Siegfried Kracauer ([1960] 1985, 127–28) argues that "sound films live up to the spirit of the medium only if the visuals take the lead in them. Film is a visual medium" and "emphasis on speech . . . strengthens this tendency away from camera-life." Similarly, Balázs ([1952] 1970, 194–95) writes that "the art of the silent film is dead, but its place was taken by the mere technique of the sound film which in twenty years has not risen and evolved into an art." In his extensive theorization of the *acousmêtre*—the voice without a visualized source—Chion ([1982] 1999, 4) suggests that cinema's ability and willingness to displace the voice characterizes the medium: "sounds and voices that wander the surface of the screen, awaiting a place to attach to, belong to the cinema and to it alone." I gather these disparate comments to highlight a consistent critical assumption that to turn away from the voice is to turn toward the *cinematic*. Realized in the flashback scenes, the threat of this formal turn is a hallmark of Argento's work overall. *Deep Red* (*Profondo rosso*, 1975) opens with the camera roving around a theater as it assumes the perspective of the as-yet-unidentified killer. Moreover, in *Suspiria* (1977) and *Inferno* (1980), Argento's photography (the former of which was also directed by Tovoli) dispenses even with the justification of a point of view, and the camera prowls around the corridors and corners of the Tanz Akademie dance school in the former, and a New York apartment building in the latter, according entirely to its "own" motivation. Argento's cinema is one of visual liberation, one in which the camera is mobile and at large.

Tenebrae's flashback scenes thus represent an explosion of the cinematic into the televisual, which is marked specifically by the camera's sudden abandonment of the voice as its guide and master. As the flashbacks demonstrate, these moments often come without warning, as the film's murders similarly intrude suddenly into the narrative. The film's shifts to a cinematic register, to an image-sound relationship where the former is no longer guided by the latter, often occur during its murderous set pieces. Most notably, Tilde (Mirella D'Angelo), a journalist and friend of Neal's, is murdered along with her lesbian partner in a scene that is famous among fans for its long take of roughly four minutes during which Tovoli uses a Louma crane. The shot recalls the final shot of Antonioni's *The Passenger* (*Professione: reporter*, 1975), also photographed by Tovoli. The scene begins with the camera surveying Tilde through a window, then crawling up the wall of her building, over its roof, and down another wall, stopping at several windows along the way, and finally settling on one through which the killer is seen beginning to break into the house. Similarly, Berti's house, the location for several of the film's murders including his own, is a polyhedral example of modernist architecture that Argento and Tovoli frequently frame in a manner that emphasizes its verticality, angularity, and glass architecture. Such framing contrasts with the pragmatic, dialogue-serving televisual framing used as a default in the film. Speech is often literally removed from the film's soundtrack during these scenes of violence, replaced by the band Goblin's instrumental synth-rock music and, ultimately, the victims' screams, which further stress the fact that these cinematic moments represent a decoupling of the camera and the speaking voice.[13] *Tenebrae* thus exhibits a careful symbiosis of content and form. As the killers abruptly trigger explosions of violence within the narrative—*at precisely* those moments—the cinematic aesthetic, characterized by an abandonment of the speaking voice as a formal linchpin, suddenly disrupts, ruptures, and does violence to the televisual order that otherwise dominates the film.[14] Indeed, in the film's final moments, Peter is impaled on a modernist sculpture and dies in a profusion of blood. As the credits roll, Anne screams, seemingly on the edge of madness; the film seems to have destroyed the possibility of any return to orderly, televisual speech (fig. 5.2).

Figure 5.2. Anne screams as she is driven to the edge of madness in the final shot of *Tenebrae* (Dario Argento, 1982). A return to orderly speech seems impossible.

In a formal game of cat and mouse, *Tenebrae* presupposes a televisual aesthetic logic only to interrupt and undermine that very model; in a sense, the film posits cinema as the Hyde to television's Jekyll. The film's form echoes its themes here: McDonagh (2010, 160) writes that Neal and Berti are dark doubles. As well as doubling Berti, Neal is internally doubled through the splitting of his personality into a smooth-operating yuppie and a psychotic killer; his ex-wife Jane (Veronica Lario), who has secretly followed him to Rome, tells Anne that she feels like she is two people in one body. These instances of thematic doubling are not just reflected but are emphasized by the tension between the televisual and the cinematic that guides the film's form. By juxtaposing the acoustic aesthetics of cinema and television as oil and water, the film defines and delineates the borders between the two by intermittently assimilating and rejecting television's voice-camera setup. *Tenebrae* explores how American(ized) commercial television infiltrates Italian sociocultural space and the neoliberal economic ideas behind this trend. The voice binds the film's sociocultural context into its form, but in doing so, it allows the film to play with that context. *Tenebrae* seems to engage with its socioeconomic and cultural setting on its own terms: the film's voices cross the border between cinema and television so that it can explore that border by both establishing and transgressing it. The film's manipulation of the image-sound or camera-speech relationship mimics the aesthetic norms of neoliberal televisual production without ever *fully* adopting them as its own. *Tenebrae* emphasizes the persistent distinction of cinema at a time when television was starting to dominate media and culture in Italy and around the world.

THE NEW YORK RIPPER AND MEDIATED ALIENATION

The title, setting, and premise of *The New York Ripper* all testify to the influence of the imported cop shows that were becoming familiar in Italy in the early 1980s. Even the film's closing theme bears a striking resemblance to that of *Kojak* (1973–78). This might also show that American films were capturing a bigger portion of the Italian market (another reason for the escalating crisis in domestic production). American imports had held a prominent place in Italian cinemas since the silent era (see chap. 3), but they became dominant throughout the 1980s: in 1980, 43.5 percent of films shown in Italy were Italian (including coproductions), while 33.7 percent were American (the rest were produced by other countries). By 1989, 21.7 percent were Italian and 63.1 percent American (Ciofalo 2011, 55). Whether viewers watched television or cinema in Italy in the 1980s, they were increasingly greeted with American products. Ciofalo (2011, 56, 159–61) states that this ubiquity led to an Americanization of the Italian imagination and a normalization of American narrative models, fashions, and cultural stereotypes. The latter is particularly evident in *The New York Ripper*. Thrower (2017, 293) describes the jaded Detective Williams as a character "we're familiar with from countless American TV cop shows," for example. Similarly, Ann-Lynne's landlady Mrs. Weissburger (Babette New) is a stereotypical busybody often seen in soaps and sitcoms of the period, and two sexually aggressive pool players are cast as two-dimensional Latino hoodlums. These are stereotypes that seem to have become intelligible to audiences in Italy as well as the United States by 1982, thanks to the increasing integration of both countries' media landscapes.

The rising ubiquity of television in the early 1980s is emphasized early in *The New York Ripper*. Mrs. Weissburger figures out when she must have last seen Ann-Lynne alive because she had "just turned on *Dallas*. You know, that TV series about that family that has money coming out their ears?" This fleeting reference to *Dallas* ties Fulci's film to the same matrix of commercial television that crisscrosses *Tenebrae* because the American soap opera was one of Italian television's most popular imports in the 1980s. Berlusconi's Canale 5 "made it the event of the season, turning it into an important weekly appointment... and promoting it with an unprecedented volume of publicity" (Buonanno 2012, 43; see also Ginsborg 2005, 41).[15] Mrs. Weissburger's statement is translated identically in the English and Italian dubs and so illustrates *Dallas*'s global cultural presence; it may be American-made, but it has cultural significance for both English- and Italian-speaking audiences. In other words, the film's reference to *Dallas* shows how commercial television was connecting the two nations' cultural reference points. Mrs. Weissburger's use of the show as a temporal marker to organize other events in her life also illustrates how neoliberalism's international commercial television project had ushered in an age when (global) media products were coming to *constitute* rather than *communicate* experience.

The overtaking of reality by media is established in the film more broadly. In an early scene, Jane Lodge (Alexandra Delli Colli), a wealthy woman and one of the duck-voiced killer's eventual victims, watches a live sex show in a grimy Times Square theater. As the show's stars have sex in front of her, Jane takes a Dictaphone out of her pocket and secretly records their utterances. Later, Jane's husband, Dr. Lodge (Cosimo Cinieri), is shown sitting in his study, pallid and erotically mesmerized, listening to the tape. Jane comes in and, with a smile that suggests the familiarity of the situation, takes the Dictaphone from him but gives him back the tape. As she leaves, Lodge drops the tape into a desk drawer where it joins a pile of other tapes containing (we assume) similar recordings: she is happy to have "made plans" for that evening, while he is happy to be alone with his tapes. This interaction is the couple's only face-to-face encounter in the film and reveals the clinical disembodiment of the sexual voice within their relationship. It is particularly stark since the vocalizations of sex might be expected to exemplify how, in Cavarero's ([2003] 2005, 177) words, "the voice belongs to the living; it communicates the presence of an existent in flesh and bone."[16] As the performers' voices are both isolated and anonymized by the recording media, and later "consumed" by Lodge in solitude, they represent not so much the *presence* but the *absence* of the tangible body from the couple's relationship.

The mediation and mediatization of the Lodges' sexual relationship is a function of the wider prevalence of audio technology in the film. The killer makes taunting calls to Williams, who records them and plays them to Davis; a radio announcer appeals for the murderer to stop his rampage; radio chatter fills the soundtrack of a shot of Times Square taken from a squad car. According to Harvey (1989, 159, 161; 2005, 47), the pervasiveness of telecommunications technology was central to the spread and success of the neoliberal paradigm; interestingly, the early 1980s saw a boom in premium-rate telephone sex lines following the breakup of AT&T's monopoly in the United States, a neoliberal gold rush similar to the surge of commercial television in Italy (Smith 2008, 237). Anthropologist Amy Flowers (1998, 1), who conducted an extensive ethnography of sex-line call centers in the early 1990s, writes that the phenomenon "illustrates a tertiary phase of human relations, one that is mediated by technology.... While facilitating distant communication, these machines minimize personal contact and mediate interactions between individuals, so that communication is conducted from person to machine, machine to person." The increasing technological disembodiment of the voice was nothing new by 1982 (see chap. 2). The accelerating commercialization of this disembodiment at the turn of the 1980s, however, integrated the voice into the neoliberal framework by detaching it from the body and turning it into an isolated product to be traded on an open market. If, as Flowers suggests, the replacement of real sex with its commercialized version became more common in neoliberal society, then the Lodges represent lonely symptoms of the wider social change that the film explores. The film's soundscape of recorded and exchangeable aural orgasms suggests that the rising tide of transactional individualism has human sexuality firmly in its grasp.[17]

In the parlance of the 1980s, *The New York Ripper* could be read as a dark depiction of the West's shift into postmodernity, neoliberalism's cultural offshoot. Although postmodernist theories have been debated since the turn of the millennium, they provide important insights into how the cultural effects of neoliberalism were understood as they developed. Fredric Jameson (1992, 9), for example, describes postmodernism in part as "the emergence of a new kind of flatness or depthlessness, a new kind of superficiality in the most literal sense," which has led to a pervasive "waning of affect" (1992, 10). Jameson's interest in flatness speaks to the dynamics at play in *The New York Ripper*'s economy of voices, which are severed from bodies in a denial of their unique physical origins and in turn perpetuate a decrease of emotional investment between the people who listen to them.[18] In a scene toward the end of the film, a sex worker named Kitty (frequented by Williams) is murdered in relentlessly graphic detail. The attack is overheard by Williams and his team when Peter phones them during the act. This might seem like a moment when the bodily origin of the voice *is* specific and understandable, but this is not the case. Williams and an army of police trace the call and then set off on a charge across the city. They discover, however, that the call is coming from an unattended phone booth where the receiver has been placed against a walkie-talkie, which relays the sounds from an unknown location. This technological relay turns Kitty's voice into a multiply mediated copy as divorced from her physical body as the voices on Jane's tapes. Although the voice on the phone is known to be Kitty's, her body seems to have disappeared. *The New York Ripper* depicts a very different relationship between the voice and the body than is seen in, for example, *The Bird with the Crystal Plumage*. In the latter, the mystery is solved because the killers' bodies can be specifically located thanks to the birdsong recorded on their phone calls. Voice, body, and place are inseparable in Argento's film, but they are almost entirely dissociated in *The New York Ripper*. This shift is one way in which the emergence of postmodernity can be seen (and heard) taking place across the giallo's lifespan.

THE VOCAL SIMULACRUM

The way *The New York Ripper* disconnects the voice from the body highlights one of postmodernism's core concepts: the simulacrum. In *Simulacra and Simulation* ([1981] 1994), published as Fulci was shooting his film, Jean Baudrillard ([1981] 1994, 83) claims that the arrival of postmodernity has led to a surge of images dominating the cultural landscape.[19] This has caused a collapse of real, medium, and message into a single "nebula." This collapse is due in part to the increasing pervasiveness of advertising and entertainment media operating through increasingly sophisticated networks of global telecommunications and has given rise to the simulacrum, the copy-without-original, or the signifier that refers only to a wider network of signifiers and has no basis in the "real." The real here is replaced by simulation. Baudrillard writes, "The era of simulation is inaugurated by a liquidation of all referentials—worse, with their artificial resurrection in the systems of signs" ([1981] 1994, 2). In the era of the simulation, in which simulacra circulate without connection to a grounding reality, society has entered a state in which "reality no more exists outside than inside the limits of the artificial perimeter" ([1981] 1994, 14). Rather, as signifiers have come to refer only to other signifiers in a referential short circuit, reality has been replaced by a simulated hyperreality: "It is a question of substituting the signs of the real for the real" ([1981] 1994, 2).

Kitty's final relayed screams, copies of copies separated from her body, are a form of vocal simulacrum. So, too, are Jane and Dr. Lodge's tapes. Lodge's drawer holds a set of near-identical voice cassettes that are connected, each sound "never exchanged for the real, but exchanged for itself, in an uninterrupted circuit without reference or circumference" ([1981] 1994, 6). In short, as aural simulacra, the voices of *The New York Ripper* point not to bodies but to other voices. Peter speaking in Donald Duck's voice is the clearest example of this idea. It is appropriate that the voice of Donald Duck uses "the buccal airstream mechanism" that forces air out of the cheeks rather than the lungs and forms words using the palette of the mouth rather than the larynx (Shell 2004, 100). Donald Duck's voice denies the corporeality it comes from; it originates from the edges of the body without involving its deeper, more intimate spaces.

Peter uses this voice to *hide* his body, to interrupt the specific sound-body relationship the voice typically implies. In this sense, Peter's duck voice serves the same purpose as the whisper used by other giallo villains to hide their identities during their threatening phone calls. Unlike the whisper, though, Peter's vocal disguise in *The New York Ripper* does not just ignore his body; it goes further and refers to a known cultural icon—Donald Duck. This is a voice that is anchored not in flesh and blood but in the vagueness of a global media landscape. Like the Lodges' tapes, this voice signals outward to an endless chain of other voices. On the film's English dub, characters say that the voice sounds like a duck, whereas the Italian dub uses the word *Paperino*, the name that Donald Duck is known by in Italian, which underscores even more clearly the network of references that makes up the character (as does the toy duck shown prominently on Susy's bedside table).[20] Peter's voice, in other words, replicates a sound that has no basis in concrete reality but is instead rooted in an ever-expanding chain of repetitions. When we hear Peter's voice, we are reminded of other times we have heard Donald Duck's voice and not the fact that the voice comes from a body. It is the film's ultimate vocal simulacrum.

As well as appearing on everything from breakfast cereal to toys to sports mascots all over the world, Donald Duck has been prominent in Italy since the early 1930s when, thanks to licensing deals between Disney and Italian publisher Mario Nerbini (and later Mondadori), he became a major character in fumetti comic books. Donald Duck's popularity in postwar Italian culture is evident in how often he appears in the background of Italian films. His image is clearly visible, for example, on the walls of a children's hospital ward in Francesco Rosi's *Hands over the City* (*Le mani sulla città*, 1963) and the bedroom walls in Enzo Milioni's pornographic giallo *The Sister of Ursula* (*La sorella di Ursula*, 1978). Indeed, Fulci's *Don't Torture a Duckling* was originally titled *Don't Torture Donald Duck* until the title was changed for legal reasons (Thrower 2017, 139). In short, when Williams is told that someone with the voice of a duck has phoned him and he asks, "A duck. . . . Where have I heard that before?" the implied answer is, clearly, "everywhere."[21]

It is easy to see Donald Duck as a symptom, or even a tool, of the American-led globalization that lies beneath the surface of both *The New York Ripper* and *Tenebrae*. Chilean-Belgian theorists Ariel Dorfman and Armand Mattelart do just that in their polemic book from 1972, *How to Read Donald Duck: Imperialist Ideology in the Disney Comic*. Dorfman and Mattelart (1991, 28) state that the (1991, 28) "Disney family" represents an almost utopian fantasy that "extends beyond all frontiers and ideologies, transcends differences between peoples and nations, and particularities of custom and language. Disney is the great supranational bridge across which all human beings may communicate with each other. And amidst so much sweetness and light, the registered trademark becomes invisible." But by their account (which is particularly attuned to Disney's role in spreading America's capitalist ideology in Latin America), this is an insidious fantasy. They argue that, in line with the principles of capitalism, every character in a Disney story is either powerful (e.g., Scrooge McDuck) or powerless (e.g., Donald Duck). Trying to subvert or challenge this natural order is futile and possibly dangerous: "Put up with what you have, or chances are you'll end up with worse" (1991, 43). Interestingly, German political and cultural theorists Theodor Adorno and Max Horkheimer (members of the Marxist Frankfurt School) had previously noted as much in their essay "The Culture Industry: Enlightenment as Mass Deception" (originally 1944). They see Donald Duck as an example of how the latent violence inherent to capitalist society is normalized for consumers through seemingly innocuous cultural objects like cartoons: "Donald Duck in the cartoon and the unfortunate in real life get their thrashing so that the audience can learn to take their own punishment" ([1947] 1997, 138, see also 136). Donald Duck's increasing presence in cultural contexts outside of America becomes a symptom of how both American culture and, perhaps, the capitalist ideology underneath it was spreading to other parts of the world. Dorfman and Mattelart (1991, 27) state that Disney comics have been exported to over a hundred countries. America's global influence is a theme in many postwar Donald Duck comics. Daniel Immerwahr (2020) points out that most of Disney's Donald Duck comics (which were written mainly by Carl Barks) involve some combination of Scrooge, Donald, and Donald's nephews traveling to (fictional) foreign lands. These foreign lands are populated by fictional races of people (usually thinly veiled stereotypes of real ethnic groups) who possess great treasures whose value they do not appreciate. Some form of danger and tension builds, and the "natives" are typically dispossessed of their treasures. It does not matter though because they never appreciated them to begin with.[22] In this reading, as both a character and a product, Donald Duck travels to other countries and cashes in on the people who live there. Immerwahr is careful not to interpret these comics as a straightforward, cut-and-dry celebration of paternalistic cultural imperialism (2020, 10), but Dorfman and Mattelart (1991, 48) are less reserved: "According to Disney, underdeveloped peoples are like children, to be treated as such."

Importantly, however, the countries where Donald Duck stories have been distributed have not been purely passive players in their relationship with America or Disney. Disney's characters are often licensed to local publishers, who are then free to use them in their own stories. In his introduction to Dorfman and

Mattelart's book, David Kunzle (1991, 15) explains that local licensees vary in how much they alter existing Donald Duck stories, how frequently they write their own stories, how accurately they translate the dialogue of the American comics, and how far they go in adding their own characters. He notes that "the Italians in particular have proven adept in the creation of indigenous characters." These domesticating processes may have allowed the "Americanness" of the comics to be toned down slightly, but in the 1970s, Disney tightened its rules for overseas franchisees and limited how much its material could be changed. The company specified, for example, that characters must be depicted within the hierarchies established by Disney—minor characters could not become stars. As a result, Disney comics in Italy could be made to seem more Italian on the surface, but they were still influenced by rules set in the US. It was imperative to preserve Disney's natural order of things, so the *Paperino* (Donald Duck) comics made in Italy can be seen as a sort of cultural Trojan horse. With these seemingly banal comics, American culture was "naturalized" as a part of Italian culture. While this process began long before the emergence of neoliberalism, the unquestioning way in which Donald Duck is referenced in *The New York Ripper* shows how far this process of naturalization had advanced by the 1980s. The rapid spread of American television and popular culture around the world intensified the development of the character to an extraordinary degree. His voice was louder than ever. Donald Duck's material importance to *The New York Ripper*'s sound design shows how Italian culture and media became more connected to global (and, for the most part, American-led) culture and media.

At least five versions of *The New York Ripper* were dubbed in different languages: English, Italian, French, Spanish, and German.[23] Each one features Peter's duck voice, showing just how globally ubiquitous Donald Duck (and his voice) had become by the early 1980s. Peter's imitation of this voice, then, can be seen as a sort of leitmotif of globalization. It invokes and signifies a cultural sphere that transcends the borders of media and countries, connecting the film to a seemingly limitless network of commercial texts. The film's use of Donald Duck's voice, like its use of racial and class stereotypes, speaks to the American-led cultural globalization that accelerated with the rise of neoliberalism. The fact that this voice consists of mostly spluttering, incoherent sounds rather than words—phonos rather than logos—makes it particularly appropriate. As pure sound, it neatly gets around the linguistic barriers that often impede the global flow of cultural objects. It is a voice that cannot be tied to a specific body in a specific place. Instead, and like Kitty's voice as she is murdered, it is everywhere, anywhere, and nowhere. The delicacy with which the narrator's voice in *The Girl Who Knew Too Much* connects that film to other texts, genres, and media explodes in *The New York Ripper*. Here, Peter's duck voice references an indiscriminate range of other texts and media the parameters of which are impossible to define. Unlike that of *Tenebrae*, Fulci's text does not try to separate itself from other media but rather joins a chain of (vocal) simulacra with no beginning or end so that the borders between media—and the borders between countries—become ever blurrier.

Tenebrae allows us to place late giallo cinema in the context of Italy's changing media landscape and the neoliberal (political) economy of commercial television that influenced those changes. Argento's film suggests that this landscape provided cinema with a new standard to redefine itself against. *The New York Ripper* features a more cacophonous global media landscape than *Tenebrae*, one characterized not by the persistent heterogeneity of media but by their growing integration. This is evidenced and perpetuated by the film's repeated assimilation of voices from cinema, cartoons, television programs, and even comics and toys that resonate internationally but are drawn from America. Despite their differences, both films show the advancement of a trend already evident in *The Girl Who Knew Too Much*. The use of voice in Bava's film signifies an Italy that was increasingly international in its economic and cultural horizons. The voices heard in *Tenebrae* and *The New York Ripper* reveal an Italy where those horizons had become international *by default*. This shift, I have argued, was mainly caused by Italy joining a neoliberal economic paradigm that was global by design and that impacted Italy through its rapidly growing, deregulated, and import-dependent media sector. These films' use of voice and sound actively engage with this disorderly media landscape and, by extension, with this time in Italy's economic history. As with each case study examined over the last five chapters, history becomes form in these gialli: in *Tenebrae* and *The New York Ripper*, the neoliberal shift that was underway in Italy at the turn of the 1980s becomes audible.

NOTES

1. The merger and hybridization of filone had always been a part of film production in postwar Italy. Mixing tropes among different filone allowed for a blend of novelty and familiarity, keeping audiences interested and so prolonging the exploitability of successful generic formulas (Albiero and Cacciatore 2015, 14). As early as 1961, for example, Bava's *Hercules in the Haunted World* (*Ercole al centro della terra*) combined the mythical *peplum* (sword-and-sandal) filone with elements of the gothic horror film emerging in Italy at that time (an emergence in which Bava also played a key role).

2. The prevalence of giallo components over poliziottesco elements in the film means that most critics consider it, foremost, a giallo.

3. The British Board of Film Classification's website contains an engaging account of the film's journey through the British censorship system. Accessed July 20, 2024, https://www.bbfc.co.uk/education/case-studies/the-new-york-ripper.

4. For a comprehensive history of neoliberalism, see Harvey 2005.

5. Argento's previous film, *Inferno*, is also set in New York City. That film, released in 1980, also touches on the city's neoliberal transformation but far less obviously than *Tenebrae*. This might be because *Inferno*, being more gothic horror than giallo, is more interested in the nightmarishly labyrinthine internal spaces where its action is set than the "real world" beyond them. See Pollard 2019.

6. Giovanni Ciofalo (2011, 96–97) notes that the term *bestseller* was itself a product of the neoliberal commodification of culture in the 1980s.

7. In 1984, Fininvest's effective violation of the ban on national commercial broadcasting led to a blackout of its stations by local courts in Rome, Turin, and Pescara. Berlusconi's political ally Prime Minister Bettino Craxi was quick to intervene, temporarily overturning the decision three days into the ban and then passing a decree to legalize Berlusconi's operations (see Balbi and Prario 2010, 392–93).

8. It is important to note, however, that many Italian viewers appreciated the increased range of programming available on commercial television in the 1980s and particularly the shift from RAI's staid, pedagogic programming to a model geared more toward entertainment (Balbi and Prario 2010, 403; Buonanno 2012, 41).

9. I have argued elsewhere that Argento's next film, *Phenomena* (1985), also registers the influence of commercial television in the way it draws on the form of the music video (Pollard 2020).

10. *Tenebrae* refers to a Christian religious ceremony held before Easter in which candles are gradually extinguished. Given how bright the film is, the word's association with darkness makes it a somewhat ironic title. Argento has repeatedly stated, however, that the darkness he is referring to is that found in the human soul.

11. A serendipitous aspect of the film's casting can be noted here: Veronica Lario, who plays Neal's ex-wife Jane, met Berlusconi in 1980, and the two were married in 1990.

12. Chion's statement can be taken literally here: Television evolved from radio rather than cinema. Many of the large broadcasters who were often responsible for developing and shaping the new medium, like the British Broadcasting Corporation (BBC) in the UK and RAI in Italy, were originally radio broadcasters.

13. See Dickinson (2008, 119–54) for an in-depth and wide-ranging analysis of the use of synthesized music in *Tenebrae* and other "video nasties." Dickinson

is particularly attentive to this music's moral ramifications and states that the cold, inhuman sound of the synthesizer encouraged these films' vilification by presenting their depictions of violence in an atmosphere of indifference.

14. Appropriately, in this context, some of the film's murders must still be edited for television in Italy (Monetti 2008, 300).

15. *Dallas* (1978–91) was hugely popular in many countries in the early 1980s.

16. In a similar vein, Ciofalo (2011, 36) argues that the Sony Walkman, a device similar to the Dictaphone, privatized and individualized the act of listening to music that had previously been collective and public.

17. For an account of how the neoliberal project was also able to co-opt feminism, see Fraser 2009.

18. For full accounts of postmodernism's characteristics and development, see Lyotard 1984; Harvey 1989; Jameson 1992.

19. There is no evidence that Fulci was aware of Baudrillard's work, however.

20. Susy's toy is similar to, but not, Donald Duck. Presumably, copyright played a part in this difference.

21. Today, Italy continues to consume huge amounts of Disney content, on-screen and in print.

22. See Immerwahr's essay in full for a nuanced analysis of how Barks's stories present a complex picture of American cultural imperialism and Barks's ambiguous attitude toward America's mission to "modernize" the Global South.

23. All are available on Shameless Entertainment's 2011 DVD release of the film.

CONCLUSION

The Voice as a Process

GIVEN THE IMPORTANCE OF THE voice to giallo cinema, it is fitting that the filone should culminate with a film that revolves quite explicitly around the power of the voice: Dario Argento's *Opera* (1987).[1] It is difficult to pinpoint the end of the giallo because Italy's cinematic filoni did not come to abrupt conclusions; they faded away through hybridization and formulaic evolution. Other films could reasonably be seen as the giallo's last stand: Vittorio De Sisti's *Crimes and Perfume* (*Delitti e profumi*, 1988) and Dario Piana's *Too Beautiful to Die* (*Sotto il vestito niente 2*, 1988), both virtually forgotten, are arguably later gialli. I consider *Opera*, then, to represent the end of the filone's generic cycle rather than its absolute chronological conclusion.[2] The film is another example of Argento's ability to pursue personal interests throughout his career; it is loosely indebted to Gaston Leroux's *The Phantom of the Opera* (1910) and the films it spawned, which Argento had been obsessed with as a child and would go on to adapt directly in 1998 (Argento 2014, 20). It was also influenced by more recent events: in 1985, Argento had been hired by the Sferisterio performance venue in Macerata to direct a staging of Giuseppe Verdi's *Rigoletto*, but once the venue's management learned that he was planning an avant-garde version that portrayed the duke as a perverted vampire, he was replaced by Mauro Bolognini. Argento was left with both an axe to grind and an interest in opera's shadowy backstage world (Jones 2016, 159). The film also taps into a wider obsession that Italian cinema has had with the country's national art since the silent days.[3] Some examples of works made during the giallo's life cycle include Pier Paolo Pasolini's *Medea* (1969), which features opera superstar Maria Callas, who, tantalizingly, is never heard singing in the film; Federico Fellini's *And the Ship Sails On* (*E la nave va*, 1983), which thematizes the death of an opera star; and Bernardo Bertolucci's *Before the Revolution* (*Prima della rivoluzione*, 1964) and *La luna* (1979), as well as Argento's *Inferno* (1980), which prominently feature operatic music.[4] If *Opera* represents the giallo's crescendo, it also stands as the filone's final reflection on the centrality of the voice to Italy's cultural heritage, its cultural industries, and, perhaps, its cultural relationships with the wider world.

The film opens during the final rehearsal for an avant-garde staging of Verdi's *Macbeth* (1847). Young singer Betty (Cristina Marsillach) inherits the role of Lady Macbeth after prima donna Mara Cekova is injured in a hit-and-run incident and, despite initial self-doubt, performs the role on opening night to rapturous acclaim. The opera's opening is also the starting point for a series of murders that take place in and around the theater: an usher is killed during the first performance, and, shortly afterward, the killer intrudes on Betty and her boyfriend Stefano after they unsuccessfully attempt to make love. The unidentified killer ties Betty up, gags her, and attaches a row of pins below each of her eyes so that she is unable to close them and is forced to watch as he stabs Stefano to death. Detective Alan Santini (Urbano Barberini), an opera lover who was enchanted by Betty's opening night performance, picks up the case, but he is unable to prevent more murders, which Betty is forced to watch with her eyes pinned open. Santini is ultimately revealed as the villain; he had been in a relationship with Betty's mother, who derived an erotic thrill from watching him kill, and he is now trying to relive that relationship with Betty. After a brief altercation, Santini appears to die in a fire at the opera house, and Betty and the show's director Marco (Ian Charleson) escape to the Swiss countryside. Santini reappears in their remote chalet, however, and kills Marco before Betty can subdue him long enough for the police to arrive and save her.

Opera presents an opportunity to compare opera and the giallo and to uncover an array of unlikely similarities between the two. By refracting opera through the formal prism of giallo cinema, the film shows that both focus on capturing the voice in its purest form. Opera's fixation on the voice as pure sound, freed from language and even from the uttering body, finds its satisfaction in the ecstatic high notes of the aria; the giallo's in the scream. The comparisons presented in Argento's film reveal that, at their extreme points, the song and the scream may amount to the same thing. As Michal Grover-Friedlander (2005, 4) writes, "Death is immanent in the operatic voice." Song and scream both explore the bodily limits of the human voice. These limits must be overcome for the voice to, fleetingly, emerge as pure sound. *Opera* focuses on the overlap between opera and the giallo and caricatures their shared pursuit of the pure voice by graphically depicting acts of violence done to characters' mouths and throats. This violence represents a pursuit of the voice to its supposed origin point, but the mutilated corpses reveal only empty and silent cavities. The voice's elusive nature is, in a sense, thematized by the film. In its mise-en-scène, *Opera* displays the gaps where the voice resounds, precariously and temporarily: the gap between lungs and mouth, body and mind, inside and outside, individual and society. These are the gaps from which the voice expands to cross borders. In line with my interests throughout this book, *Opera*'s juxtaposition of opera and the giallo highlights how, in both, the human voice resonates far beyond the diegetic body. The negotiations performed by the voice tie textual aesthetics to contextual imperatives at different levels, turning vague sociocultural ideas into tangible artistic forms. The complexity of the voice in *Opera* highlights its significance in giallo cinema, showing that the voice can clearly express the historicity of any audiovisual text. Viewing the voice as an ongoing and dynamic interaction between text and context means analyzing audiovisual texts for how they engage with their broader social, cultural, economic, or political environments.

GIALLO AND OPERA, GIALLO AS OPERA

Opera opens with an extreme close-up of a raven's eye, with the auditorium of the Reggio di Parma opera house reflected across its surface.[5] This shot signals the film's interest in spectatorship, an interest further demonstrated by the pins Santini uses to ensure that Betty witnesses his crimes. Just as emphatically, however, this overture indicates the film's interest in the voice—the pure voice as unadulterated sonority. The camera lingers on the raven as it perches above the stage. Unseen, a male baritone and female soprano (Cekova) rehearse, while the bird caws an unwanted accompaniment. The involvement of birdsong in the operatic aria hints at how the voice is idealized in both opera and the giallo. The bird's cry is vocalization freed from any connection to the word (suggesting, perhaps, the cry of the birdlike sirens in Homer's *Odyssey*). The theorization of opera clearly highlights the importance of the pure voice to its form, above and beyond the libretto (story), physical performances, costumes, or mise-en-scène. According to Grover-Friedlander (2005, 23), "Opera is essentially about the wish for the autonomization of voice or an attempt to approach voice as detached object." What is most fundamentally at stake in opera is the human voice freed from the shackles of language. The presence of the ravens in *Opera* becomes particularly relevant here. It is hard not to see a connection to Alfred Hitchcock's *The Birds* (1963), especially because they eventually peck out one of Santini's eyes after identifying him as the killer. Regarding *The Birds*,

Figure 6.1. Betty onstage and producing pure voice in *Opera* (Dario Argento, 1987).

Lee Edelman (2004, 135) writes, "Hitchcock's birds, in the specificity of their embodiment, resist, both within and without the film, hermeneutic determination." They resist interpretation: Hitchcock's birds are all form, and that form exists entirely for its own sake. They hold no meaning. Argento's birds might also represent the operatic dream of pure sound that exists entirely for its own sake. The operatic voice is the voice returned to birdsong.

Both singers remain unseen in this opening shot as cinematographer Ronnie Taylor's camera lingers on the raven. Mara Cekova is never on-screen at all: her argument with Marco and exit from the theater are shown from her point of view; a later scene where she screams at a television broadcast of Betty's performance shows only her plaster-casted leg. It is as if, as a prima donna star, her voice has transcended her body to exist in a permanently acousmatic state and achieve total purity. When Betty is onstage, her effort to produce a pure, ecstatic voice is emphasized visually as well as aurally (fig. 6.1). But *Opera*, like all gialli, also strives toward another form of pure voice: the scream. Following the Torranis' first murder on the Spanish Steps in *The Girl Who Knew Too Much*, countless giallo scenes of suspense and death reach their peaks in nonverbal outbursts of pure vocal affect. These are screams that shatter language and break free from the bodies they come from as if physically extracted by violence. The closing moments of Argento's *Tenebrae*, in which Anne screams uncontrollably, unstoppably, and endlessly as the film fades out, highlight the scream as the giallo's final destination. In this way, the giallo is built around what Chion ([1982] 1999, 77) terms "the screaming point," which he defines less as a specific sound than a "black hole" to which a film is narratively drawn and that manifests "the fantasy of an auditory absolute." The giallo's murder scenes and opera's arias are both formal set pieces designed to achieve pure vocalization. The affinity of the scream and the song is perhaps unsurprising when one considers that several theorists of the voice have noticed their concurrence. Brandon LaBelle (2014, 58) suggests that "all shouts, songs, and cries in general ... no doubt have as their ultimate horizon that of the scream." Michel Poizat, whose *The Angel's Cry* (1992) stands as one of the seminal theorizations of the voice in opera, argues at length that everything in opera moves "toward that supreme mark of the failure of speech and the signifying order, the cry" (1992, 39). *Opera* suggests the fragility of the border between song and scream when, during the opening performance, Santini's murder of an usher causes a light to fall from a box into the stalls below. Betty's voice slides from the note she is holding to a short scream of surprise and back again, emphasizing the thin and permeable border between the two vocal modes.[6]

In both opera and the giallo, vocal excess is closely associated with the collapse of the visual. Poizat (1992, 33–34) points out that "there is something inescapably paradoxical about opera: producers sink enormous sums of money into ... creating sumptuous sets and costumes only to have the spectators, in those great moments, close their eyes to the display, the better to be ravished by the diva's singing. The collapse of the visual order in these instants ... is constitutive of opera." The coincidence between the pure vocality of the scream and the collapse of the visual is equally typical of the giallo, a fact that *Opera*'s main conceit consciously and self-reflexively comments on. Argento explains, "I film these images because I want people to see them and not avoid the positive confrontation of their fears by looking away. So I thought to myself, 'How would it be possible to achieve this and force someone to watch the most gruesome murder and make sure they can't avert their eyes?' The answer I came up with [the pins attached beneath Betty's eyes] is the core of what *Opera* is about" (quoted in Jones 2016, 158). Despite significant aesthetic (not to mention financial) investments in the visual, both opera and the giallo focus so intently on pursuing the pure voice that they may completely overshadow the image. At a fundamental level, they share a self-destructive fixation on the voice. *Opera* is not simply *about* opera, then. Rather, the film and the giallo more widely ask to be understood *as* operatic.[7] Alan Jones (2016, 167) describes the film as "virtually plotless ... an excuse to garnish one glittering set piece after another." The same may be said for many operas. What matters for opera is the attainment of the high note; what matters for *Opera* is the attainment of the scream. In each case, the (acoustic) end justifies the (narrative and visual) means.

The power of the voice in *Opera* is so great that it starts to dominate the images that the audience *does* see. In several scenes, Taylor's camera captures close-ups and extreme close-ups of the sound equipment in Betty's bedroom, where she prepares for her performance by listening to operatic recordings and spoken-word relaxation tapes. As she does so, the camera explores these devices: a green light labeled "voice" that illuminates when a tape is played; moving equalizer bars on her stereo's display; the turning spools of a tape; play, fast-forward, and rewind buttons. Like an opera fan, the camera desperately reaches out for the voice, but the voice is always out of reach, concealed from the film's view by technologies that translate it into abstract visual symbols and analogs.[8] As if in recognition of this futility, the film conducts its search for the voice at a far more visceral level as well. Much has been said about the violence done to characters' eyes in *Opera* and the giallo in general: Adam Knee (1996, 218) argues that "the eye itself is particularly privileged, figured as a site of both potential victimization and violation," while James Gracey (2010, 105) notes that in *Opera*, the shots of the raven's eye, the attack on one of Santini's eyes, Betty's eye pins, and the frequent inclusion of opera glasses emphasize the eye's soft vulnerability. (Betty's friend Mira [Daria Nicolodi] is also shot through the eye by Santini after looking through the peephole in Betty's door.) The focus on violence done to characters' mouths and throats in this film and the entire giallo filone, however, has not been stressed as much. In *Opera*, Stefano is killed partly by being stabbed through the bottom of his mouth. As Stefano screams, Taylor's camera reveals the blade of Santini's knife sticking up through his tongue and filling his mouth. Later, costumer Julia (Coralina Cataldi-Tassoni) accidentally swallows an incriminating bracelet as Santini kills her. He first attempts to recover it by wedging open her mouth, but when that fails, he cuts open her throat and retrieves it directly from the area around her voice box. This recurrent throat and mouth violence is foreshadowed when Cekova sends Betty a bottle of perfume as an opening night gift. As Betty pours the evil-smelling liquid down the drain, Stefano grabs his throat and boisterously pretends to choke. *Opera* caricatures the pursuit of the voice staged by both opera and giallo cinema by treating that pursuit on a ruthlessly literal level.[9]

PROCESS OVER PRODUCT

Opera's grimly absurd suggestion that the voice might be physically cut from the body results in nothing but brutalized cadavers. The film uses the giallo's typically extreme style to show the ephemerality that charges the voice with its emotive power. Grover-Friedlander (2005, 4) writes, "Moments of beautiful singing are always already being mourned, since one knows that they will have gone by at the very moment they appear." The scream's emotional power comes from the suggestion that it will soon end, forever (see chap. 4). The voice has no true afterlife; it exists in an ungraspable present that evaporates instantly. The voice cannot be pinpointed (perhaps an appropriate metaphor regarding this film) because it exists as a process rather than a product. As Connor (2000, 4) writes, "My voice is not something that I merely have, or even something that I, if only in part, am. Rather, it is something that I do." The idea of the voice as a *process* is already present in the setup for the film's murder scenes. In addition to attaching pins to Betty's eyes, Santini gags her. The film draws a clear link between the sights "entering" Betty through her eyes and the voice "leaving" through her mouth and recognizes that by flooding Betty with certain stimuli, Santini will elicit a certain type of utterance. The film acknowledges the voice's inseparability from the wider context that bears it. Stefano jokes with Betty that opera singers are known to have sex before important performances because "it relaxes the voice, sweetens it up a little." His joke implies that the voice represents an ongoing negotiation among the stimuli (visual, aural, physical, and emotional) that precede it. In other words, the voice's true origins must be sought before the utterance itself. As an ephemeral process of mediation and negotiation, the voice exists in suspension between input and output, cause and effect. Although in the most physiological terms it may temporarily resound in certain spaces of the body, the voice always overreaches those borders. Even the lone utterance stands as a sort of conversation among the various influences that give rise to it and influence its form. As *Sound and Horror in the Giallo Film* has sought to show, the *cinematic* voice uncovers the many contextual conversations taking place within the film text. These conversations combine the aesthetic, commercial, and social, revealing a film's status as an aesthetic document, commodity, and cultural object.

The contextual negotiations presented by the voice in opera and the voice in giallo cinema bear a striking similarity. As is the case with the giallo, the voice in opera straddles the national and the international. *Opera* draws attention to this fact by featuring a work by Verdi. Opera is widely believed to have originated with Florentine court performances of the early seventeenth century. Many consider it to be the closest thing to a national Italian art form, but its national(ist) themes peak with Verdi.[10] Donald Grout and Hermine Weigel Williams (2003, 402) write, "Italy during the *Risorgimento*—the Italian nationalist movement (c. 1815–70)—was seething with revolution, and Verdi's early operas came to play an important part in the patriotic movements of the 1840s and 1850s. Though their scenes and characters ostensibly had no connection with contemporary events, the librettos were filled with conspiracies, political assassinations, appeals to liberty, and exhortations against tyranny, all of which were readily understood in the intended sense by sympathetic audiences" (see also Crisp and Hillman 2002). Luchino Visconti's *Senso* (1954) is an excellent example of the national and nationalist respect shown to the composer by Italian culture. The film is set in 1866 and opens with a staging of Verdi's *Il Trovatore* (1853) that inspires clashes in the stalls between Italian nationalists and Austrian troops. Even in Argento's film, Julia claims that she is carrying out Marco's belligerent backstage orders not for him but "for Verdi," a love of whose work she expresses several times in a clear sign of the veneration he seems to inspire in Italy. And yet, for all its Italian specificity, opera soon became an international artistic and cultural form. Daniel Snowman (2009, 3) writes that "by the late nineteenth century, a typically 'Anglo-Saxon' patron of the New York Metropolitan Opera, that archetypal product of Gilded Age America, might have caught a French work sung by a Czech, Polish and Italian cast led by a German conductor." Opera was both Italian in origin and transnational in practice, and the giallo follows this pattern. Snowman's description of the operatic performance suggests that the singing voice becomes a sort of sonorous melting pot, a meeting point for multiple nationalities. As discussed in chapter 3, this reflects the structure of many gialli, in their reliance on both the universally recognizable scream and the use of dubbing. Argento (2014, 279–80) has stated that *Opera* was shot in English to facilitate an international cast and distribution.[11] The voice in both the giallo and the opera resounds in national and international contexts, and it addresses, in the same breath, Italy and the world beyond it. The voices in both opera and the giallo underscore the cultural porosity of Italy's borders at times when Italy's self-image and relationship to the rest of the world (as a unifying country, as a rapidly industrializing member of an integrating world) were shifting profoundly. The voice in opera and the giallo turns context into text.

Like the giallo, opera also spans high and low culture and questions that distinction. John Storey (2002, 36–37) describes how in the early stages of its development opera was frequently enjoyed by large numbers of the working classes in Italy and abroad. He explains that "opera as 'high culture' is therefore not a universal given, unfolding from its moment of intellectual birth; rather, it is an historically specific category institutionalized (depending on which cultural historian you find most convincing) by the 1860s, 1900s, or 1930s . . . it did not become unpopular, rather it was *made* unpopular. . . . In short, opera was transformed from *entertainment* enjoyed by the many into *Culture* to be appreciated by the few" (original emphasis).[12]

Throughout the history of opera, the voices of its stars have resounded across supposed cultural boundaries. *Opera* portrays this quite clearly. As Betty performs on opening night, the film cuts to a young girl who lives in her apartment building and is watching Betty live on television, as, elsewhere, is an irate Cekova (and, later, Santini, who strokes Betty's televised image with a knife). The diegetic television broadcast shows how Betty's voice extends simultaneously through the spaces of so-called high culture (the opera house) and those of popular culture (the television in the private apartment).[13] Allied to both yet loyal to neither, the voice transcends the supposed border between high and low, elite and popular, and mediates their interaction. The giallo also challenges the border between elite and popular culture; this trend is most evident in Argento's work. As discussed in chapter 2, Argento's esoteric pursuit of his own styles and themes seems to align him with his art film contemporaries. Yet his many commercial successes and his role as a sort of godfather to the giallo place him simultaneously in the filone system. The point of interest is not which side of the high/low cultural boundary Argento occupies but how he and the giallo challenge the solidity of that boundary. Indeed, the giallo has been welcomed into several institutions often associated with high culture. For example, Mark Betz (2009, 48) describes having screened gialli, including *The Bird with the Crystal Plumage*, while working as a programmer at New York's George Eastman House in the late 1990s, and in 2016, London's Barbican ran a four-week program titled "She's So Giallo: Women of 1970s Italian Thrillers," which screened gialli by Argento, Fulci, Sergio Martino, and Piero Schivazappa. Similar works were shown at the Gallery of Modern Art in Queensland, Australia, in 2018 (Kannas 2020, 63), and an Argento retrospective was shown at New York's Lincoln Center in 2022. *Opera* itself was partly funded by Radiotelevisione italiana through television presales, though it premiered at the Cannes Film Festival; its distribution straddled popular appeal and prestige from the outset.

The voice offers a clear way to understand how the giallo mixes the elite and the popular on a more material level. Although the dialogue that accompanies Marsillach's on-screen performance was dubbed by various voice actors for the various releases, the vocal tracks for Betty's songs were provided by the well-established Norwegian-Italian soprano Elizabeth Norberg-Schulz. Betty's "voice" ("voices" might be more appropriate) is a complex composite of elements derived from both "popular" and "elite" culture. When Betty speaks, her voice is influenced by financial expediency and the search for a wide distribution market (it literally carries this resonance in the hollow, studio-recorded tone that characterizes much of her dubbed dialogue). When Betty sings, however, her voice contains artistic or musical influences drawn from a narrower cultural sphere. By interweaving Norberg-Schulz's song with the utterances of

Marsillach's uncredited voice double(s), Betty's voice calls into question the mutual distinction between high/elite and low/pop culture.[14]

As an active, dynamic *process*, the voice in both the giallo and the opera mediates between a range of aesthetic, commercial, social, cultural, and economic imperatives. Opera and the giallo are both well placed to emphasize this aspect of the voice because both foreground their textuality through their eccentric form and they are both so sensitive to commercial and social concerns. Grout and Weigel Williams (2003, 577) explain, "Of all the musical forms, opera is the most immediately sensitive to changes in political, economic, social, and general cultural conditions. Its very nature as a complex and costly public spectacle largely dependent on official patronage or private subsidy makes it especially vulnerable to political dictates and economic vicissitudes ... its form, content, and idiom are all affected by changing ideals." For both opera and the giallo, the economic motivations behind a production and the social phenomena from which they stem emboss themselves on the form of the text. A final example of this fact, drawn from *Opera*, makes for a neat summary. James Gracey (2010, 102) explains, "When the film premiered at Cannes, it wasn't well received due to the atrocious dubbing—especially that of Detective Santini.... His voice was re-looped and, as a result, much of his dialogue sounds echoic and quite odd." In Santini's "echoic" voice, one thus hears a negotiation among aesthetic models of what an appropriate voice sounds like for a certain character type, the multiple flows of labor performed in multiple sound studio sessions, and the institutional influence wielded by a prestigious film festival and marketplace. In Santini's voice—as in both the giallo and the opera—form *is* context.[15]

LAST WORDS

Sound and Horror in the Giallo Film aims to enhance our understanding of the giallo's historical significance by pushing back against the visual-narrative focus that dominates existing research on these films. As I have suggested by comparing the giallo to opera, the image is often overwhelmed by sound in these films. In Sergio Martino's *All the Colors of the Dark* (*Tutti i colori del buio*, 1972), a man is killed in his car, and his lifeless form falls against the steering wheel, causing the horn to sound. Its screech parodies a human scream, and, in this way, the film plays with our expectation that certain types of (vocal) sound dominate the giallo's violent set pieces. Paired with a relatively static shot of the victim, the relentless and eerily almost human sound does, in fact, command the audience's attention. From a vantage point several decades after the conclusion of the giallo cycle, Peter Strickland's *Berberian Sound Studio* (2012) demonstrates that giallo cinema's use of sound continues to captivate and remain in audiences' memories. The film tells the story of a sound engineer named Gilderoy (Toby Jones) who, at some point in the 1970s, travels from the UK to Italy to work on the sound effects and dubbing for a violent giallo film. As his work progresses, tensions rise between cast and crew, and the line between reality and the film being made is blurred. *Berberian Sound Studio* is obsessed with both the process of giallo soundtrack creation and the mesmerizing, surreal effect of those soundtracks. There are several shots of Gilderoy destroying vegetables to create the sounds of stabbings, and, at one point, he starts speaking Italian in a voice that is very clearly dubbed, by Strickland's sound team, onto Jones's performance. We see little of the fictional giallo, though. *Berberian Sound Studio* highlights the uncanniness of the giallo's voices and recognizes their centrality to the form and the appeal they hold for audiences. These voices are oneiric and unsettling yet inextricable from the time and place in which they were recorded—the sound studios of 1970s Italy. Strickland emphasizes how voices haunt the giallo; they are both here and there, part of the film but not part of the on-screen spaces and performances. They can never quite be contained or controlled. They stem from the film text yet reach beyond it, acting as conduits for forces and imperatives that may enter the text from outside.

The voice is invaluable for understanding the giallo's historicity because it is aesthetically pivotal; central to the expression of themes; and, often, unabashedly shaped by commercial concerns. As the cinematic voice moves from utterance to utterance, sonorous mode to sonorous mode, the nature of the relationship it presents between text and context changes. It is in this way that I have tried to present the voice as both a *conversation* and a *negotiation* between text and context, film and society. The voice's ever-shifting dynamism gives it a complexity capable of matching the intricacy of the text-context interaction. Crucially, in the case of the giallo, these text-context negotiations not only register films' historicities but also actively contribute to the historical times when the texts were produced. The overt use of dubbing in *Short Night of Glass Dolls* reflected a period when Europe was becoming more economically and politically integrated, but it also participated in and therefore perpetuated that process. In *The Girl Who Knew Too Much*, the erratic voice-over indicated the increasingly multinational and multimedia character of Italy's postboom cultural landscape and, in doing so, helped to create that complex environment. At the other end of the giallo cycle, *Tenebrae* and *The New York Ripper* highlighted the televisual cacophony that accompanied the neoliberalism of Italian media and added their own voice tracks to make it even louder. More conservatively, *Don't Torture a Duckling*, in its focus on silence, not only continued picturesque artistic traditions concerning the Italian South but also helped to strengthen sociogeographical distinctions during a time of change in the country. *Torso* more subtly perpetuated the long-standing, extractive relationship between urban Italy and rural Italy. Vitali (2016, 26) emphasizes "the issue of how [one may] read historical dynamics in films beyond the allegorical model ... as the very pressures at work in the film-text." In *Sound and Horror in the Giallo Film*, I hope to have shown that one productive way of doing this is through the attentive study—at once formal and historical—of sound and the voice.

I have tried to provide film studies and the humanities with a helpful approach to listening to the cinematic voice. Anthropologist Amanda Weidman (2014, 38) writes, "As a phenomenon that links material practices with subjectivity, and embodied sound with collectively recognized meanings, the voice is a crucial site where the realms of the cultural and sociopolitical link to the level of the individual." When humans use their voices, the intimately personal and the fundamentally social—the mouth of the utterer and the ears of the listener(s)—are invoked and interlocked. The individual utterer automatically takes up position in a range of wider networks. The voice is always in multiple places and yet, somehow, in none of them. It is always "at" and "between" each point in the networks that it mediates. The voice's diffuse nature is particularly clear in cinema, where it serves as a cornerstone of a film's acoustic aesthetic, reinforces the depictions of social relationships that so often give life to films' themes, and stands as the tangible product of the sound studio. The commercial priorities at play in soundtrack construction are in turn frequently shaped by wider social, cultural, economic, and political phenomena. The voice's negotiation of three levels of resonance—formal, thematic, and industrial—*gives voice* to the context(s) from which a film emerges and to which it might talk back. The comparison of the giallo to opera briefly discussed in this chapter aims to show the portability of this theorization of the voice. By exploring and challenging the borders between text and context(s) across the spectrum of audiovisual art and culture, the voice provides a way to open those borders as part of the critical process. This approach is especially useful to the study of horror cinema since horror is so often—as the giallo demonstrates—aesthetically extreme, socially attuned, and commercially driven. My hope is that other films and genres (or, indeed, filoni) will be listened to closely, and perhaps comparatively, so that a conversation can continue to grow. Like the giallo, other horror genres—and other films and audiovisual texts generally—cannot be read comprehensively when they are treated only as images. They must be heard.

NOTES

1. Some versions of the film were released in English as *Terror at the Opera*.

2. From the 1990s onward, Argento shifted toward literary adaptations, fantastical horror, and increasingly banal thrillers. *Sleepless* (*Non ho sonno*, 2001) is a possible exception, as it clearly shows how Argento tried to rekindle the giallo format for which he was most famous. However, the film is essentially a pastiche, which precludes it from being part of a style of filmmaking that had disappeared by that point.

3. See Ladd 2018.

4. Interestingly, *Opera* was released in the same year as Don Boyd's *Aria* (1987), which "consists of ten segments drawn from different operas, each filmed by a different director ... any way they wished" (Citron 2010, 58). Argento's film intersects not only the interest in opera extending throughout Italian cinematic history but also one that spans multiple countries.

5. Argento had wanted La Scala, but the success of the 1986 season there meant there was no available downtime (see Argento quoted in Maiello 1996, 63).

6. Argento's use of nondiegetic heavy metal music, replete with highly distorted vocals, during the murder scenes also challenges the divide between song and scream.

7. Intriguingly, the affinity between opera and horror cinema has been leveraged by more recent theatrical ventures. Jeongwon Joe (2013, 180) writes, "Fresco Opera Theatre's intriguing piece, *Ding Dong, the Diva's Dead* (2010), seems to be a theatrical enactment of the cliché of opera's kinship with cinematic death.... Premiered at Overture Center Playhouse in Madison, WI, in October of 2010, this imaginative work stages famous death scenes in opera as those in celebrated horror films."

8. This might align with Argento's claim that "in *Opera* love is haunted by the specter of AIDS ... relations between people are generally cold, people are distant with each other. This is surely the personification of the AIDS nightmare" (quoted in Palmerini and Mistretta 1996, 16). If the voice is a primary structure of human reciprocity and togetherness, its ungraspable quality in the film speaks to Argento's wider concern with human alienation.

9. It is worth noting that operatic singing carries a risk of trauma to the throat. In his *Treatise on Singing* written in 1857, Italian singing teacher Paolo Pergetti (1857, 3) repeatedly warns that "to force the voice by excess of study on

that part forming the 'break,' produces the so-called 'cracking' or 'breaking' of the voice ... it might thereby be completely lost." In a sense, the operatic voice contains the potential for violence.

10. A comment by Federico Fellini establishes Italy's vital relationship to opera: "It is a kind of Italian ritual, an emblem of Italianness, our most accurate reflection. It has gone on throughout Italian history: the Wars of Independence, the struggle for Unification, Fascism, the Resistance. It is the form of spectacle that most resembles us, that most directly expresses our psychology, our mentality, our sense of style. It's as inaccurate, superficial, shoddy, distracting, stupefying—that is to say, as Italian—as one can imagine" (quoted in Costantini 1995, 123–24).

11. The film's final soundtrack was dubbed, however, even in English.

12. Snowman (2009, 44) quotes the British eighteenth-century tourist Samuel Sharp's observation, written in 1767, that "it is so much the fashion ... through all Italy, to consider the opera as a place of rendezvous and visiting ... they do not seem in the least to attend to the musick [sic], but laugh and talk through the whole performance, without any restraint." The resemblance of this description to Wagstaff's of the postwar *terza visione* cinema (see the introduction) is remarkable.

13. As mentioned in the introduction, I am wary of using the term *popular* in cases like this because it is so difficult to define. Following the critics I am drawing on, I use it here to denote cultural products that aspire to draw large audiences from across the social spectrum.

14. Snowman (2009, 310) notes that, as it expanded in the 1920s and 1930s, cinema "offer[ed] millions of Italians an inexpensive version of the warm, romantic fare their parents used to seek—rather more expensively—in the opera house. The cinema was to become an even more potent rival to the opera house in Italy after the arrival of the 'talkies.'" It is perhaps no surprise, then, that parallels between opera and popular cinema present themselves so clearly.

15. There are several other intriguing parallels between opera and the giallo that are beyond the scope of this discussion as they do not pertain directly to the voice. These include a shared interest in baroque spectacle; a shared interest in scenes of death, particularly female; a shared fascination with innovative technology; a shared history of finding themselves on the receiving end of moralistic censure; and a shared celebration of the narratively ridiculous.

BIBLIOGRAPHY

Ackerman, James S. 1990. *The Villa: Form and Ideology of Country Houses.* London: Thame and Hudson.

Adorno, Theodor, and Max Horkheimer. (1947) 1997. *Dialectic of Enlightenment.* Translated by John Cumming. London: Verso.

Albiero, Paolo, and Giacomo Cacciatore. 2015. *Il terrorista dei generi. Tutto il cinema di Lucio Fulci.* Palermo: Edizioni LEIMA.

Alfaro, María Jesús. 1996. "Intertextuality: Origins and Development of the Concept." *Atlantis* 18, nos. 1/2: 268–85.

Allen, Graham. 2011. *Intertextuality.* London: Routledge.

Altman, Rick. 1980. "Moving Lips: Cinema as Ventriloquism." *Yale French Studies* 60: 67–79.

———. 1992. "The Material Heterogeneity of Recorded Sound." In *Sound Theory, Sound Practice,* edited by Rick Altman, 15–31. London: Routledge.

Argento, Dario. 2014. *Paura.* Turin: Einaudi.

Balázs, Béla. (1952) 1970. *Theory of the Film: Character and Growth of a New Art.* Translated by Edith Bone. New York: Dover.

Balbi, Gabriele, and Benedetta Prario. 2010. "The History of Fininvest/Mediaset's Media Strategy: 30 Years of Politics, the Market, Technology and Italian Society." *Media, Culture and Society* 32, no. 3: 309–410.

Balmain, Collette. 2002. "Mario Bava's *The Evil Eye*: Realism and the Italian Horror Film." *Post Script—Essays in Film and the Humanities* 21, no. 3: 20–31.

Barra, Luca. 2013. "Un'americana a Roma. Intrecci televisivi tra Italia e Stati Uniti." In *Storie e culture della televisione italiana,* edited by Aldo Grasso, 305–316. Milan: Mondadori.

Barthes, Roland. 1977. "The Grain of the Voice." In *Image, Music, Text,* translated by Stephen Heath, 179–89. London: Fontana.

Bartolini, Claudio. 2017. *Il cinema giallo thriller italiano*. Rome: Gremese.
Baschiera, Stefano. 2016. "The 1980s Italian Horror Cinema of Imitation: The Good, the Ugly and the Sequel." In *Italian Horror Cinema*, edited by Stefano Baschiera and Russ Hunter, 45–61. Edinburgh: Edinburgh University Press.
Baschiera, Stefano, and Francesco Di Chiara. 2010. "A Postcard from the Grindhouse: Exotic Landscapes and Italian Holidays in Lucio Fulci's *Zombie* and Sergio Martino's *Torso*." In *Cinema Inferno: Celluloid Explosions from the Cultural Margins*, edited by Robert G. Weiner and John Cline, 101–23. Lanham, MD: Scarecrow.
———. 2010. "Once Upon a Time in Italy: Transnational Features of Genre Production, 1960s–1970s." *Film International* 8, no. 6: 30–39.
Baudrillard, Jean. (1981) 1994. *Simulacra and Simulation*. Translated by Sheila Faria Glaser. Ann Arbor: University of Michigan Press.
Bazin, André. (1957) 1985. "On the *politiques des auteurs*." In *Cahiers du Cinéma, the 1950s: Neo-Realism, Hollywood, New Wave*, edited by Jim Hillier, 248–59. Cambridge: Harvard University Press.
Berardi, Franco. 2018. *Breathing: Chaos and Poetry*. South Pasadena, CA: Semiotext(e).
Berardi, Franco, Marco Jacquemet, and Gianfranco Vitali. 2009. *Ethereal Shadows: Communications and Power in Contemporary Italy*. Translated by Jessica Otey. New York: Autonomedia.
Bergfelder, Tim. 2006. *International Adventures: German Popular Cinema and European Co-Productions in the 1960s*. New York: Berghahn Books.
Betz, Mark. 2009. *Beyond the Subtitle: Remapping European Art Cinema*. Minneapolis: University of Minnesota Press.
Bondanella, Peter. 2009. *A History of Italian Cinema*. New York: Continuum.
Brophy, Philip. 1999. "I Scream in Silence: Cinema, Sex and the Sound of Women Dying." In *Cinesonic: The World of Sound in Film*, edited by Philip Brophy, 51–78. North Ryde: Australian Film, Television and Radio School.
Brown, Fredric. (1949) 1958. *The Screaming Mimi*. London: Corgi.
Brown, Keith H. 2012. "Gothic, *Giallo*, Genre: Hybrid Images in Italian Horror Cinema, 1956–82." *Ihla do Desterro* 62: 173–94.
Bruschini, Antonio, and Antonio Tentori. 2013. *Italian Giallo Movies*. Translated by Roberto Curti. Rome: Profondo rosso.
Buonanno, Milly. 2005. "The 'Sailor' and the 'Peasant': The Italian Police Series between Foreign and Domestic." *Media International Australia* 115, no. 1: 48–59.
———. 2012. *Italian TV Drama and Beyond: Stories from the Soil, Stories from the Sea*. Translated by Jennifer Radice. Bristol & Chicago: Intellect.
Burke, Frank. 2002. "Intimations (and More) of Colonialism." *Kinoeye* 2, no. 11. Accessed August 15, 2023. http://www.kinoeye.org/02/11/burke11.php.
Buscombe, Edward. (1973) 2008. "Ideas of Authorship." In *Auteurs and Authorship: A Film Reader*, edited by Barry Keith Grant, 76–78. Oxford: Blackwell.

Cavarero, Adriana. (2003) 2005. *For More Than One Voice: Toward a Philosophy of Vocal Expression*. Translated by Paul A. Kottman. Stanford, CA: Stanford University Press.

Chianese, As, and Gordiano Lupi. 2010. *Filmare la morte. Il cinema horror e thriller di Lucio Fulci*. Piombino: Edizioni il Foglio.

Chion, Michel. 1994. *Audio-Vision: Sound on Screen*. Translated by Claudia Gorbman. New York: Columbia University Press.

———. (1982) 1999. *The Voice in Cinema*. Translated by Claudia Gorbman. New York: Columbia University Press.

Christie, Agatha. (1936) 2013. *The ABC Murders*. London: Harper Collins.

Church, David. 2015. "One on Top of the Other: Lucio Fulci, Transnational Film Industries, and the Retrospective Construction of the Italian Horror Canon." *Quarterly Review of Film and Video* 32, no. 1: 1–20.

Ciofalo, Giovanni. 2011. *Infiniti anni Ottanta. Tv, cultura e società alle origini del nostro presente*. Milan: Mondadori Università.

Citron, Marcia J. 2010. *When Opera Meets Film*. Cambridge: Cambridge University Press.

Connor, Steven. 2000. *Dumbstruck: A Cultural History of Ventriloquism*. Oxford: Oxford University Press.

———. 2014. *Beyond Words: Sobs, Hums, Stutters and Other Vocalizations*. London: Reaktion Books.

Copjec, Joan. 1993. "The Phenomenal Nonphenomenal: Private Space in Film Noir." In *Shades of Noir: A Reader*, edited by Joan Copjec, 167–97. London: Verso.

Corbin, Alain. 2018. *A History of Silence: From the Renaissance to the Present Day*. Translated by Jean Birrell. Medford, MA: Polity.

Corsi, Barbara. 1996. "Eutanasia di un'unione." In *Identità italiana e identità europea nel cinema italiano del 1945 al miracolo economico*, edited by Gian Piero Brunetta, 69–86. Turin: Edizioni della Fondazione Giovanni Agnelli.

———. 2020. "Italian Film Producers and the Challenge of Soviet Coproductions: Franco Cristaldi and the Case of *The Red Tent*." *Historical Journal of Film, Radio and Television* 40, no. 1: 84–107.

Costantini, Costanzo. 1995. *Conversations with Fellini*. Translated by Sohrab Sorooshian. London: Harcourt Brace.

Costantini, Daniele, and Francesco Dal Bosco. 1997. *Nuovo cinema inferno. L'opera di Dario Argento*. Milan: Nuova Pratiche Editrice.

Crisp, Deborah, and Roger Hillman. 2002. "Verdi in Postwar Italian Cinema." In *Between Opera and Cinema*, edited by Jeongwon Joe and Rose Theresa, 155–76. London: Routledge.

Curti, Roberto. 2019. *Blood and Black Lace*. Leighton Buzzard: Auteur.

Dauenhauer, Bernard P. 1980. *Silence: The Phenomenon and Its Ontological Significance*. Bloomington: Indiana University Press.

De Gaetano, Domenico, and Marcello Garofalo, eds. 2022. *Dario Argento: The Exhibit*. Milan: Silvana Editoriale.

Di Chiara, Francesco. 2013. "Looking for New Aesthetic Models through Italian-Yugoslavian Film Co-Productions: Lowbrow Neorealism in *Sand, Love and Salt*." *Illuminance* 25, no. 3: 37–49.

Di Chiara, Francesco, and Paolo Noto. 2023. "Timber Horses and Dollars in Free Currency: Film Policy Cycles and the Italian-Yugoslavian 1957 Co-Production Agreements." *Journal of Italian Cinema and Media Studies* 11, nos. 3/4: 647–66.

Dickie, John. 1997. "Stereotypes of the Italian South 1860–1900." In *The New History of the Italian South: The Mezzogiorno Revisited*, edited by Robert Lumley and Jonathan Morris, 114–47. Exeter: University of Exeter Press.

Dickinson, Kay. 2008. *Off Key: When Film and Music Won't Work Together*. Oxford: Oxford University Press.

Doane, Mary Ann. 1980. "The Voice in the Cinema: The Articulation of Body and Space." *Yale French Studies* 60: 33–50.

Dolar, Mladen. 2006. *A Voice and Nothing More*. Cambridge, MA: MIT Press.

D'Onofrio, Robert. 2015. "Torso and More So." *Fangoria* 340: 44–46.

Dorfles, Piero. 1998. *Carosello*. Bologna: Il Mulino.

Dorfman, Ariel, and Armand Mattelart. 1991. *How to Read Donald Duck: Imperialist Ideology in the Disney Comic*. Translated by David Kunzle. New York: International General.

Downing, John. 2001. *Radical Media: Rebellious Communication and Social Movements*. London: Sage.

Dunnett, Jane. 2010. "*Supergiallo*: How Mondadori Turned Crime into a Brand." *The Italianist* 30, no. 1: 63–80.

Eco, Umberto. 1984. "A Guide to Neo-Television of the 1980s." Translated by Robert Lumley. *Framework* 25: 18–27.

Edelman, Lee. 2004. *No Future: Queer Theory and the Death Drive*. Durham, NC: Duke University Press.

Ehrenreich, Andreas. 2017. "No Niche At All: The Distribution and Marketing of the Giallo Genre." *Bianco e Nero* 587: 113–26.

Eidsheim, Nina Sun. 2015. *Sensing Sound: Singing and Listening as Vibrational Practice*. Durham, NC: Duke University Press.

———. 2019. *The Race of Sound: Listening, Timbre, and Vocality in African American Music*. Durham, NC: Duke University Press.

Esposito, Roberto. 2011. *Immunitas: The Protection and Negation of Life*. Translated by Zakiya Hanafi. Cambridge: Polity Press.

Fisher, Austin. 2016. "Political Memory in the Italian Hinterland: Locating the 'Rural *Giallo*.'" In *Italian Horror Cinema*, edited by Stefano Baschiera and Russ Hunter, 160–74. Edinburgh: Edinburgh University Press.

———. 2019. *Blood in the Streets: Histories of Violence in Italian Crime Cinema*. Edinburgh: Edinburgh University Press.
Flowers, Amy. 1998. *The Fantasy Factory: An Insider's View of the Phone Sex Industry*. Philadelphia: University of Pennsylvania Press.
Foot, John. 1999. "Television and the City: The Impact of Television in Milan, 1954–1960." *Contemporary European History* 8, no. 3: 379–94.
Forgacs, David, and Stephen Gundle. 2007. *Mass Culture and Italian Society from Fascism to the Cold War*. Bloomington: Indiana University Press.
Fraser, Nancy. 2009. "Feminism, Capitalism and the Cunning of History." *New Left Review* 56: 97–117.
Freud, Sigmund. (1919) 2001. "The Uncanny." In *The Standard Edition of the Complete Psychological Works of Sigmund Freud*, vol. 17, edited and translated by James Strachey, 217–56. London: Vintage.
Galt, Rosalind. 2011. "On *L'Avventura* and the Picturesque." In *Antonioni: Centenary Essays*, edited by John David Rhodes and Laura Rascaroli, 134–53. London: BFI.
Ginsborg, Paul. 1990. *A History of Contemporary Italy: Society and Politics, 1943–1988*. London: Penguin Books.
———. 2001. *Italy and Its Discontents: Family, Civil Society, State 1980–2001*. London: Penguin Books.
———. 2005. *Silvio Berlusconi: Television, Power and Patrimony*. London: Verso.
Glynn, Ruth, Giancarlo Lombardi, and Alan O'Leary. 2012. "Introduction: Terrorism, Italian Style." In *Terrorism, Italian Style: Representations of Political Violence in Contemporary Italian Cinema*, edited by Ruth Glynn, Giancarlo Lombardi, and Alan O'Leary, 13–25. London: IGRS Books.
Gomarasca, Manlio. 2008. "Una bottega rinascimentale. La produzione." In *Argento vivo. Il cinema di Dario Argento tra genere e autorialità*, edited by Vito Zagarrio, 246–52. Venice: Marsilio.
Gracey, James. 2010. *Dario Argento*. Harpenden: Kamera Books.
Gramsci, Antonio. (1926) 2000. *The Gramsci Reader: Selected Writings 1916–1935*, edited by David Forgacs, translated by various. New York: New York University Press.
Gribaudi, Gabriella. 1997. "Images of the South: The Mezzogiorno as Seen by Insiders and Outsiders." In *The New History of the Italian South: The Mezzogiorno Revisited*, edited by Robert Lumley and Jonathan Morris, 83–113. Exeter: University of Exeter Press.
Grout, Donald, and Hermine Weigel Williams. 2003. *A Short History of Opera*. New York: Columbia University Press.
Grover-Friedlander, Michal. 2005. *Vocal Apparitions: The Attraction of Cinema to Opera*. Princeton, NJ: University of Princeton Press.
Gundle, Stephen. 1990. "From Neo-Realism to *Luci Rosse*: Cinema, Politics, Society, 1945–85." In *Culture and Conflict in Postwar Italy: Essays on Mass and Popular*

Culture, edited by Zygmunt G. Barański and Robert Lumley, 195–224. London: Macmillan.

———. 2006. "Adriano Celentano and the Origins of Rock and Roll in Italy." *Journal of Modern Italian Studies* 11, no. 3: 367–86.

Harvey, David. 1989. *The Condition of Postmodernity: An Enquiry into the Origins of Cultural Change.* Oxford: Basil Blackwell.

———. 2005. *A Brief History of Neoliberalism.* Oxford: Oxford University Press.

Higson, Andrew. 2000. "The Limiting Imagination of National Cinema." In *Cinema and Nation*, edited by Mette Hjorte and Scott MacKenzie, 57–68. London: Routledge.

Howarth, Troy. 2014. *The Haunted World of Mario Bava.* Godalming: FAB.

———. 2015. *Splintered Visions: Lucio Fulci and His Films.* Baltimore: Midnight Marquee.

Hunt, Leon. 1992. "A Sadistic Night at the *Opera*: Notes on the Italian Horror Film." *Velvet Light Trap* 30: 65–75.

———. 2016. "Kings of Terror, Geniuses of Crime: *Giallo* Cinema and *Fumetti Neri.*" In *Italian Horror Cinema*, edited by Stefano Baschiera and Russ Hunter, 145–59. Edinburgh: Edinburgh University Press.

———. 2022. *Mario Bava: The Artisan as Italian Horror Auteur.* New York: Bloomsbury.

Hutchings, Peter. 2016. "Bavaesque: The Making of Mario Bava as an Italian Horror Auteur." In *Italian Horror Cinema*, edited by Stefano Baschiera and Russ Hunter, 79–92. Edinburgh: Edinburgh University Press.

Immerwahr, Daniel. 2020. "Ten-Cent Ideology: Donald Duck Comic Books and the U.S. Challenge to Modernization." *Modern American History* 3: 1–26.

Jäckel, Anne. 2003. "Dual Nationality Film Productions in Europe after 1945." *Historical Journal of Film, Radio and Television* 23, no. 3: 231–43.

Jameson, Fredric. 1992. *Postmodernism, or, the Cultural Logic of Late Capitalism.* London: Verso.

Joe, Jeongwon. 2013. *Opera as Soundtrack.* London: Routledge.

Jones, Alan. 2016. *Dario Argento: The Man, the Myths & the Magic.* Godalming: FAB.

Kannas, Alexia. 2017. "All the Colours of the Dark: Film Genre and the Italian Giallo." *Journal of Italian Cinema and Media Studies* 5, no. 2: 173–90.

———. 2020. *Giallo! Genre, Modernity, and Detection in Italian Horror Cinema.* Albany: State University of New York Press.

Karpf, Anne. 2006. *The Human Voice.* London: Bloomsbury.

Knee, Adam. 1996. "Gender, Genre, Argento." In *The Dread of Difference*, edited by Barry Keith Grant, 213–30. Austin: University of Texas Press.

Koven, Mikel J. 2006. *La Dolce Morte: Vernacular Cinema and the Italian Giallo Film.* Oxford: Scarecrow.

Kracauer, Siegfried. (1960) 1985. "Dialogue and Sound." In *Film Sound: Theory and Practice*, edited by Elisabeth Weis and John Belton, 126–42. New York: Columbia University Press.

Kunzle, David. 1991. "Introduction to the English Edition." In *How to Read Donald Duck: Imperialist Ideology in the Disney Comic*, edited by Ariel Dorfman and Armand Mattelart and translated by David Kunzle, 11–23. New York: International General.
LaBelle, Brandon. 2014. *Lexicon of the Mouth: Poetics and Politics of Voice and the Oral Imaginary*. New York: Bloomsbury.
Lachetti, Stefani. 2017. *La paura cammina con i tacchi alti*. Piombino: Cinetecca di Caino.
Ladd, Marco. 2018. "Film Music Avant La Lettre? Disentangling Film from Opera in Italy, c. 1913." *Opera Quarterly* 34, no. 1: 29–64.
Lado, Aldo. 2012. "Aldo Lado about *Short Night of Glass Dolls* Aka *La Corta Notte Delle Bambole Di Vetro* (1971)." Accessed August 7, 2024. https://www.youtube.com/watch?v=GIc5xOMBuXs.
Leavitt IV, Charles L. 2020. *Italian Neorealism: A Cultural History*. Toronto: University of Toronto Press.
Lucas, Tim. 2007. *Mario Bava: All the Colors of the Dark*. Cincinnati: Video Watchdog.
Lumley, Robert. 1990. *States of Emergency: Cultures of Revolt in Italy from 1968 to 1978*. London: Verso.
Lyotard, Jean-François. 1984. *The Postmodern Condition: A Report on Knowledge*. Translated by Geoffrey Bennington and Brian Massumi. Manchester: Manchester University Press.
Maiello, Fabio. 1996. *Intervista a Dario Argento. L'occhio che uccide*. Naples: Edizione Scientifiche Italiane.
Martino, Sergio. 2016. "'The Ruthless Logic of Commercial Production' . . . The Sergio Martino Interview." Accessed April 7, 2021. https://houseoffreudstein.wordpress.com/2016/12/04/the-ruthless-logic-of-commercial-production-the-sergio-martino-interview/.
———. 2017. *Mille Peccati . . . Nessuna virtù?* Milan: Bloodbuster.
Massey, Doreen. 2005. *For Space*. London: Sage.
McDonagh, Maitland. 2010. *Broken Mirrors/Broken Minds: The Dark Dreams of Dario Argento*. Minneapolis: University of Minnesota Press.
Mendik, Xavier. 2015. *Bodies of Desire and Bodies in Distress: The Golden Age of Italian Cult Cinema 1970–1985*. Newcastle upon Tyne: Cambridge Scholars.
Mereu Keating, Carla. 2016. *The Politics of Dubbing: Film Censorship and State Intervention in the Translation of Foreign Cinema in Fascist Italy*. Oxford: Peter Lang.
Mitric, Petar. 2018. "The European Co-Production Treaties: A Short History and a Possible Typology." In *European Film and Television Co-Production: Policy and Practice*, edited by Julia Hammett-Jamart, Petar Mitric, and Eva Novrup Redvall, 63–82. Cham: Palgrave Macmillan.

Monetti, Domenico. 2008. "Un crudele gioco metalinguistico. *Tenebre.*" In *Argento vivo. Il cinema di Dario Argento tra genere e autorialità*, edited by Vito Zagarrio, 299–301. Venice: Marsilio.

Narremore, James. 2014. "Authorship, Auteurism, and Cultural Politics." In *An Invention without a Future: Essays on Cinema*, 15–32. Berkeley: University of California Press.

Needham, Gary. 2002. "Playing with Genre: An Introduction to the Italian *Giallo.*" *Kinoeye* 2, no. 11. Accessed August 7, 2024. http://www.kinoeye.org/02/11/needham11.php.

Nowell-Smith, Geoffrey. 1968. "Italy Sotto Voce." *Sight and Sound* 68, no. 3: 145–47.

O'Leary, Alan. 2010. "Italian Cinema and the 'Anni Di Piombo.'" *Journal of European Studies* 40, no. 3: 243–57.

Olivier, Marc. 2020. *Household Horror: Cinematic Fear and the Secret Life of Everyday Objects*. Bloomington: Indiana University Press.

Olney, Ian. 2013. *Euro Horror: Classic European Horror Cinema in Contemporary American Culture*. Bloomington: Indiana University Press.

Orr, Mary. 2003. *Intertextuality: Debates and Contexts*. Cambridge: Polity.

Palmerini, Luca M., and Gaetano Mistretta. 1996. *Spaghetti Nightmares: Italian Fantasy-Horrors as Seen through the Eyes of Their Protagonists*. Translated by Gilliam M. A. Kirkpatrick. Key West, FL: Fantasma Books.

Pergetti, Paolo. 1857. *Pergetti's Treatise on Singing*. London: Robert W. Ollivier.

Perkins, V. F. (1972) 1993. *Film as Film: Understanding and Judging Movies*. Boston: DeCapo.

Pezzotta, Alberto. 1997. *Mario Bava*. Milan: Il castor.

———. 2008. "La modernità imperfetta." In *Argento vivo. Il cinema di Dario Argento tra genere e autorialità*, edited by Vito Zagarrio, 83–89. Venice: Marsilio.

Picard, Max. 1961. *The World of Silence*. Translated by Stanley Godman. Chicago: Henry Regency.

Poizat, Michel. 1992. *The Angel's Cry: Beyond the Pleasure Principle in Opera*. Translated by Arthur Denner. Ithaca, NY: Cornell University Press.

Pollard, Damien. 2019. "'I'm Blind, Not Deaf!': Hegemonic Soundscapes and Resistant Hearing in Dario Argento's *Suspiria* and *Inferno*." *Journal of Italian Cinema and Media Studies* 7, no. 1: 55–73.

———. 2020. "Coherently Incoherent? Dario Argento's *Phenomena* and the Influence of the Music Video." *L'Avventura: International Journal of Italian Film and Media Landscapes* 6, no. 2: 193–206.

———. 2021. "Radio Alice and Italy's Movement of 1977: Polyvocality, Sonority and Space." *Sound Studies* 7, no. 2: 151–72.

Rafaella. (1983) 1991. "More Silences than Lies." In *Italian Feminist Thought: A Reader*, edited by Paola Bono and Sandra Kemp, 173–77. Oxford: Blackwell.

Reich, Jacqueline. 2001. "The Mother of All Horrors: Witches, Gender, and the Films of Dario Argento." In *Monsters in the Italian Literary Imagination*, edited by Keala J. Jewell, 89–106. Detroit: Wayne State University Press.

Restivo, Angelo. 2002. *The Cinema of Economic Miracles: Visuality and Modernization in the Italian Art Film*. Durham, NC: Duke University Press.

Rhodes, John David. 2017. *Spectacle of Property: The House in American Film*. Minneapolis: University of Minnesota Press.

Romanelli, Claudia. 2016. "French and Italian Co-Productions and the Limits of Transnational Cinema." *Journal of Italian Cinema and Media Studies* 4, no. 1: 25–50.

Sabelli, Giacomo, ed. 2013. *Argentophobia. Caratteristiche e peculiarità nella filmografia di Dario Argento*. Rome: UniversItalia.

Sanjek, David. 1994. "Foreign Detection: The West German *Krimi* and the Italian *Giallo*." *Spectator* 14, no. 2: 83–95.

Saunders, George R. 1998. "The Magic of the South: Popular Religion and Elite Catholicism in Italian Ethnology." In *Italy's "Southern Question": Orientalism in One Country*, edited by Jane Schneider, 177–202. Oxford: Berg.

Scaglioni, Massimo. 2013. "Verso un'Italia a colori. La pubblicità televisiva fra *Carosello* e lo spot." In *Storie e culture della televisione italiana*, edited by Aldo Grasso, 337–51. Milan: Mondadori.

Schneider, Jane. 1998. "Introduction: The Dynamics of Neo-Orientalism in Italy (1848–1995)." In *Italy's "Southern Question": Orientalism in One Country*, edited by Jane Schneider, 1–23. Oxford: Berg.

Schoonover, Karl. 2018. "What Do We Do with Vacant Space in Horror Films?" *Discourse* 40, no. 3: 342–57.

Sevastakis, Michael. 2016. *Giallo Cinema and Its Folktale Roots: A Critical Study of 10 Films, 1962–1987*. Jefferson, NC: McFarland.

Shell, Marc. 2004. "Animals That Talk." *Differences: A Journal of Feminist Cultural Studies* 15, no. 1: 87–104.

Shipka, Danny. 2011. *Perverse Titillation: The Exploitation Cinema of Italy, Spain and France, 1960–1980*. Jefferson, NC: McFarland.

Siegel, Michael. 2010. "Roma De Profundis: Post-Economic Miracle Rome and the Films of Dario Argento (1970–1982)." PhD diss., Brown University.

———. 2011. "The Non-Place of Argento: *The Bird with the Crystal Plumage* and Roman Urban History." In *Taking Place: Location and the Moving Image*, edited by John David Rhodes and Elena Gorfinkel, 211–30. Minneapolis: University of Minnesota Press.

———. 2014. "*Tenebre*, or, On Neoliberalism and Violence." Accessed August 16, 2023. http://www.academia.edu/9796852/Tenebre_Or_On_Neoliberalism_and_Violence.

Silveri, Umberto Gentiloni. 2019. *Storia dell'Italia contemporanea 1943–2019*. Bologna: Il Mulino.

Silverman, Kaja. 1988. *The Acoustic Mirror: The Female Voice in Psychoanalysis and Cinema*. Bloomington: Indiana University Press.

Sisto, Antonella C. 2014. *Film Sound in Italy: Listening to the Screen*. Basingstoke: Palgrave Macmillan.

Smith, Jacob. 2008. *Vocal Tracks: Performance and Sound Media*. Berkeley: University of California Press.

Snowman, Daniel. 2009. *The Gilded Stage: A Social History of Opera*. London: Atlantic Books.

Sorlin, Pierre. 1996. *Italian National Cinema, 1896–1996*. London: Routledge.

Storey, John. 2002. "'Expecting Rain': Opera as Popular Culture." In *High-Pop: Making Culture into Popular Entertainment*, edited by Jim Collins, 32–55. Oxford: Blackwell.

Straub, Jean-Marie, and Danièle Huillet. 1985. "Direct Sound: An Interview with Jean-Marie Straub and Danièle Huillet." In *Film Sound: Theory and Practice*, edited by Elisabeth Weis and John Belton, 150–53. New York: Columbia University Press.

Telotte, J. P. 1989. *Voices in the Dark: The Narrative Patterns of Film Noir*. Urbana: University of Illinois Press.

Thrower, Stephen. 2017. *Beyond Terror: The Films of Lucio Fulci*. Guildford: FAB.

Tortaro, Donato. 2011. "A Genealogy of Italian Popular Cinema: The Filone." *Off/Screen* 15, no. 11: 2011.

Truffaut, François. [1954] 2008. "A Certain Tendency of the French Cinema." In *Auteurs and Authorship: A Film Reader*, edited by Barry Keith Grant, 9–18. Oxford: Blackwell.

Vitali, Valentina. 2016. *Capital and Popular Cinema: The Dollars Are Coming!* Manchester: Manchester University Press.

Wagstaff, Christopher. 1992. "A Forkful of Westerns: Industry, Audiences and the Italian Western." In *Popular European Cinema*, edited by Richard Dyer and Ginette Vincendeau, 245–61. London: Routledge.

———. 2013. "Italian Cinema, Popular?" In *Popular Italian Cinema*, edited by Louis Bayman and Sergio Rigoletto, 29–51. New York: Palgrave Macmillan.

Warnke, Martin. 1994. *Political Landscape: The Art History of Nature*. Translated by David McLintock. London: Reaktion Books.

Weidman, Amanda. 2014. "Anthropology and Voice." *Annual Review of Anthropology* 43: 37–51.

Whittaker, Tom. 2020. *The Spanish Quinqui Film: Delinquency, Sound, Sensation*. Manchester: Manchester University Press.

Whittaker, Tom, and Sarah Wright, eds. 2017. *Locating the Voice in Film: Critical Approaches and Global Practices*. Oxford: Oxford University Press.

Wood, Mary. 2007. "Italian Film Noir." In *European Film Noir*, edited by Andrew Spicer, 236–72. Manchester: Manchester University Press.

INDEX

1968 protests, 19–20, 125

Ackerman, James, 110–12, 115n12
acousmêtre, 15, 67, 129
air travel, 66
Alfred Hitchcock Presents (1955–62), 74
All the Colors of the Dark (Martino, 1972), 151
Altman, Rick, 28, 82, 92
American International Pictures (AIP), 49–50
Antonioni, Michelangelo, 29, 39, 84, 86, 129, 130
Argento, Dario, 4, 6, 8, 22, 24, 26, 27, 33, 53, 54–57, 59–61, 62, 63, 69, 71, 73–74, 95, 117, 118, 119, 125–30, 140n5, 140nn9–10, 142–43, 146, 149, 150, 154n2, 154nn5–6, 154n8. *See also individual films*
Argento, Salvatore, 56–57
art films, 4, 6, 8, 16, 20, 84, 129
artisanal filmmaking, 4–5, 48–49, 55, 60
auteurism 4, 22, 24, 54–55, 57–61, 63, 69, 72
autostrada. *See* highways

Balázs, Béla, 99, 100, 129
Baudrillard, Jean, 26, 119, 135. *See also* the simulacrum
Bava, Mario, 4, 6, 9, 10, 23, 31n20, 33, 37, 39, 40, 42, 43, 48–49, 50–51, 52n7, 55–56, 59. *See also individual films*

Baxter, Les, 51
Bay of Blood (Bava, 1971), 95
Berberian Sound Studio (Strickland, 2012), 152
Berlusconi, Silvio, 123–24, 132, 140n7, 140n11
Bertolucci, Bernardo, 57, 86, 143
Bird with the Crystal Plumage, The (Argento, 1970), 24, 53–57, 61–63, 65–66, 68–72, 73, 77, 80, 81, 134, 150
birds, 61–62, 63, 81, 93n3, 135, 144–45
Birds, The (Hitchcock, 1963), 144–45
birdsong. *See* birds
Black Sabbath (Bava, 1963), 31n20
Black Sunday (Bava, 1960), 42
Blood and Black Lace (Bava, 1964), 1–2, 9–10, 27–30, 33, 53, 70, 110
Bolkan, Florinda, 96, 103

Cahiers du Cinéma, 57-58, 59
cannibal films, 3, 117, 126
Cannibal Holocaust (Deodato, 1980), 126
Carosello (1957–77), 45–47, 48, 52n6, 52n7, 125
Catholic Church. *See* Catholicism
Catholicism, 17, 19, 30n6
Cavarero, Adriana, 13–14, 35–36, 37, 41
Celentano, Adriano, 23, 50–51
central Italy, 96, 105
Chion, Michel, 14–15, 67
Christian Democrat Party, 17–18, 19

INDEX

Christie, Agatha, 34, 40
cinema attendance in Italy, 20–21, 117
comedy, 3, 5, 8
comics. *See* fumetti comics
communism, 17–18, 77
Connor, Steven, 13, 14, 67, 148
cop shows, 125, 132
coproduction, 4, 8, 11, 24, 29, 30n5, 75–76, 83–87, 91–92, 93nn4–5, 115n13, 132
coproduction treaties, 83–84, 86, 93n5
Craxi, Bettino, 140n7
crime dramas. *See* cop shows
crime novels. *See* literature
Crimes and Perfume (De Sisti, 1988), 142
cult cinema, 4, 6, 10, 59
Czechoslovakia, 76–78, 84, 89, 91

Dallas (1978–91), 132–33, 141n15
Dania Films, 3
Deep Red (Argento, 1975), 22, 129–30
deregulation of broadcasting in Italy, 20, 26, 124–25, 139
Dictaphone, 133, 141n16
Disney, 136–38, 141n21
Doane, Mary Ann, 63–64
Dolar, Mladen, 13
La dolce vita (Fellini, 1960), 43–44, 50
Don't Torture a Duckling (Fulci, 1972), 25, 94–104, 105, 106, 112, 113, 114n3, 136, 153
Donald Duck, 26, 116, 119, 135–38, 141n20
Door into Darkness (1973), 126. *See also*, "The Tram"
Dorfman, Ariel, 136–37
dubbing, 16, 22, 24–25, 29–30, 49, 74–76, 82–83, 85–92, 138, 149, 150, 151, 152

Eco, Umberto, 127
economic miracle, 18–19, 20, 29, 37, 44, 45, 46, 105, 113, 114n3, 122, 152
Ehrenreich, Andreas, 6
Eidsheim, Nina Sun, 40–41, 78
Esposito, Roberto, 90
European Economic Community (EEC), 76, 87
European Union of Film, 87

Fascism, 16, 17, 19, 20, 25, 37, 39, 72n1, 89–92
Fellini, Federico, 20, 43–44, 129, 155n10
film exhibition in Italy, 5, 6, 30nn6–7, 89, 117, 132. *See also* cinema attendance in Italy; third-run cinemas
Film Noir, 23, 34, 39–40, 46, 74
filone cinema, 2–8, 11, 30n1, 30n4, 30n8, 40, 54–55, 74, 84, 85, 95, 108, 139n1, 142, 150
Fisher, Austin, 11–12
France, 83
Freud, Sigmund, 88, 91
Fulci, Lucio, 4, 6, 95, 98, 101–03, 114n2, 114n7, 118, 121, 136. *See also individual films*
Fulvia Films, 3
fumetti comics, 7, 136–39

Galatea, 3, 34
Galt, Rosalind, 102
gender, 9, 13–14, 18, 21–22, 35, 52n4, 64, 80, 104, 116, 117, 150
Germany, 7, 29, 40, 77, 83–85
Giallo (Camerini, 1933), 33
Ginger and Fred (Fellini, 1986), 126
Girl Who Knew Too Much, The (Bava, 1963), 8, 11–12, 23, 33–51, 53, 63, 66, 74, 92, 118, 119, 138, 139, 145, 152
globalisation, 16, 20, 119, 120, 124–25, 136–138, 139
Goblin (band), 130
gothic, 3, 42–43, 118, 139n1, 140n5

highways, 96, 97–98, 99, 101, 104
Hitchcock, Alfred, 7. *See also individual films*

Icicle Thief, The (Nichetti, 1989), 126–27
Inferno (Argento, 1980), 118, 130, 140n5, 143
intertextuality, 23, 33–35, 39–40, 41–42, 47, 48, 49, 51, 51n1, 56, 74, 93n3
Istituto Luce, 37
Italian Communist Party, 17–18
Italian Fascist Party. *See* Fascism

Kannas, Alexia, 10–11
Koven, Mikel, 10–11, 29
krimi films, 7

INDEX

Lado, Aldo, 25, 76, 84. See also *Short Night of Glass Dolls*
language, 12, 13, 29, 48, 61, 76, 82, 85, 89–90, 91, 93n6, 94, 114n9, 132, 136, 138, 143, 144, 145. *See also* dubbing
Leone, Sergio 4, 6, 53, 54, 57
literature, 7, 8, 23, 33, 34, 37–38, 39–40, 41, 56, 118
logos, 13–14, 35–36, 37, 40, 43, 47, 48, 52n4, 62, 138
Lonely Villa, The (Griffith, 1909), 109, 111

Man Who Knew Too Much, The (Hitchcock, 1934 & 1956), 33, 56
Marshall Plan, The, 17-18,
Martino, Sergio, 6, 59, 85, 95, 108, 109–10, 112, 113, 114n8, 150. See also *Torso*
Massey, Doreen, 68
Mattelart, Armand, 136–37
Mezzogiorno. *See* southern Italy
modernity, 2, 10, 17, 20, 29, 44, 46–48, 95, 98, 99, 101, 104, 114n7
Mondadori, 7, 41, 136
Moro, Aldo, 19
motorcars, 52n8, 98, 104, 105, 109, 111. *See also* highways
Murderrock (Fulci, 1984), 126
music, 7, 46, 50–51, 78, 113n1, 130, 140n13, 143, 150–51, 154n6. *See also* song
Mussolini, Benito, 16, 17, 72n1, 89
mutism, 80, 106

nationalism, 76, 89–91
NATO (North Atlantic Treaty Organization), 76, 86
neoliberalism, 20, 26, 119–25, 127, 128, 131, 133–34, 138–39, 153
Neorealism, 20, 31n6,
New York City, 26, 116, 117, 118–23, 140n5, 150
New York Ripper, The (Fulci, 1982), 26, 116–17, 119–23, 132–36, 138–39, 152–53
Nightmare City (Lenzi, 1980), 126

opera, 27, 142–44, 146–51, 153, 155n7, 155n10, 155n12, 155nn14–15

Opera (Argento, 1987), 27, 142–51, 155n4, 155n8

Pasolini, Pier Paolo, 20, 86, 93n3, 142
Perugia, 104, 105–06, 111, 112, 114n8
petrochemicals, 18, 29, 52n8
phones. *See* telephone
phonos, 13–14, 35–37, 39, 40–41, 52n4, 138
picturesque, 95, 102–04, 106, 110, 153
police dramas. *See* cop shows
poliziottesco films, 3, 8, 117
popular cinema, 3, 7, 11, 39, 49, 116–17, 139n1, 150, 155nn13–14
pornography. *See* sex
postmodernism, 20, 26, 119, 134–35
Prague Spring, 76, 89
Psycho (Hitchcock, 1960), 33, 50, 56

Radiotelevisione italiana (RAI), 45, 123, 126, 127, 140, 150
RAI. *See* Radiotelevisione italiana
Risorgimento, The, 98, 148
Roman Holiday (Wilder, 1953), 33
Rome, 9, 19, 44–48, 52n8, 56, 70, 72n1, 92, 93n3, 112, 114n7, 126
Running Man, The (Glaser, 1987), 127

scream, 25, 27, 43, 80, 94, 96, 110–11, 115n11, 130, 131, 135, 143, 146, 147–48, 149, 151, 154n6
Second World War, The, 17, 24, 84
Seda Spettacoli, 3, 56
set piece, 5, 26, 119, 130, 146, 151
sex, 7, 8, 9, 65, 73, 106, 114n9, 116, 133, 134, 136, 148
sexploitation films, 106
Short Night of Glass Dolls (Lado, 1971), 25, 73–89, 91–92, 119, 152
silence, 1, 25, 27, 29–30, 33, 68, 73, 80–81, 82, 94–96, 99, 100, 101, 103–04, 106–07, 108, 109–11, 113, 113n1, 114nn9–10, 115n11, 115n14, 153
Silverman, Kaja, 64
simulacrum, The, 26, 119, 135–36, 139
singing. *See* song
sirens (myth), 94, 110, 144

socialism, 17
song, 23, 40, 50–51, 78, 142, 143, 145, 146, 147, 149, 150, 154n6, 154n9. *See also* Adriano Celentano; opera
Sorel, Jean, 73, 82. *See also Short Night of Glass Dolls*
southern Italy, 10, 19, 25, 95–96, 97–102, 103, 104, 114n7, 153
Soviet Union, 76, 77, 78, 89
space, 13, 14, 15, 24, 28, 44, 47–48, 55–56, 61–72, 78, 83, 95, 96, 98, 104, 106–12, 113, 120, 126, 129, 152
Spaghetti Western films. *See* Western films
Spain, 15--16, 86
subtitling, 16, 85, 89, 91, 93n6
Sunset Boulevard (Wilder, 1950), 74
suspense, 8, 25–26, 28, 80, 96, 108–11, 145
Suspiria (Argento, 1977), 63, 118, 130

Tagliacozzo, 95, 104, 105, 111
talk shows, 125, 128
technology of voice, 24, 56, 61, 69–71, 98, 104, 125, 133–34, 147. *See also* telephones
telephones, 1, 2, 10, 22, 26, 27–30, 31n20, 36, 69–71, 98, 109, 133, 134, 135
television, 5, 18, 21, 23, 26, 30n1, 34, 45–47, 70, 91, 119, 123–29, 131–33, 138, 139, 140nn8–9, 140n12, 150
television advertising, 23, 34, 45–48, 52n7, 124, 125, 129, 135
television imports, 26, 123–25, 127, 132–33, 140nn8–9
Tenebrae (Argento, 1982), 26, 63, 116–21, 122–23, 125–32, 139, 140n10, 145, 152–53
terrorism, 19
terza visione cinemas. *See* third-run cinemas
third-run cinemas, 5–6, 30n7, 155n12
Titanus, 56
Too Beautiful to Die (Piana, 1988), 142

Torso (Martino, 1973), 25, 72n6, 95, 96, 104–13, 115n13, 153
"Tram, The" (Argento, 1973), 128
translation, 88–91, 132, 138. *See also* dubbing; language; subtitling
transnational filmmaking, 4, 11, 83–85, 87–88, 89, 91. *See also* coproduction
Treaty of Rome, 86
Truffaut, François, 57

uncanniness, 9, 67, 88, 92, 152

Verdi, Giuseppe, 142, 143, 148–49
vernacular cinema, 10
Videodrome (Cronenberg, 1983), 127
villa, 25, 95–96, 106–13, 115n12, 115n14
Vitali, Valentina, 11–12, 40, 153
voice (and film form), 1, 12, 14–17, 22, 23–27, 28, 34–43, 46–48, 49–51, 55–56, 61, 63–69, 73–75, 76–80, 94, 100–101, 128–29, 130, 131, 136, 144–46, 147–48, 151–53
voice (and film production), 10, 24–25, 29–30, 48–51, 75, 81–92, 103, 138–39, 151, 152
voice (and film theory), 28, 64, 67, 99, 100, 129
voice (and philosophy), 12-14, 35-36, 40–41, 148,
voice (and social, cultural and political significance), 10, 12, 15–17, 21, 22, 23–27, 35, 40, 48, 69–72, 76–80, 81–92, 95, 98–99, 100–01, 104, 119, 131, 134–36, 139, 149–51, 152–53

West Germany. *See* Germany
Western films (genre), 3, 5, 6, 7, 8, 31n9, 85

Yugoslavia, 84–85, 86, 87

zombie films, 3, 117, 126

DAMIEN POLLARD is Lecturer in Film at Northumbria University. He is editor (with Edward Bowen) of *Film Exhibition: The Italian Context*.

For Indiana University Press

Sabrina Black, Editorial Assistant
Allison Chaplin, Acquisitions Editor
Anna Garnai, Production Coordinator
Sophia Hebert, Assistant Acquisitions Editor
Samantha Heffner, Marketing and Publicity Manager
Katie Huggins, Production Manager
Darja Malcolm-Clarke, Project Manager/Editor
Dan Pyle, Online Publishing Manager
Michael Regoli, Director of Publishing Operations
Jennifer L. Wilder, Senior Artist and Book Designer

www.ingramcontent.com/pod-product-compliance
Lightning Source LLC
Chambersburg PA
CBHW030655230426
43665CB00011B/1106